KT-479-809

THE SCOTTISH GARDENER

SUKI URQUHART

BEING

Observations made in
a Journey through the
Whole of Scotland from
1998 to 2004
Chiefly Relating to
the Scottish Gardener
Past & Present

PHOTOGRAPHS BY
RAY COX

 Birlinn

This edition published in 2005 by Birlinn Ltd
West Newington House
10 Newington Road
Edinburgh EH9 1QS

www.birlinn.co.uk

Copyright © Suki Urquhart 2005
Photographs copyright © Ray Cox 2005

All rights reserved. No part of this publication may be reproduced, stored, or transmitted
in any form, or by any means, electronic, mechanical or photocopying, recording or otherwise,
without the express written permission of the publisher

ISBN10: 1 84158 363 4
ISBN: 978 1 84158 363 1

British Library Cataloguing-in-Publication Data
A catalogue record for this book is available from the British Library

The publisher acknowledges subsidy from the

Scottish
Arts Council

towards publication of this book

Design and art direction by James Hutcheson
Design, layout and typesetting by Sharon McTeir
Book set in 10/14pt Adobe Garamond

Printed and bound in Slovenia

To the High Scrivener
and the Unicorns

CONTENTS

ACKNOWLEDGEMENTS

Thanks are due to the gardeners who have helped me make gardens over the last 30 years in Scotland, and who made me realise that the more I learnt the less I knew about both plants and people, especially: Jock McGregor in Kinross-shire; Donald Campbell in The Inner Hebrides; George Stables and John Kidd in Aberdeenshire and Tom Christian and James Evans in Highland Perthshire.

As to writing, help and encouragement has come from many including: Merlin Holland, Roddy Martine, Archie MacKenzie, Gerald Laing, Alastair Robertson, Collette Douglas Home and Giles Gordon, who (although he maintained that journalists couldn't write books) acted as my agent and was in the process of negotiating with Birlinn over this book when he died.

For help during my research and writing of *The Scottish Gardener*, I would like to thank all those generous people who assisted by giving me the run of their libraries, lent me books, allowed me to share their own research and quote from published works, for encouragement, for proof reading and advice, in particular: Henry Steuart Fothringham, Anna Buxton, James Irvine Robertson, Christopher Dingwall, Charles McKean and Fiona Jamieson; Hugh Andrew, Andrew Simmons and the staff at Birlinn who have produced this book; Ray Cox the photographer whose spelling (and photography) is much better than mine.

To my family and in particular my three daughters who put up with my inattention over long periods but gave unstinting encouragement.

Last but not least, the 'Gardeners' themselves who feature in this book for giving me their time and for telling me about themselves and their gardens.

PREFACE

To choose just a few gardens from the many thousands in Scotland, as illustrations for a book about the Scottish Gardener, is a challenge. The sixty or so gardens and gardeners featured in this book are taken in the main from around three hundred published articles that I wrote about Scottish gardening and gardeners over a period of six years. The gardens I have chosen have as much to do with people and history as they do with the exact science or art of gardening. Gardens evolve and those that I visited in the 1990s will not necessarily look the same today. To my mind, an individual's garden reflects the character of that person, thus giving individuality to that space in a way that public gardens can rarely do. No National Trust gardens (with the exception of Crarae, which I visited two years before it was handed over to the National Trust) are included for this reason and also because they form a collection in their own right.

As for the gardeners, I have tried to place them in relevant chapters, although their diversity of origin, training and interests, the different paths that led them into various branches of horticulture, botany, plant collecting, propagation, design, taxonomy, illustration and writing, together with the fact that many engage in more than one discipline, make them difficult to separate into individual categories.

Suki Urquhart
Dull Schoolhouse
September 2005

Introduction

Balloch Castle (now Taymouth) in Perthshire showing the elaborate formal gardens. Attributed to James Norie, the painting hangs in the National Portrait Gallery, Edinburgh.

INTRODUCTION

'The Voyage of Discovery consists not in seeking new landscapes, but in having new eyes.' MARCEL PROUST

The phrase 'point of view' comes from the French *point de vue*, which is horticultural in origin and is in fact about the place from where you are looking. It all depends where you are looking from as to what you see and in gardening there is no greater truism. It would seem likely that dismissing early gardening as not having happened probably had much to do with not rating the plants that were being gardened. Today there is hardly a plant in the world that you cannot buy for your garden. It would also have to do with the use of the space; two thousand years ago the choice north of the wall, as described by Procopius in the sixth century AD, would be mainly limited to wild plants and their practical uses. He wrote a scant description from Constantinople of the 'lost' Roman provinces of Britain. Of Scotland he said:

Part of the island nearest Gaul was still inhabited and fertile, but it was divided from the rest of the island by a wall, beyond which was a region infested by wild beasts, with an atmosphere fatal to human life, wherefore it was tenanted only by the spirits of the departed.

The practice of deriding the perceived barbaric nature of Scotland continued in history. In 1531 Robert Lindsay of Pitscottie wrote about a visit to Scotland by the Pope's ambassador:

For, I heard say, this noble earl [of Atholl] gart make[1] a curious palace to the king, to his mother and to the ambassador [of the Pope]; where they were so honourably eased and lodged, as though they had been in England, France, Italy, or Spain ... a fair palace of green timber, wound with green birks[2] ... and also this palace within was hung with fine tapestries and arrases of silk, and lighted with fine glass windows in

all the airths ... The Ambassador of the Pope seeing this great banquet and triumph ... thought it a great marvel, that such a thing could be in Scotland, considering that it was named the Arse of the World by other countries.

Another writer, Fynes Moryson, conjectures along the same lines in 1598:

As in the Northerne parts of England, they have small pleasantness, goodnesse, or abundance of Fruites and Flowers, so in Scotland they must have lesse, or none at all.

Dr Johnson, well known for his contempt of Scotland, wrote in his *Journey to the Western Islands of Scotland* in 1773:

To the southern inhabitants of Scotland, the state of the mountains and the islands is equally known with that of Borneo and Sumatra: of both they have only heard a little, and guess the rest.

Perhaps he was just rehashing Martin Martin's words of 1695:

Foreigners, sailing thro the Western Isles, have been tempted, from the sight of so many wild Hills ... and fac'd with high Rocks, to imagine the Inhabitants, as well as the Places of their residence, are barbarous; ... the like is suppos'd by many that live in the South of Scotland, who know no more of the Western Isles than the Natives of Italy.[3]

Searching through the gardening books written about Scottish gardens since the first, John Reid's *Scots Gard'ner* of 1683, it seems that it really does all depend on your point of view. That one type of gardener will dismiss another's garden because it is not his idea of a garden has been going on since the beginning of time. The prolific writer John

Claudius Loudon, a Scot from Lanarkshire, devotes a section to the history of Scottish gardening in his famous *Encyclopaedia of Gardening* in 1834. Having spent his working life in London, he is quite disparaging about his fellow Scots gardeners:

Gentlemen in Scotland have no idea of the care and expense taken and incurred in England to protect the blossoms of wall fruit trees. If they have laid out a kitchen-garden and built the walls, they think it quite enough, just as a planter of forest trees thinks the work is finished when he has filled the ground with so many thousand plants per acre. By not cropping the borders, by thatching peach borders occasionally in rainy autumns to prevent the rain from penetrating them, thereby checking the growth and ripening the wood, and by careful covering with canvass during the blossoming season, crops of wall fruit might be rendered nearly as certain and as abundant as crops of gooseberries. But very few country gentlemen in Scotland would go to the necessary expense.

For most writers of Scottish garden history since the mid-nineteenth century, Loudon was the main authority and one finds his version cropping up time and again in books written since. For instance, he describes James I (of Scotland), who

admired the gardens of Windsor, in 1420; and having been in love there, and married an Englishwoman, … an excellent man … he would sometimes instruct them [the Scots] in the art of cultivating kitchen and pleasure gardens … This proves the advanced state of horticulture in England at that period; as it was in England that James must have obtained his knowledge.

Loudon continues bewailing the lack of gardens in the fifteenth and sixteenth centuries and concedes that 'during the 17th century, a few gardens must have been formed in Scotland'. He complains that in the eighteenth century the Scots failed to follow Lord Kame's improvements to his landscape at Blair Drummond in Perthshire, but instead employed mediocre 'itinerant pupils of Brown,[4] or professors in his school, who resided in Scotland; and

thus it is, that after commencing in the best taste, Scotland continued for many years to patronise the very worst'.

How a garden was shaped by the human condition of the time is quite another matter. Planting in gardens is a continuously moving art form, a matter of taste and fashion, of necessity and of availability. But if the garden visitor wishes to trace the history of Scottish gardens from the medieval period to the present day, he will find more relevance in the structures than in the plants. In wandering around these gardens, it is possible to imagine the pageant of history unfolding in the landscape. Re-creations will always lack the vital element in a garden – the people of the time that worked and lived in that space.

When travellers first started to tour Scotland to observe the people and the countryside and to visit houses and gardens, they recorded their impressions in journals, or 'observations', and many are mentioned in this book.[5] Whether they were ambassadors, spies, historians, geologists, botanists, poets, writers, artists, birdwatchers, evangelists or merely tourists, if they noticed gardens, they noted the status of the owner, the relative beauty of the work and its relationship to the surrounding countryside and how fashionable it was at the time. In my own travels from north to south and from east to west, I am sometimes amazed at how an impression, written three or four hundred years ago, appears the same even now. Faujus de St Fond[6] gives gripping descriptions of his journeys in driving rain and dark, trying to reach an inn for the night and about storm-tossed trips in the Hebrides. All of these are very familiar to me even though I had the comfort of a car; I have been stuck in floods and snowdrifts or been in a boat where the engine died in a force-eight gale.

The glens, lochs and mountains are easily identified and, as John Macky[7] wrote, 'Wherever you see a Body of Trees, there is certainly a Laird's House; most of them old Towers of Stone, built strong, to prevent a Surprize from Inroads.' This is still the case today. In 1901 Sir Arthur Mitchell, in his paper entitled *A List of Travels, Tours, Journeys, Voyages, Cruises, Excursions, Wanderings, Rambles,*

Visits, etc., Relating to Scotland,[8] prefaces the list with the following remark:

> *Many of the travellers who have left accounts of their journeys appear either to have had eyes which did not see, or not to have known what they should look for and what ought to be described or recorded in view of its ultimate value.*

These impressions are full of different points of view[9] that were often coloured by what they thought they had come to see, or by the fact that it was different from what they had expected. Garden visiting was never the main purpose of their journey, but the practice of visiting 'Gentlemen's Seats' and commenting on the house, the contents, the gardens and policies was often central to the tour and occasionally they peeped over the garden fence of humbler abodes.

Some arrived with pre-conceived ideas like the Rev. William Gilpin, who had come to Scotland to revel in the picturesque. In his book[10] he rebukes Dr Johnson, who also had a pre-conceived point of view, and is probably the best known of these chroniclers, saying:

> *Dr Johnson has given us a picture of Scotch landscape, painted, I am sorry to say, by the hand of peevishness. It presents us with all its defects; but none of its beauties. The hills, says he, are almost totally covered with dark heath; and even that appears checked in its growth. What is not heath is nakedness; a little diversified, now and then by a stream, rushing down the steep. An eye accustomed to flowery pastures, and waving harvests, is astonished, and repelled by this wide extent of hopeless sterility ... How much more just, and good-natured is the remark of another able writer on the subject [Gregory]: 'We are agreeably struck with the grandeur, and magnificence of nature in her wildest forms – with the prospect of vast, and stupendous mountains.'*

Gilpin had equally strong views on Drumlanrig, seat of the Duke of Queensberry:

> *The garden front of Queensberry-house opens on a very delightful piece of scenery ... It is amazing what contrivance hath been used to deform all this beauty. The descent from*

the house has a substratum of solid rock, which has been cut into three or four terraces at an immense expence. The art of blasting rocks by gunpowder was not in use, when this great work was undertaken. It was all performed by manual labour; ... How much less expensive is it, in general, to **improve** the face of nature, than to **deform** it!*

Gilpin goes on to describe the canal and the cascade, both man-made, and concludes: 'So vile a waste of expence, as this whole scene exhibits, we rarely meet with. Deformity is spread so wide through every part of it, that it now exceeds the art of man to restore it again to nature.'

Whereas Macky, when visiting the same Drumlanrig records:

> *The ancient paternal seat of the Dukes of Queensbury ... The Offices below are very noble; and the hanging Gardens cut out of the Rock down to the River side, with Water-works and Grottos, to every way answer the great Genius of William Duke of Queensbury, its first founder ... There is a vast Plantation of Trees round the Palace, and the Surprise of seeing so fine a Building in so coarse a Country adds to its Beauty.*

Gilpin continued almost as 'peevish' as Johnson on the subject of Blair Atholl: 'At present it is much injured by vistas, and a kitchen garden, which tho extraordinary in its way, is still a nuisance.' While another traveller, Robert Heron,[11] visiting the same place twenty years later, noted that 'the [kitchen] garden, properly so called is large and well laid out, although perhaps not so very well kept, as might be wished. In the middle is an artificial piece of water which has no disagreeable effect.'

Travelling on to Taymouth,[12] Heron is more critical:

> *One of the most admired objects is an avenue of venerable limes; extending four hundred and fifty yards in length. The tops of these unite with a spherical angle, like that which marks the roof, doors, and windows of a Gothic palace ... I am rather inclined to suspect, that the arch in which the trees of this avenue join their summits, may be artificial, in a good measure ... They are of that age in which is was esteemed the perfection of Taste in Gardening to prune vegetables into the fantastic figures of Animals, and of all the oddest*

productions of Art. Had I met such an avenue in the middle of an extensive, natural forest, I might have supposed what is peculiar in it to have been the untutored work of nature accidentally imitating art. But, in this situation, one cannot, without extreme simplicity, conceive such a fancy of it.

Thomas Pennant, who had viewed the same feature in 1769 at Taymouth, had this to say about it:

The Berceau walk is very magnificent, composed of great trees, forming a fine gothic arch; and probably that species of architecture owed its origin to such vaulted shades.

In my travels around Scotland my main purpose was to seek out gardens, but my fascination is also with 'the human condition', so the people in the gardens are as much of interest as the gardens themselves. The plants within these gardens may have changed over the centuries. Some plantings have tried to remain true to their history while others have simply been gardened within the historic boundaries and around the historic buildings. The relationship of a garden to the house and the immediate environment is also a crucial element for aesthetic appeal.

Scotland is divided, not north by south, but east by west, and by the height of the land above sea level. Many plants grown on the west coast of Scotland would curl up and die in the land-locked counties of central England. It is a very good place to garden in spite of the capricious nature of the climate; that four seasons can be experienced in one day is not so much the boast, but the reality. (Billy Connolly goes further, saying that in Scotland there are only two seasons – May and winter.) The coolness and the rain in fact favour many plants. Drought is rarely a factor and the long summer days create extra growing time, albeit offset by the short dark winter days. The main enemies of the gardener in Scotland today are the biting wind, the rabbits and the deer. These factors, along with geographic differences in soil and rainfall, dictate the variety and types of gardens to be found. Weather and predators also account for the huge numbers of walled gardens [13] that have been made from the earliest times to enclose everything from a small physic garden to very grand layouts covering many acres.

So what constitutes a garden? Who were the Scottish gardeners? How can you define gardening? What is history? The scraps of written evidence give clues, in diaries and accounts. But these are embellished with anecdote, hearsay, gossip and spin. So I would like to add my own interpretation of events and hope that it is not spin but conjecture based on research that has produced these ideas and observations while marrying them to gardens that exist today.

Notes

1. 'Gart make' = caused to be made.
2. Trees, usually birch.
3. Thomas Pennant wrote much the same thing in his *Tour of Scotland 1769*, saying 'a country almost as little known to its southern brethren as Kamschatska'.
4. Lancelot 'Capability' Brown – pioneer of the English Landscape Movement.
5. Gardens start to be mentioned from the sixteenth century by Alesius, by Donald Monro (1549), Martin Martin (1695), John Macky (1723), Daniel Defoe (1725), Thomas Pennant (1769), Dr Johnson and James Boswell (1775), William Gilpin (1776), Faujus de St Fond (1784), Robert Heron (1792), Elizabeth Grant (1794), with many more in the nineteenth century.
6. *Travels in England and Scotland* (1784).
7. *Journey Through Scotland*, vol. III: 1723.
8. Published in the *Proceedings of Society of the Antiquaries of Scotland 1900–1901*, vol. xxxv, third series, vol. xi.
9. The earliest travellers published start in 1296, with 45 listed before 1600, 57 in the next century, rising to 150 for the eighteenth and 600 during the nineteenth century.
10. *Observations on Several Parts of Great Britain, particularly The Highlands of Scotland, relative chiefly to picturesque beauty, made in the year 1776.*
11. *Observations made in a Journey through the Western Counties of Scotland in the Autumn of M,DCC,XCII* (1793).
12. Seat of the Earls of Breadalbane in Perthshire.
13. Over 3,000 according to the Garden History Society.

CHAPTER ONE

Physic, Monastic and Royal

Twenty-first century physic garden, Pitnacree Garden Cottage.

PHYSIC, MONASTIC AND ROYAL

'Gardening was at first a useful art: but there is beauty in utility.'
HENRY HOME, LORD KAMES

Apart from royal and monastic records, historical evidence for gardening prior to the twelfth century has traditionally been dismissed and the assumption made that it simply was not going on. Maybe denying the husbanding of wild plants as a form of gardening has something to do with the limitless choice of plant material that we have to choose from today. Lupins and nemesia are pretty commonly grown but these were originally exotic imports. So gardening native plants, now more commonly classified as weeds, was historically ridiculed. Most of our edible roots, fruits and vegetables started out as wild plants. Why force the tips of nettles when you can grow an import like spinach; or pick early shoots of bracken instead of asparagus?

Growing herbs for medicines is equally dismissed by many as not proper gardening, but in the twenty-first century one third of all drugs are based on herbs and a further third are composed of chemical equivalents. If you can weave fine cloth from nettles, which we did in Scotland, you would need to cultivate them. Equally, protecting places where the best dye plants grew, and searching out rocks and branches where the lichens were abundant is a form of gardening – gathering a harvest within nature's own rich garden.

Strabo records the legal necessity among the Gaels of maintaining a trim figure: 'The following is a further peculiar trait: they try not to become stout and fat-bellied, and any young man who exceeds the standard length of the girdle is fined.'

The Gaels were the mercenary armies of choice used by the Romans for hundreds of years. Various Roman writers describe the Celts:

Almost all are of tall stature, fair and ruddy, terrible for the fierceness of their eyes, fond of quarrelling, and of overbearing insolence. In fact a whole band of foreigners will be unable to cope with one of them in a fight, if he calls in his wife, stronger than he by far and with flashing eyes; least of all when she swells her neck and gnashes her teeth, and poising her huge white arms, begins to rain blows mingled with kicks like shots discharged by the twisted cords of a catapult.

An army marches on its stomach and it would seem that the Celts' diet contributed to their physiques. The Celtic races that included the Picts, the Scots and the Gaels mixed with Viking and Norse, survived on the fringes of Britain and Europe where their culture largely escaped Romanisation. This allowed their unique form of holistic herbal medicine to continue into the early twentieth century in remote parts of the Hebrides and the Highlands. The early Celts may not have gardened for pleasure, but they would have gardened for food, medicine and dye-stuffs. This last reason for cultivating plants was necessary to create the bright colours that the Celts so loved. Even before the Roman invasion there was a thriving trade with Europe in wool and also in *sagi,* long woollen cloaks. Vegetable dyes were used, not just to create the stripes and checks woven into clothes, but for painting their bodies and faces in battle. The best known body paint was woad, *Ivatis tinctoria,* a plant that has to be grown from seed annually and requires a rich loam. The Celtic practice of hair dying is also recorded – abundant hair was considered a mark of great beauty and often three different shades would be applied, the dye giving extra volume.

The strong pagan religious superstitions, many of which have passed into the Christian religions, revered such plants as heather, rowan, elder, holly and ivy, mistletoe, yew and silver birch, some also having medicinal and practical uses.

While most of these plants could be dismissed as growing naturally in the wild, more recent archeo-botanical research at ancient settlements, via pollen samples, has thrown up all manner of more exotic herbs and spices for both medicinal and culinary use: coriander, opium poppy, caper, spurge, figs, mace, onions, peas, broad beans, raisins, fruits and dye plants along with the different woods, animals, fish and birds.

As for more (or less) evidence of gardening in the Islands, Donald Monro's *A Description of the Occidental i.e. Western Islands of Scotland*, written around 1549, records (off the southwest coast of Barra): 'St. Colmis Ile. Within this Ile. Mccloyd of the Leozus [Lewis] hes ane fair Orcheard, and he that is Gardiner hes that Ile frie.' Many of the islands that Monro visited are described as 'inhabite and manurit'.

Martin Martin writes, in his 1695 account of his native Western Isles of Scotland,

In many places the soil is proper for wheat; and their grass is good … If the natives were taught and encouraged to take pains to improve their corn and hay, to plant, enclose, and manure their ground, drain lakes, sow wheat and peas, and plant orchards and kitchen gardens, etc. they might have as great plenty of all things for the sustenance of mankind as any other people in Europe.

By the end of the following century much had changed. In 1790 Sir John Sinclair of Ulbster in Caithness wrote to every minister in the 938 parishes of Scotland enclosing a questionnaire on 166 aspects of daily life. This became the Statistical Account of 1799. In the replies there are descriptions of gardening as a pastime as practised by everyone, from crofters to lairds. The minister of Birsay and Harray in Orkney wrote: 'The gardens will produce early cabbage and colliflower; as also onions, leeks, garlick, parsnips, carrots, turnips, and small salad herbs; very fine flowering will in some years likewise blow, which I have tried.' Another respondent from Orkney stated that 'perhaps the finest and largest artichokes in the world are to be found in this country, in the common kail-yards'.

Shetland, too, grew 'artichokes of delicate taste … and most of the garden flowers that grow in the north of Scotland'.

From Wick came the news that they were growing 'common apples and pears', which, 'together with cherries, strawberries, and currants, answer well when properly attended to; cucumbers are raised in hot beds; artichokes are found here in highest perfection'. This reply goes on to list a comprehensive range of vegetables as well as 'pot, aromatic, and medicinal herbs, by due attention'. These were in the minister's own garden, while the gentry at Castairs House in Lanarkshire were growing grapes, pineapples and melons as well as tea and coffee plants. Lord Lovat, near Inverness, meanwhile had a walled garden of seven Scotch acres[1] with eighteen-foot high brick-lined walls built in the fashion of 'a crinkle, crankle wall'.[2] The poor, for the most part, seemed doomed to a kail-and-cabbage diet but there were exceptions in areas like Forgandenny, Perthshire, where villagers were growing a variety of vegetables, herbs, flowers and fruit bushes – these 'chiefly for shelter to their hives

The Palace of Birsay, former seat of the Bishops of Orkney, was already a ruin by the seventeenth century (Crown copyright © RCAHMS).

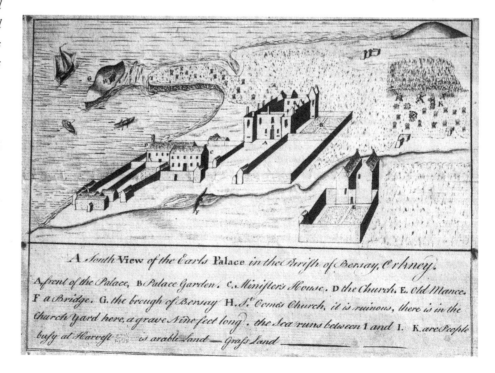

A South View of the Earls Palace in the Parish of Bensay, Orkney. A front of the Palace, B Palace Garden, C Minister's House, D the Church, E Old Mance, F a Bridge, G the brough of Bensay H St Comes Church, it is ruinous, there is in the church yard here, a grave Nine feet long. the Sea runs between I and I. K are People busy at Harvest is arable Land — Grass Land

of bees, of which there is no inconsiderable number'. The minister at Scone reports: 'And not only the handicraftsmen, at their leisure hours, but the farmers, begin to pay more attention to their gardens than formerly; a certain indication of the thriving state of this country, men commonly attending, first, to what is necessary, and then to what is commodious and ornamental.' From Banff came a description of early allotments, to provide the townsfolk with herbs and vegetables.

Few links havfe been made between the ancient Celtic practices of herbal medicine and gardening. The Celtic belief in preventative medicine that maintained health through diet, exercise and hygiene and the use of herbs to cure ills has in turn links with Greek and Arabic sources as early as AD 78. Pliny the Elder describes them in his *Natural History*. The holistic practice of the early Celtic physicians is interesting in that both the mind and the body were addressed so that herbal remedies, combined with rituals, song and dance provided a cure. These healers mainly used 'simples', a decoction of a single herb, for their potions.

Tradition has it that every Scottish king from Robert Bruce to James VI employed a 'Beaton' physician. Seventh- and eighth-century Gaelic law tracts accorded physicians the privileges of nobles, by virtue of their professional skills that were passed down through families. The MacBeths were thought to have come from Ireland at the end of the thirteenth century, as part of the retinue of

Jacqui Hazzard preparing a jar for a herbal tincture at Garden Cottage, Pitnacree.

Áine when she married Angus Og, Lord of the Isles. By the sixteenth century they had become known as Beaton. Numerous branches of the family practised medicine throughout Scotland over a period of 400 years. In 1629 one Fergus Beaton, who lived at Balinabe in Islay, was chief physician to the Lord of the Isles. Behind the site of the original house is an old walled garden where he presumably cultivated his herbs. Other Beaton houses are recorded as having herbal gardens attached to them: Ardeoran in Lorn and Pennycross on Mull, where the sites of the herb gardens were still evident in the nineteenth century.

Herbalism, banned by law in 1941 under the Pharmacy and Medicine Act, was repealed in 1968 and, though again threatened under EU legislation, is on the increase. As an example, there is the garden of Jacqui Hazzard in Perthshire, beside the River Tay. On entering the small courtyard of Garden Cottage in Pitnacree, the visitor is greeted by a group of brightly coloured flowers, growing in pots by the wall. A notice on the door says: 'I'm in the garden.' This is the old walled garden of a former dower house which Jacqui is transforming into a twenty-first century 'garden of simples', the name applied to medieval physic gardens.

When Peter Rabbit's mother gave him a cup of camomile tea after his frightening adventures in Mr McGregor's garden (based on a garden in nearby Dunkeld), she was using the most ancient of medicines. In Jacqui Hazzard's mail-order catalogue the entry for camomile tea reads: 'traditionally used to ease tummy aches and soothe restlessness … gentle enough for infants …'

The word 'drug' comes from the Anglo Saxon word 'drigan' meaning 'to dry' and dried herbs used as medicines have been used for millennia. *The Greek Herbal*, written by Dioscorides in the first century AD, was the main textbook used all over Europe and the Middle East for 1,500 years. It was translated into Arabic in the ninth century but not into English until the sixteenth century when the first gardening books started appearing in England. These included John Gerard's *Herbal*, written in the 1633 and still used today. By contrast the earlier twenty-nine medieval Gaelic medical tracts in the National Library of Scotland make mention of Greek and Arab practices. Highland physicians studied in Paris and Bologna from the beginning of the twelfth century. These centres of learning were in turn developing the legacies of ninth-century Salerno, near Naples, where women were encouraged to study and distinctions of race, class and colour were irrelevant. The aim was to concentrate on preventative medicine in terms of lifestyle, diet and exercise. De-toxifying herbal teas were much in use.

Jacqui Hazzard is concerned with growing, drying, mixing and prescribing herbal cures in the form of teas, compounds and creams at her dispensary where she specialises in gynaecological treatments. 'Best breast tea', for instance, 'produces an abundant flow of rich milk infused with dill and fennel to lessen colic in baby'. While raspberry leaf tea 'restores tone to the female system'. For PMT, Jacqui recommends a blend of motherwort and vervain to combat mood swings and cramps. Horsetail mineral tea (also containing nettle and sticky willy) combats structural fragility (osteoporosis) and fatigue during and after menopause. So cherished patches of what most gardeners would regard as pernicious weeds are cultivated with loving care. This accords with the principles of permaculture, an organic method of gardening, which is as much about growing people as growing gardens. Rudolph Steiner, an early pioneer of the philosophy, maintained that people are much healthier if they eat the right food and that by growing things without chemicals you end up with all the necessary minerals inside – which in turn increases your mental powers.

Where earlier physic gardens would have had raised beds, because the art of drainage had not been invented, here raised beds are used for other reasons. First, the method of construction uses curving walls of stone or wood that are lined with newspaper and cardboard to suppress weeds. On top of this is a thick layer of straw followed by a similar layer of manure. Compost is put on the top and seeds and plants can then be grown while the whole lot rots down into an incredibly rich loam. The other reason for these high raised beds is that Jacqui Hazzard, who suffered from polio as a child, was awarded two grants to create a garden that is easily accessible for the disabled. The old

Medicinal plants that most gardeners would consider weeds growing in Jacqui Hazzard's garden.

Jacqui Hazzard's scarecrow contemplates the peaceful surrounding hills of Strathtay.

traditional straight paths delineated with box hedges are giving way to curved, more organic shapes. The ancient gnarled espaliered apple trees seem to hunch their knobbly shoulders in amazement at their under-planting of lupins, brambles, foxgloves and nettles. An area is given over to ground elder, once imported into this country by Italian monks who used to cook it like spinach and eat it to cure their gout (hence its other name, 'bishopwort').

Patients are encouraged to wander around Jacqui's garden where they can enjoy a variety of sights including some contented chickens scratching amongst the raspberries. Day lilies grow inside their enclosure while a scarecrow in a pink gingham shirt presides over some new planting further down the sloping ground. Visitors can meditate in a spot that looks out of the garden towards an ancient burial mound where Scots pines surround a standing stone. The healing provided here is a holistic experience embracing the spiritual, emotional and physical – washed down with a cup of 'simple' tea.

Sandra Masson at Rubha Phoil Forest Garden and Herb Nursery, Armadale, Isle of Skye.

Home made tepee for climbers and herbs growing at Rubha Phoil.

Sandra Masson, it would seem, is continuing a long tradition of Hebridean herbal gardening at her Rubha Phoil Forest Garden at Armadale on the Isle of Skye. It has come a long way since she bought, unseen, the fifteen-acre peninsula with its ancient larch woods in 1983 from the laird, Lord Macdonald of the Isles.

Sandra wanted to live near mountains and sea and says that Skye is a magical island, which pulls people towards it, particularly 'strong women'. Rubha Phoil itself seems to attract people because of the energy generated by the ley lines running through it. Since starting the garden and herb nursery, Sandra has studied the Gaelic tradition of using plants to heal and the folklore attached to them. All the herbs in the nursery are labelled with their Gaelic names, the common English ones and explanations of their use and properties. She has some ingenious ways of looking after her plants without modern aids. To combat rabbits, she keeps cats. To get rid of slugs, she uses salt. And, by boiling up camomile, she makes a very effective spray against 'damping off' for seedlings. The silica in horsetail strengthens plant cells if sprayed onto the leaves and she makes her own fertiliser from comfrey.[3]

Run on the permaculture principle, the garden is totally organic and useful weeds are as celebrated as useful plants. Like Jacqui Hazzard, Sandra is a devotee of Rudolph Steiner and his belief in 'what you put in you get out'. Steiner also ascribed spiritual value to natural processes so that even bodily waste should be integrated into the natural cycle. Going further than just organic methods, he advocated crop planting in accordance with moon cycles, a principle that is followed at Rubha Phoil during seed-plantings.

Sandra and her partner Sam practise what they preach and live in an eco house that they built themselves from a kit. It is wooden and has no nails, and no mains services. A windmill generates electricity and water is collected from the roofs via gutters and pipes and stored in tanks. It has a compost toilet and a reed bed system for treating the waste, which in turn is used to fertilise the comfrey bed. There is an eco shower and a twenty-first century computer – this is Skye power.

Beyond the nursery, the garden and the growing spaces there is a woodland walk. It is well to smother your hands, wrists and neck with the Rubha Phoil special midge oil. Not only does it work, it smells delicious with its combination of tea tree, lavender and citronella mixed with an almond base oil. Ecologically protected as you follow the many meandering bark paths through the trees and stop to sit on the benches and seats strategically placed to admire the views of the sea and the hills, time slips away. Silver birch trees, ferns and wild honeysuckle grow next to oaks and rowans; it is peaceful and healing. Everything is recycled: there are squash and pumpkins growing in the compost heap that is covered with carpet. Fish boxes are used as beds and nasturtiums grow up fishing nets. Ropes and buoys are made into swings in the picnic area. In the wooden shop Sandra sells home-made herb lotions and oils as well as colourful salads containing flower petals, herbs and leaves. These are distributed by the Skye Organic Box Scheme and supplied to local restaurants. Herb teas for sale include one made from the bog myrtle; it works as

The Eco House on Skye illuminated by a rainbow.

a tonic and restorative to revive the spirits. In children it cures ill temper and in the old it aids poor memory and helps with confusion.

———— ❧ ————

Apart from records of royal gardens, it is the gardens of the powerful bishops, monasteries and religious houses that can tell us more about gardening from the twelfth century onwards. By the canon, '*De decimis hortorum*', it was decreed in 1269 that 'the tithes of gardens in cities and burghs should belong to the vicars, and that the tithes of gardens in villages wherein corn was cultivated should belong to the parson; but for other articles cultivated in such gardens the tithes should remain to the vicar'. From this it would seem that they were gardens attached to ordinary lay properties, but what 'other articles cultivated in such gardens' implies, is impossible to tell.

More information is available further afield. In Germany in the ninth century there was a flourishing tradition of monastery gardens at the time of the Emperor Charlemagne, who wrote his famous *Capitulare de Villis* as an instruction to his subjects on what they should be planting. The *Capitulare* is a plant list that includes herbs, fruit, vegetables and flowers. The herbs were further sub-divided into pot herbs, industrial herbs and nuts, pulses and roots, salads and physical herbs. The flowers at the head of the list were lily, rose and flag iris.

So what did these enclosed monastic gardens look like and what were their uses? Benedictine plans for the ideal layout of the monastery with enclosed gardens dating from

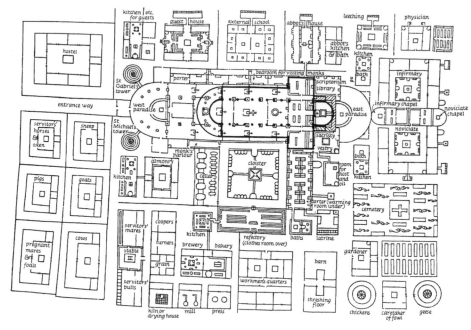

The ninth-century Benedictine's St Gall plan showing the ideal layout for a monastic garden.

the early ninth century are still preserved at St Gall in Switzerland and show a high degree of order. A series of walled gardens placed around the church included, in the centre, a cloister garden where the monks could walk and meditate. A physic garden and an infirmary cloister adjoined the infirmary; here, specialised plants and flowers were to be grown in separate beds intersected with paths for use by the apothecary and a peaceful space where convalescing monks could recover. At the west entrance to the church is shown an enclosed curved 'paradise' garden while the monks' cemetery doubled as an orchard surrounded by walls.

Sir Robert of Molesme, founder of the Cistercian order, encouraged his monks to study medicine, but as late as AD 1020, fear of contamination by the pagan superstitions associated with plants caused Burchard, Bishop of Worms, to warn his people that while they were harvesting 'medicinal herbs' they must keep their minds firmly focused on 'the creed and the paternoster'. St Bernard forbade any study of herbal medicine at all, in case the monks became tainted by paganism. He ordered only prayers and love for the healing of the sick, which must have been tough on the patient.

Not surprisingly, the first thirteen centuries AD saw little or no advance in medicine. The Christian religion had a strange idea that being sick was to do with being sinful, although the monks did feel moved to help the poor and needy with as much herbal care that they could muster along with generous dosages of prayer.

The great abbeys and monasteries of Scotland are well recorded and there are descriptions of their gardens and orchards. Place names also give a clue to where gardens most probably were situated. Indeed the island of Lismore, an ancient religious centre, is a classic example for Lismore itself means 'a big enclosure or garden'. A trawl through the place names of Scotland throws up plenty of examples: Luss, 'herb' (Luss is connected to the Celtic missionary Kessog who bought Christianity to the area around Loch Lomond in the sixth century); Liff, 'herb' (*lus* is Gaelic for herb; and Fs and Ss were often interchanged and spelling could frequently be erratic); Luffness, 'place full of little herbs'; Roslin, 'moor of hollies';[4] Rossie, 'rose place, shrubbery'; Garth and Gart, 'garden, enclosure'; Gartnavel, 'enclosure with apples'; and Glenluce, 'the glen of herbs'.

The Cistercian Abbey of Glenluce was founded in 1190. It had a twelve-acre garden and orchard, visited in 1507 by James IV who, it is recorded, gave four shillings to the gardener.

One monastic settlement that has remained almost untouched (albeit ruined) is Inchmahome Priory. Inchmahome means 'the isle of rest' or 'the island of my dear little Colman'. The island is, as one flowery-tongued Victorian visitor exclaimed, 'romantically embowered amid umbrageous, patriarchal trees'. Today's visitor to the tranquil and atmospheric island, while admiring the beauty of the ruined priory buildings, is also struck by the abundance of ancient and huge trees. Some have spectacular hollow trunks while others have tumbled over exposing the gnarled tracery of their roots that seem full of spirits and fairies. Most notably there are three sweet chestnuts which have been dated to the second half of the sixteenth century and are associated with places that were visited by Mary, Queen of Scots. The five-year-old Mary was brought to Inchmahome after the battle of Pinkie in 1547 and she spent three weeks there before being shipped off to France for safety.

Walter Comyn, first Earl of Menteith, founded the Augustinian Priory on his island of Inchmahome in 1238

as an ecclesiastical insurance policy for his afterlife. It was dedicated to St Colman, Bishop of Dromore, Co. Down – who had died around AD 500 – and was built on the site of earlier churches on the largest of the three islands on the Lake of Menteith.[5] The smallest, Inchcuan (the dog island) was involved in some way with the breeding of tenacious fox-killing terriers, which were famous enough to be sought by James VI.

Rather fancifully known as Queen Mary's bower, there is the remains of a boxwood-enclosed mount in the grounds where she is supposed to have gardened. Given her tender age and the brief period of her stay, it is much more likely that she gambolled there instead and as this mount faces the ruins of the Menteith stronghold on the third island of Inchtalla (Island of the great house), it could have been used for signalling or just for admiring the view. Tantalising traces now remain of the herb and medicinal gardens that there undoubtedly would have been alongside the infirmary where old or sick monks were housed and treated with herbal remedies. Then, the layout of the herb beds would have followed strict symmetrical rectangles and squares, so that anyone could be sent there by the physician to find ingredients for the tisanes and compounds with the instruction to 'look in the third bed on the top right-hand side'. After the reformation it was used as a pleasure garden by the Earls of Menteith, so what was where is hard to tell.

Another important area in a monastery garden was the orchard, which would contain both fruit and nut trees and often doubled as a burial ground for the monks. Some old fruit and nut trees are noted on the island by Thomas Hunter in his book *Woods, Forests, and Estates of Perthshire*, published in 1883. Fresh fruit was a ready source of vitamins and was made into various beverages, some alcoholic. Water could be contaminated and monks would be given a jug of home brew: cider from apples, perry from pears and liqueur from plums and cherries to drink with their meals. Preserves – made after the import of sugar in the eighteenth century – and jellies livened up the diet. Bees, kept in the orchard to

pollinate the blossom, produced honey for sweetening food and for the manufacture of mead and the mixture of whisky and honey known as Atholl brose. Whisky was widely used, flavoured with herbs, as a medicine.

Historic Scotland has made a detailed survey of the trees and, because no animals graze the island, there is continuous regeneration in progress with specimens planted from the sixteenth century right through to the present day. Among the oldest are the hazel that were used for 'coppicing'. This involved cutting down the trees at regular intervals to provide poles and sticks. These would be used for fencing and hurdles in the gardens and as supports for the vegetables and in basket making. As the monks on Inchmahome would have mostly eaten the fish and eel that inhabit the Lake of Menteith in great quantity, the hazel sticks would have been woven into fish traps as well.

The ruins of Inchmahome Priory on the Lake of Menteith.

In early summer the ruins at Inchmahome are decorated with the alpine purple fairy foxglove that has seeded itself into the crevices.

The ruins of the cloister garth [6] can be clearly seen adjacent to the church. In early summer the mellow grey stones are decorated all over with the small purple fairy foxglove, *Erinus alpinus*, that has seeded itself into the crevices. This plant is native to North Africa and southern Europe, showing that visitors had come from far afield. Medieval monastic gardens were highly organised and practical as well as having a spiritual and healing role to play. Inside the cloister was traditionally a green space surrounded by open stone corridors that linked the various buildings and provided a sheltered place in which to walk and meditate. Indeed, a journey around the cloister was compared to the 'journey through life', while the central space was invariably set out 'like the garden

of Eden'. In some cases a pond and four crossed paths dissected the green turfed area with little or no planting, symbolising the four rivers that flowed out of Eden and the four gospels contained in the New Testament. Around these the monks would sit and contemplate and pray. The light from the open space invaded the dark stone corridors of the monastery and this was referred to as 'God's light which lightens the darkness'. In the twelfth century, St Hildegard of Bingen points to the healing aspect or 'greening' power of the enclosure in a passage which could be justly applied to the whole island of Inchmahome:

> *… greening love hastens to the aid of all.*
> *With the passion of heavenly yearning,*
> *people who breathe this dew produce rich fruit.*

The perception that Scottish gardening is just a poor relation of the English version was obviously uppermost in the mind of James VI when he ordered an overhaul of the gardens at Holyrood in 1617 prior to his visit with the English court. He gave instructions that they be 'reformit with all expedition of maissons and wrycht wark in respect he wald be convayit and conducted to certain noblis of Ingland he wald let them know that this cuntrie was nothing inferior to thers in anie respect'.

James VI and his wife Anne of Denmark had embarked on a huge gardening programme at their palaces in and around London when he became James I of England in 1603. Anne was a prodigious spender and vast sums were lavished on gardens at Somerset House, Greenwich, and, for their son Prince Henry, at Richmond. They employed the help of Salomon de Caus, a French hydraulic engineer who delighted his clients with elaborate water effects and fountains influenced by the great Italian Renaissance gardens. Later Inigo Jones, back from travels in Italy, worked on Somerset House and St James's Palace, creating gardens of sculpture and allegory, while de Caus' younger brother Isaac created grottoes and more water works for the nobility, moving gardening into the realms of science and magic. So it was hardly surprising that James was worried that the simple 'yardis' at Holyrood might look old-fashioned or shabby.

The Stuarts were related to all the great gardening royal families of Europe. Henry VIII's sister Margaret Tudor had married James IV in 1503 in the famous marriage of the 'Thrissil and the Rose'.[7] Henry's garden-building at Hampton Court, Nonsuch[8] and Whitehall were on a stupendous scale. So James lost no time in upgrading the gardens at Stirling Castle and much preparation was made for his Tudor bride:

In his gardens there he planted vast numbers of fruit trees of various kinds, and vines which were cultivated by his French gardener. Herbs of various kinds were brought from several places, and seeds of different kinds of vegetables were occasionally bought for them. Here also the King formed fishponds, and had live fish, namely, perches, trouts, pikes, etc., brought from Loch Leven and other waters and put into his ponds.

These gardens were said to rival the ones at Richmond Palace at the time. A painting in the Smith Art Gallery, Stirling, by J. Vosterman shows extensive gardens around Stirling Castle in the time of the Stuarts in the 1670s. The King's Knot Garden below Stirling Castle can still be seen in outline and at its centre there would most probably have been a mount with a banqueting hall – not as grand as the three-storey one that his brother-in-law Henry had made at Hampton Court, but probably decorated with symbols of the heraldry so beloved of the age.

References to royal gardens go back further. Edinburgh Castle has the earliest, dating from the twelfth century describing gardens that stretched down along Stables Wynd, up until the seventeenth century. In 1128 the king, David I, granted a charter to the Abbey of Holyrood '…with another land which lies below the castle, viz: from the well which rises next to the corner of my garden, by the road which goes to the church of St Cuthbert …' The King's Garden[9] lay to the south and west of the castle,

with the kitchen garden roughly where Johnston Terrace is now situated. The great orchard known as Orchardfields[10] contained not just fruit trees but fishponds, rabbit warrens and doocots and was also used for events such as tilting competitions and entertainments for visiting dignitaries. The area stretched out towards the king's farm at Dalry where the border was the north side of Morrison Street. Castle Barns and King's Stables were, literally, the granaries where grain from the farm was stored and the stables for the King's horses.

There are records of the King's Garden at the Castle of Elgin in 1261 during the reign of Alexander III :

… concerning the garden of the lord king and the land pertaining to the said garden; to which garden and land Robert Spinc of Elgin and Margaret his wife have a right and claim tenancy, that they may enjoy the same peacefully; rendering herbs and aleam [onions] to the household of the lord king while he resides in the castle of Elgin …

The Palace of Linlithgow was built in 1425 by James I on a site in royal use since David I's time. Little is known about the gardens. However, additions were made by James III, who continued the cultured European pursuits of the Stuart kings and was described by the historian Robert Lindsay of Pitscottie as 'delighting more in music and policie [pleasure grounds] and building' than in the governing of his kingdom, so the terraces to the north overlooking the loch (as described by a visitor in 1480) could have been made by his orders. More building went on under James IV and again under James V, who ordered the King's fountain for the forecourt of his birthplace and that also of his daughter, Mary, Queen of Scots.

Mary's first mother-in-law, when she married the Dauphin of France in 1558, was Catherine de Medici. The Medicis' power and wealth in their native Florence made them powerful patrons of the arts and the creators of Renaissance gardens. Catherine was one of the great gardeners in sixteenth-century France. In 1600, Marie de Medici married Henri IV and together they created gardens of marvel at Fontainebleau and St Germain-en-Laye.

The ruined abbey at the Palace of Holyrood House, Edinburgh.

Mary's grand-daughter Elizabeth of Hanover presided over the creation of one of Europe's grandest gardens, the Hortus Palatinus in Heidleberg, laid out by de Caus in 1613. Generations of royal gardeners spanning the continent of Europe linked Italy, France, England, Denmark and Germany with Scotland. The cross-fertilisation of ideas, plants and gardeners was immense.

Holyrood became the principal royal palace in 1503 and it is there, in the sixteenth and seventeenth centuries, that Scottish gardening rose to prominence. The gardens were looked after by the monks at the abbey until the time of James IV, and throughout the sixteenth and early seventeenth centuries there is evidence of much gardening activity with great flurries of effort being expended

for royal marriages and events. As at Stirling, James IV undertook massive building and gardening works in preparation for his marriage to Margaret Tudor in 1503 at the abbey. Accounts for the period just before mention Sir John Scharpe 'who makis the garding in Edinburgh by the King's command'. He continued doing so for James V also. He drained the loch beside the abbey to make more room 'for the garding to be maid' and organised work on the Lion 'Yardis' where in common with other royal households, they kept lions, tigers and 'strange spotted beasties'.[11] Scharpe gardened for John Stewart, Duke of Albany who governed Scotland until James V took over at the age of sixteen when, like his father, he too made much of the gardens before his marriage to Madeleine de Valois, importing more French gardeners and craftsmen to Holyrood.

James V's second marriage, to Marie de Guise, continued the Franco–Scottish alliance, but this cultural age was bought to an abrupt end by the English invasions, with their scorched-earth policies in 1544 and 1547 and the ravaging of Holyrood. The kingdom was put in order fairly quickly afterwards and two regents acted for the child Queen Mary: the Earl of Arran and subsequently Marie de Guise.[12] At this time, John Ochter was the gardener at Holyrood and after him Johnne Morisoun, who was charged with providing daily two servants for 'rewling [rolling] and dressing' of the said yards [gardens] and to find 'caill [kale or greens], herbis and sellatis to oure soverane ladyis'. It is interesting to note that Morisoun spent a lot of his time providing produce and services for Arran's own estate gardens and these were regularly charged up to the royal accounts. In 1558 the fishponds were drained and the Dean's garden was purchased for £20 to add to the other 'yardis' – the privy gardens, Queen's garden and the King's orchard or garden.

When Mary, Queen of Scots returned to Scotland in 1561, her principal residence was the Palace of Holyrood. For the next six years she used the gardens here and at Stirling

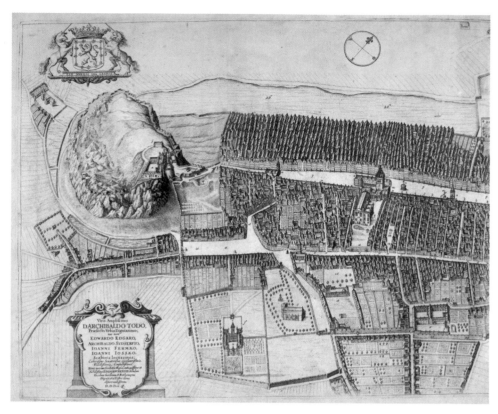

James Gordon of Rothiemay's plan of Edinburgh, 1647 published by De Wit in 1695, showing the gardens around the Castle (Trustees of the National Library of Scotland).

for previously unheard-of festivals, fêtes and picnics – the taste for which she would have acquired in France – to the amazement of the locals. Jousting, tournaments and hawking, hunting and archery, tennis, bowls and billiards all feature in accounts of the gardens. Mary's gardener was called Williame Broune and he looked after all her gardens between the palace and the Leith gate in the north as well as those on the west and east. Johnne Morisoun returned to look after the south orchards, which provided space for both food and recreation.

Following the Union of the Crowns in 1603, the gardens were maintained by the Crown and so they flourished into the 1640s. Gordon of Rothiemay's plan[13] in 1647 shows extensive knot gardens, orchards, walks and allées and it is known that the layout for Pitmedden Garden in Aberdeenshire was taken from some of the Holyrood parterres. This plan shows the palace and gardens before the disastrous sacking and fire inflicted by Cromwell's troops in 1650. Charles II reconstructed the palace buildings in 1671 and they remain much the same today.

The decline of the gardens would appear to date from the second half of the seventeenth century and it seems that this

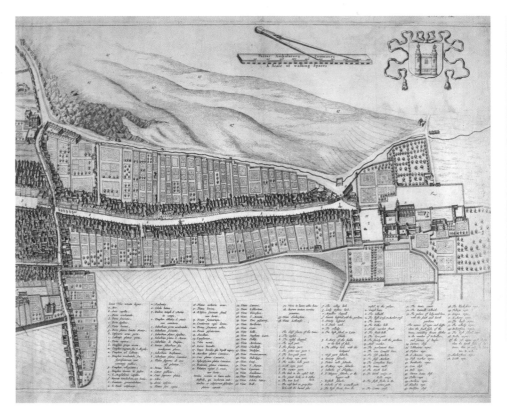

The head gardener at Holyrood, Alan Keir, now known as the 'service manager'.

A section of Gordon's map of Edinburgh showing the extensive gardens around Holyrood in the seventeenth century.

neglect carried on for the next two hundred years until Prince Albert re-designed and created the present-day gardens in 1857. His overall plan has changed little over the last century and a half, apart from a rockery extended by King George VI here, and a seat for the present Queen, there. Her Majesty takes a positive interest, but the recent changes in planting and maintenance are dictated by financial injections – steadily diminishing and now no longer the responsibility of the crown – from Historic Scotland. Gardeners are down to five, from the fifteen that looked after the gardens twenty years ago. The head gardener, Alan Keir, a highly trained and dedicated veteran of twenty-four years in the job, is now described officially as the Service Manager. Will royal garden parties henceforth be known as 'Service Parties'?

What is left at Holyrood is a pleasing but inappropriate Victorian garden, in the most dramatic location. Its sole purpose now is to surround a lawn big enough to give a garden party twice a year. It would be fitting to restore part of it in keeping with the building and the history – after all its new neighbours have spent £18 million landscaping their four-acre plot around the new Scottish Parliament building. [14]

Science was gaining ground and medicine was split into three different disciplines, producing a rivalry between physicians, surgeons and apothecaries. An effort to reconcile them into one body led Sir Robert Sibbald, together with fellow physician and botanist Andrew Balfour, to create the first Edinburgh Botanic Garden [15] in 1670, at Holyrood. Sibbald had studied medicine at both Leiden and Paris, while Balfour had studied at Caen in France.

Edinburgh was already renowned for its advances in medicine. Although mainly

a garden of 'simples' to aid the teaching of medicine, the new physic garden included many other plants to create a visual 'encyclopaedia', in an effort to encourage the craft of gardening in Scotland generally. The Chelsea Physic Garden was made three years later in London. Closely associated with the Society of Apothecaries, it too was mainly a garden of simples and Adam was referred to as 'the great simpler'. John Evelyn, gardener and diarist, states that 'without some tincture in Medicine' gardening lost its purpose. A great muddling up of religion, science and nature seemed to be going on. Many believed that the value of the botanic garden in studying and collecting every plant that God had created would, because a part of God was revealed in each creation, reveal God himself.

Work in the botanics was likened to Adam as the gardener in God's own paradise. There was a widespread

The lawns at Holyrood have to be large enough for the Royal garden parties.

Christ shows himself as Adam the Gardener after the Resurection. Print of David's 'Duodecim Specula', 1610.

feeling that it would be through studying nature, 'the work of God', that knowledge would be gained, rather than by studying the Bible.[16] William Prynne wrote that 'if Bibles faile each garden will descry the works of God to us', while the *Anthracius Botanophilus* told of 'kind nature always having held forth her Book'.

The sixteenth and seventeenth centuries marked the beginnings of modern scientific studies and botany was no exception. With the discovery of America, a new continent had been added to the map of the world that previously had depicted only three. Columbus and his fellow explorers had failed to find the earthly paradise of Eden, but instead they found new plants to bring back to Europe – including the potato. The age-old layout of gardens as four squares now seemed more logically to represent these four continents, as they had done in ancient Persian gardens. A famous fête in the Boboli Gardens outside Florence, in 1661, represented the four continents in its 'Atlas' theme with the participants costumed to represent Europe, Africa, Asia and America, while statues of the European horse, the Asian camel, the African leopard and the American parrot are amongst those in the gardens of Versailles. There were those who thought that God had withheld the discovery of America at the creation until man was good enough to merit the fruits, flowers and beasts it contained.

So the Garden of Eden became translated into a quest to gather examples of everything growing in the four continents and bring them together within the sheltering walls of one garden. As G. Porro, author of *L'horto de i semplici de Padova* (1591), said of the first botanic garden at Padua, they were 'collecting the whole world in a chamber', creating an encyclopaedia of creatures, plants and fruits in imitation of the original Eden and as Noah tried to do in his ark. Religion and gardens met science and so the motivation to create the early botanical gardens was born. Milton describes them in *Paradise Lost*:

> *Whatever Earth all-bearing mother yields*
> *In India east or west, or middle shore*

And:

> *The Indies for the Balm and Spice*
> *Rifle the treasures of old Paradise*

The small forty-foot-square plot at Holyrood had around nine hundred plants crammed into it, so that within a decade it not only expanded into the King's garden nearby but also found a larger space (where Waverley Station is now) next to the Trinity Hospital. Unfortunately, for the seemingly hard-working but underpaid keeper James Sutherland, this was badly flooded and largely desecrated when the Nor' Loch was drained during the siege of Edinburgh Castle in 1689. Sutherland struggled on and later the whole garden was moved to a new site.

Founded by Sir John Hope in 1760, the new garden occupied five acres in the area between Annandale Street and Macdonald Road, backing onto Hopetoun Crescent, at the very edge of the New Town. There were once rows of elm trees adorning Leith Walk, much admired by the great architect William Playfair who described the developments taking place at the upper end of the street during the 1820s as 'a happy union of foliage and building'. However, as the final buildings of Edinburgh's Georgian New Town encroached, the stock was removed to the site of the present Royal Botanic Garden at Inverleith in the same year. Maybe Playfair was referring to this event, described in Sir Henry Steuart's *Planters Guide*[17] published in 1828. Steuart writes of the trees progress from Leith Walk, 'some of them from thirty to forty feet high', through Edinburgh:

In removing the Trees,[18] *owing to the immense friction, occasioned by the lowness of the wheels, ten and twelve horses were occasionally employed; so that the procession through the suburbs for many days, consisting of men, and horses, and waving boughs, presented a spectacle that was at once novel and imposing. The citizens of Edinburgh were surprised and delighted with the master of an Art, which seemed more powerful and persuasive than the strains of Orpheus, in drawing after it, along their streets, both grove and underwood of such majestic size.*

The Physic Garden at Trinity Hospital, Edinburgh.

Sir Henry Steuart's 'tree moving machine' from Steuart's Tree Planter's Guide, *1828.*

PLATE III.

VIEW OF THE MACHINE IN MOTION, AND OF
A TREE DURING TRANSPORTATION.

The only remaining link with Sir John Hope's garden is the quaint head gardener's cottage on Shrub Place. Today the Royal Botanic Garden in Edinburgh ranks as one of the most comprehensive and important in the world. It includes woodlands, an arboretum, demonstration gardens, peat gardens, water, rock, and alpine gardens, together with definitive collections of plants and rhododendron species growing outside. Two huge palm houses built in the nineteenth century contain massive collections of exotics under glass. A library of more than 100,000 books and a vast collection of dried botanical specimens all draw in a million visitors each year.

Water Garden at the Royal Botanic Garden, Edinburgh.

The Palm House, Royal Botanic Garden, Edinburgh.

Notes

1. One Scotch acre = 6150.5 square yards.

2. Serpentine, which was believed to catch more sunlight.

3. Two kilos of leaves mixed with twenty litres of water which you close with a lid and leave for six to eight weeks before using the liquid.

4. The Scots word for holly is 'hollins'; 'lin' or 'lan' is also used for enclosure.

5. Various crannogs have been discovered in the lake that is whimsically the only stretch of water in Scotland not called a loch. In fact it is marked on old maps as Laich of Menteith, which means the 'lower land', a name often given to low-lying boggy places, but it later became anglicised, Laich becoming Lake.

6. The word cloister comes from the Latin *claustium* – a closed-in place.

7. Scotland does not have a monopoly on the thistle, since they are amongst the most ancient of known plants used for food and for medicine and they appear in Greek and Roman writing as well as in Scottish heraldry. However, the thistle was the cap badge of the House of Stuart and this humble plant came to be regarded as the emblem of Scotland when, in 1458, it was depicted on an embroidered banner for James III. The 1503 phrase 'The Thrissill and the Rose' was in turn followed by the creation of the 'Order of the Thistle' in 1540, by James V. There is a debate as to which thistle is the true 'Scotch' one, but it is generally accepted that it is the cotton or woolly thistle (*Onopordon acanthium*). Others argue that it is the melancholy thistle (*Carduus heterophyllus*) as this variety is more common in Scotland than in England and, what is more, Culpeper swore that: 'being drank expels superfluous melancholy out of the body and makes a man as merry as a cricket' – which would seem as good a reason as any for choosing it.

8. So called because 'none such' wonder had ever been seen before …

9. Later uses for these gardens are discussed in Chapter 8.

10. Bread Street was formally known as Orchardfield Place and Orchardfield Street became Spittal Street.

11. Somewhat comically, it was across this yard that the earls of Atholl, Bothwell and Huntly fled, Errol Flynn-like, after climbing out of a window following the murder of Riccio, secretary of Mary, Queen of Scots.

12. Marie de Guise mainly lived in lodgings further along the Royal Mile but would have overseen the gardens at the palace.

13. The plan was drawn for the Town Council by James Gordon in 1647 and engraved by W & J Blaeu in Amsterdam, 1649. After Blaeu's death in 1673, the engraved plates which had survived the fire at his business in 1672 were sold in auction. The plate was acquired by Frederick de Wit and published in 1695. Subsequent editions with revisions and alterations have appeared, mostly published by Andrew Johnston between 1709 and 1719.

14. See Epilogue.

15. The first complete botanic gardens were founded at the University of Padua, which served the thriving trading city of Venice, in 1545 and around the same time at Pisa in Italy. There were many more that followed, including Leiden in Holland (in 1587) and Robin's and the Jardin du Roi in Paris (both founded in 1626). Meanwhile, in England, herbalist John Gerard's attempts to persuade the University of Cambridge to establish one during the same period came to nothing. In

1621 the Earl of Danby founded the Oxford Botanic Garden and by 1658 this was growing 2,000 plants of which only 600 were English.

16. 'Restore to us in part what Adam knew before.'

17. 'This is in every way a very valuable and meritorious work; abounding with curious learning and ingenious remarks, but still more full of practiacal information, useful precepts, and necessary cautions, delivered with an earnestness, copiousness, and precision, that must recommend them to readers everywhere.'

Sir Walter Scott: Book review in The Edinburgh Review, *vol.49 (1829).*

18. Sir Henry invented a 'tree moving machine' which is illustrated in his book and reproduced here.

CHAPTER TWO

Grand Designs

The garden at Kinross House.

GRAND DESIGNS

'Delicat gardine with walls sumptuously built of hewen stone polisht, with pictures and coats of armes in the walls, with a fine summer house with a hous for a bath on the south corners thereof far exceeding any new work of thir times. Excellent Kitchine gardine[1] and orcheard with diverse kynds of most excellent fruits and most delict … It is an extrordinaire warme and ear place so that the fruits will be readie there a fourthnight sooner than in any place of the shyre.' OCHTERLONY OF GUYND[2]

It is difficult to know where to place the garden that survives at Edzell in Angus. Although it was built in 1604, it is really part of a building programme that was begun in the middle of the previous century. Often described by writers as unique, this uniqueness lies more in its survival than in its building, although none with such elaborate stone carvings have been noted anywhere else,

outside royal palaces. I suspect that there were others like it but, like wallpaper, the fashion changed and new ideas came along that superseded the old. Many houses built at the time had courtyard gardens attached to them with banqueting houses or summer houses incorporated into the corners. These privy gardens, or *jardins clos*, provided just that: a private place to walk and talk outwith the sometimes overcrowded interiors of the house. Bath houses too were not uncommon, while sundials were very common indeed as centrepieces in gardens of this period. Maybe some had grottoes and elaborate mechanical fountains, as was the fashion on the continent, although most writers seem to agree that it took far longer for the Renaissance garden ornament to reach our shores. Roy Strong[3] asserts that as this cra was coming to a close around 1570 across the English Channel, it was just beginning in England. So what was happening in Scotland?

Architectural historian, Charles McKean[4] makes a compelling case for the lively and artistic Renaissance court of James V and his second wife, Mary of Guise, during the first half of the sixteenth century. Sir David Lindsay, the builder of the garden at Edzell, had travelled widely and was largely educated in Europe in the second half of the sixteenth century; he would have observed at first hand the prevailing garden ideas there. A contemporary of James VI, he was a Templar and a scholar, the embodiment of the cultured and aesthetic gentleman. This garden was made at the beginning of James VI and I's reign when religious belief was in turmoil, torn between Catholic and Protestant. The

The ruined Edzell Castle with walled garden and parterre.

The banqueting house in the corner of the walled garden at Edzell. The box hedging is clipped into the mottoes of the Lindsays – DUM SPIRO SPERO (While I breathe I hope) and ENDURE FORTE (Endure Firmly).

fascination with sundials, the symbolic shapes of hearts, crescents, suns and circles, the importance of astrology, geometry, religion, the arts and science and their relationship to nature and therefore gardens, is hard to fathom in the twenty-first century. That Lindsay's Mannerist-style garden was at the heart of all this there is no doubt, he so incorporated his beliefs and ancestry into the decorations. He placed carvings of the Planetary Deities on one wall, while representations of the Liberal Arts decorate another. A third wall contains a more Christian message – the Cardinal Virtues. Some are missing, some have been restored and there would have been more images as well with statues in the niches. Maybe some would have been placed in between the carvings that were divided into compartments by 'clasped pilasters'. But if you look at the clasped pilasters that are on the north side of the Palace of Stirling[5] you will see an uncanny similarity. It would not be unreasonable to suppose that similar statues stood on the top of the Edzell pilasters. Speculation as to what they were like and also about the exact use of the 'fess chequy' – the armorial device of the Lindsays, represented in chequered recesses in the walls – continues.

Raised and recessed devices, as well as the imagery in the carving, also bear a marked resemblance to those at Stirling. Imagine how all these stone features would have stood out when the walls were harled and lime-washed, as they would have been when originally built. Above the squares are carved stars (pierced with holes thought to be for nesting birds), another heraldic symbol, indicating a third son, from the Lindsay coat of arms. They

Carvings of the Planetary Deities, the Liberal Arts and the Cardinal Virtues decorate the walls at Edzell.

are also the seven-pointed stars of the Knights Templar. Another interpretation for the stars, though, lies in Roman mythology, where the presence of stars showed that the gods were smiling on your enterprise. So how can we read these? The simple answer would be heraldry, because that was an important part of gardens of the period, but maybe it is more complicated. The profoundly spiritual approach of Mannerist garden design explored nature with a view to learning about the divine, so different interpretations can be placed on the allegorical features at Edzell. These Mannerist gardens were hymns to the new sciences.

It would be logical to assume that in the centre of the garden there would have been a raised sundial or fountain, again with symbolic carving. Could there have been a labyrinth of clipped box around it? The fourth, plain wall may well have had a covered arbour running down its length, again a favourite from medieval times. Sometimes these were built with osiers (willows) that supported climbing fruits and flowers. The other walls are so 'decorated' that it would be strange to leave one completely bare. Maybe the bath house was in fact a grotto, decorated with shells and nymphs … Dreams are free, but Lindsay died with debts – some suggest because of the garden, but more plausible is the age-old and, in his case, documented, problem of bailing out his son and heir from legal entanglements.

During the same decade – in 1611 – Sir George Bruce moved into his fine new house, Culross Palace. Although this was indeed a grand house for the period, the use of the word palace or place simply defined the building as a 'courtyard house' rather than bestowing any grand rank on the occupant. For at least fifty years before Lindsay and Bruce, gentlemen's residences were being built with privy gardens attached. They would have been quite like Edzell. Charles McKean describes Melgund in Angus, the house built by Cardinal David Beaton in 1543 for Marion Ogilvy, his mistress and the mother of his many children:

Approximately U-plan, this house has a tower at the west end, a palace block in the middle and a projecting wing with a circular tower containing an oratory at the east end.

It was once magnificent. A walled garden lay to the east, and a garden stair led up to Marion Ogilvy's chamber.

McKean's convincing demolition of the concept that the architecture of buildings of the sixteenth and seventeenth centuries were for defence throws much light on the gardens that would have been attached to these Renaissance châteaux. In the nineteenth and twentieth centuries, pundits all averred that they would not have had gardens because they were defensive. If you redefine the architecture as a style and the use as purely domestic, the gardens too make sense.

As Edzell is one of the few remaining examples intact, it was considered a curiosity rather than the norm. Marion Ogilvy's first-floor entrance at Melgund was not uncommon, but previously, where they were found, they were believed to be defensive. Many houses of this period had wooden balconies overlooking the garden, entered from upper floors as well as by stairs from the garden. Viewing pavilions and platforms were not confined to garden corners, but were deliberately built on the tops of the towers so that a good view could be had of the policies and yards. When Hugh, Lord Somervill, went to live in his mad elder brother's tower at Carnwath in Lanarkshire, he was embarrassed by 'the barenesse of the tower of Carnwath, having noe planting, yea, not soe much then as a kaill-yard'.

There are many more references to gardens of this period. A contemporary description of Balloch (later Taymouth

Castle Lyon (now Huntly) drawn by Slezer (RCAHMS).

Castle), built in 1559, the home of the infamous lairds of Breadalbane, says that it was 'environed by plantations and formal gardens'. The remains of terraces excavated next to early houses and castles such as Neidpath and Aberdour also show that elaborate gardens not only existed, but were integral to the plans for the house as a whole.

It seems extraordinary that today it is necessary to argue that these gardens existed. They were to be found all over Europe and in England so why was the perception that Scotland was so backward and uncivilised that it could do no better than a kail-yard before the seventeenth century? The educated Scot probably travelled as much as his English counterpart and brought home the fruits of his travels. The influences in Scotland were far more European than English. Just consider the number of Scots gardening terms that are the same in French.[6]

By the seventeenth century the building boom was gathering momentum and many more records are available about gardens. The middle classes were also embellishing their living spaces, with tradesmen and smaller lairds making houses and gardens in both town and country. The House of Partick was built in 1611 for Glasgow merchant George Hutcheson, founder of Hutcheson's Hospital. It was described as a 'very handsome house, well finished and adorned with curious[7] orchyards and gardens, stately avenues and large enclosures, sheltered with a great deal of planting so that it has become one of the sweetest seats upon the River Clyde in the shire'.

Apart from the relentless march of fashion, another reason why so few gardens of this period remain can be laid at the door of the Roundheads. There was wholesale destruction of both houses and gardens during the disastrous sacking and burning inflicted on estates by Cromwell and his troops when they invaded Scotland. In 1640,

John Spalding, Commissary Clerk of Aberdeen, wrote of the troops' destruction of Lord Banff's palace (later Duff House) in Banff: 'The soldiers fell quickly too to cutting and hewing down the pleasant planting and fruitful young trees, bravely growing within the laird of Banff's orchards and gardens (pitiful to see!) …' before moving on to destroy the 'haill houses'. The Earl of Argyll was organising similar acts of vandalism in Angus, while anything left was burnt and looted by the Covenanting General Baillie on his march into Atholl country.

Times, though, became more peaceful and we learn that in 1654 a Mr Thomas Stewart got married and retired to Coltness in Lanarkshire, where he 'set himself to planting and enclosing, and so to embellish the place'. Having made many new rooms and outbuildings he made:

A high front wall towards the east, with an arched entry or porch, [which] enclosed all … The gardens were to the south of the house, much improved and enlarged; and the nursery-garden was a small square enclosure to the west of the house. The slope of the grounds to the west made the south garden, next the house fall into three cross terraces.

Stewart laid out parterres with a strawberry border down one side and an orchard of cherries, walnuts and chestnut trees. Further orchards and a kitchen garden had a 'high stone-wall on the south, for ripening and improving finer fruits'. Even the fishponds 'for pikes and perches' were enclosed with 'a strong wall and hedgerows of trees'.

McKean reckons that he can identify the remains of a thousand 'seats' built in Scotland between 1500 and 1680, but asks, 'How many more were built of which no trace remains?' Gardens disappear faster than houses. The first Jacobite uprising of 1715 was to have a curious effect on many of the fine gardens made in the seventeenth century. Anyone who was proved to have been a supporter of the Old Pretender had their property forfeited and such properties were put up for sale, with many being bought by the York Building Company.[8] Edzell was one of these, its assets stripped by the company; John Macky, travelling through Scotland in 1723, records others – such as the palaces of Seaton, Penmure and Winton – where the houses were empty but 'where the spacious gardens were well kept having been let out to a gardener'.[9] He visited Alloa, where the disgraced Earl of Mar had made magnificent gardens; today there is no trace, as the town of Alloa is built where the gardens once were.

The Plantation round the House of Alloway, is the largest, and the finest, laid out by the unhappy Earl that commanded in the Rebellion, of any in Britain; it far exceeds either Hampton-Court, or Kensington; the Gardens consisting of Two and Forty Acres; and the Wood, with Vistoes [sic] cut through it, of One Hundred and Fifty Acres.

Macky goes on to describe parterres, from which 'you have Thirty Two different Vistoes, each ending on some remarkable Seat or Mountain, at some Miles Distance', terraces, ornamental ponds, statues, wildernesses and grottoes. Drummond Castle in Perthshire was another forfeited estate where the gardens were let out as a nursery by the York Building Company.

For the general public, however, gardening was on the rise and many would have made use of John Reid's book *The Scots Gard'ner*[10] that had been published in 1683 and was the first of its kind in Scotland. Reid liked order and his often-quoted passage about placing the house in the centre of the garden 'as the nose the centre of the face' with 'all the Walks, Trees and Hedges running to the House' was certainly being carried out at Kinross House.

The owner and architect of Kinross House and gardens, Sir William Bruce, was born in 1630 during the turbulent period in Scottish history when Charles I was on the throne. After the overthrow of Cromwell, Bruce was rewarded for his royalist sympathies with a knighthood and the post of Surveyor-General, or Master of the King's Works. As such he was responsible for the re-building of Holyrood Palace between 1671 and 1679, which had been sacked by Cromwell's troops. Bruce bought the Kinross Estate in

Carving on the Fish Gate, Kinross House, showing the different species of fish swimming in Loch Leven.

1675. What is significant is the fact that Bruce designed and built the garden layout at Kinross before he built the house. From 1679 he was enclosing, draining, levelling and planting the gardens and the rides.

Loch Leven at this time was higher than it is now and the water would have been almost up to the elaborately carved Fish Gate in front of the 'jettie for the bierge'. In common with the great gardens of this age, Bruce designed parterres, fruit gardens, a bowling green, 'Bow Butts' (for archery), a boat house, ice house, kitchen garden, nursery, a 'Bletcherie in Weemen's Court' (bleaching green in the women's enclosure), a mill and a hay yard. In one drawing there is provision too for an amphitheatre, a 'Jouet court' (for tennis), kitchen bath court and 'closets'. Today many of Bruce's vistas from the central part of the garden are obscured by mature trees but originally, wherever you walked, the eye would have been led to a distant point in the park.

The influence on the great Scottish gardens at this time came very much from France where the great designer Le Nôtre was creating the formal gardens at Versailles in the second half of the seventeenth century. The philosophy was that the elaborate formality was part of a single composition that included the house while reflecting the wealth and the control of the environment by the owner. Bruce was not only the most important Scottish architect of his day, but also the most talented garden designer, and he fully understood the need to integrate the design of the house and the garden. By using Loch Leven Castle as the focal point of the garden vista, apart from introducing

*The view from the front of the house through the garden to the Fish
Gate and onto Loch Leven Castle on the island.*

a romantic element, he was also linking the house and garden to the wider landscape – thus creating a unified composition of the whole. If you stand on the roof of Kinross House and turn 360 degrees, it is possible to appreciate the massive scale of this design and its perfect proportions. As you enter the gates at the top of the avenue (which measures '1434 foots long and 120 broad'), if the front door of the house is open, it is possible as you drive down to see through a corresponding door on the other side of the house. The line continues right down the centre of the garden, through the Fish Gate, across the water to Loch Leven Castle, all in perfect alignment. It is the ultimate example of 'borrowing' the landscape and setting the house and garden within it, which is the job of every good garden design.

In 1681 Bruce's son John started sending him boxes of plants, roots, shrubs and seeds from Paris. The first box contained slender laurel, *Lychnis hirsuta*, double jonquils and ranunculus. The horse chestnut trees that Sir William had requested could not be sent at first because, as John wrote, the trees were 'verie dear' and difficult to transport, and also because 'the nuts are verie scarce this year'. Added in the box were detailed instructions to Sir William and his gardener James Shanks on how to grow and maintain all these rare treasures. Later he sent single anemone roots, seeds of amaranthus and double poppy seeds in many colours for the parterre. Finally a 'little barrel' arrived with 300 horse chestnut conkers packed in sand and the instruction: 'They must be presentlie set in the places where you have a mind to have them grow; they take best with a hot sandy soil.' One of these trees still stands at Kinross, although over the years many more have been planted.

Bruce's life, however, was to be changed by the 'Glorious Revolution' in 1688. His Jacobite sympathies and allegiances caused his arrest and he was imprisoned first in Stirling Castle and later in Edinburgh Castle. While in the latter, he signed over the Estate of Kinross to his son John in 1708, but he only survived for another two years and died in 1710.

Kinross House passed to the Graham family, who purchased it in the late eighteenth century, and via a Graham daughter to the Montgomery family, into which she married, who still own the house today. The house stood empty between 1819 and 1881 and it was Sir Basil Montgomery who began the restoration of the house and the re-making of the gardens in 1902. His influence on the gardens can be clearly seen in the temples he added and the layout, but Sir William Bruce would have no trouble finding his way around as his original plan was quite closely followed and still dominates. The fine ogee-roofed pavilions

James and Lizzie Montgomery, the current owners of Kinross House.

Daniel Defoe described Kinross House as 'the most beautiful and regular piece of architecture … in all Scotland, perhaps in all Britain'.

from 1686, the two Doric summer seats and the Fish Gate still provide focal points for the walks and cross axis. The gardens and policies remain the perfect complement to what Daniel Defoe[11] described as 'the most beautiful and regular piece of architecture [for a private gentleman's seat] in all Scotland, perhaps in all Britain'.

'Studiously avoid the manner that is mean and pitiful, and always aim at that which is grand and noble', wrote John James in his translation of *The Theory and Practice of Gardening*, published in 1712. Amongst the list of subscribers to the first edition was the first Duke of Atholl. James Murray, the second Duke, who began landscaping in 1732, would have read this book in his library at Blair Castle in Perthshire, while

James Murray, second Duke of Atholl, who created the Hercules Garden in 1744.

Blair Castle: statue of
Hercules, by John Cheere
of London.

he was creating landscapes in the style of the *ferme ornée*. In 1744 he had completed the Hercules Walk and begun work on the walled garden. Covering nine acres, it was ten years in the making and now, two hundred and fifty years later, it has taken ten years to restore what is probably the largest walled garden under cultivation in Scotland today.

Painstaking research by Christopher Dingwall of the Garden History Society and a partnership consisting of the Atholl Estates, Scottish Conservation and Scottish Enterprise came together to fulfil this ambitious project, originally started by Ian Murray, the tenth Duke. After his death, his half sister Sarah Troughton inherited the restoration along with responsibility for the Blair Trust, which runs the castle (visited by 130,000 each year), a private army and 140,000 acres. Two world wars, crippling death duties in 1917 and an unsuccessful attempt at using it as a market garden in the 1940s, resulted in a fate common to many such gardens

in the 1950s – the dreaded Christmas-tree plantation. Unfortunately no one bothered to harvest them, so that by 1980 this extraordinary creation was virtually obliterated by thousands of thirty-foot Norway spruce trees.

The history of the gardens at Blair in a way reflects the history of grand-scale gardening generally in Britain. Walled gardens attached to houses were in the main swept away in the eighteenth century and vistas and rides created to connect to the wider landscape. As a focal point for one of the main 'walks' that he instructed his gardener John Wilson to construct, Duke James bought the statue of Hercules (a copy, executed by John Cheere of London, of the Roman original at the Palazzo Farnese) for twenty-five pounds. When you reach the statue you can look down on what was a wet meadow to the north of this walk. This is the visitor's first glimpse of the 'surprise' garden, which James planned around the two huge ponds, containing a series of

Blair Castle: view of the ponds in the Hercules Garden.

Blair Castle: a few of the remaining statues in the garden.

islands and peninsulas. Teams of men and women dug these by hand over several years. The peaty nature of the soil contained the water that was fed into them through stone-lined underground channels with the depths regulated by a system of sluices. Walls were built incorporating a head-gardener's house in the northwest corner and two small pavilions (one of which survives today as a potting shed) in the west wall. On the east wall was an alcove that was later replaced by McGregor's Folly: used over the years as a summer house and a curling house, it now houses a display on the history and restoration of the garden. A century later the north wall was rebuilt further out to make room for glasshouses and herbaceous borders, divided by yew buttresses.

Duke James, however, did not stop here. In 1752 he indulged the current passion for Chinoiserie[12] with brightly painted gates and 'Chinese Chippendale' railings together with a Chinese bridge designed by Abraham Swan in 1753. Just as fashionable, though, were the many statues he placed on the tops of the walls and around the garden. Some from John Cheere included a figure supporting a sundial, the 'four seasons' in marble, and seventeen lead figures brightly painted in natural colours – as was then the fashion – representing rustic and sailor folk, musicians and dancers. One anonymous visitor commented that

> *The gardens are not so curious as at the Duke's house at Dunkeld; but here are statues, which the other has not; which are, an Hercules, a Diana, Bacchus, and a Temple of Fame, filled on every side with bustoes of the ancient philosophers and poets; that of the Duke himself being placed in the middle, in lead gilt.*[13]

Classical representations of Mercury, Baccus and Pomona gazed across at theatricals such as Scaramouche, Harlequin and Columbine and two skaters were placed at the edge of the Hercules Pond. Along with dancing Highland lads and lassies inside, outside the walls a realistic gamekeeper firing a gun caused much comment.[14] It must have been an extraordinary sight that greeted the walker who arrived at the Hercules statue and looked down upon this very upmarket version of today's gnome gardens. On the islands were built 'swan houses' thatched with reeds to protect the swans' nests.

Sadly, few of the figures remain, but the Chinoiserie bridge and the original planting of the gardens have been carefully re-created in a simplified form. Rows of fruit trees, as shown in early plans, have been planted but they now grow in grass whereas before they would have been divided up with vegetables, soft-fruit beds and paths. The archives in the castle have produced lists of the plants and trees together with shipping notes from the Atholl estates and nurseries in the south of England. Along the gravel walks running around the garden were, and are again, borders edged with low box hedges containing 'many sorts of perennial flowers' backed by climbing roses and honeysuckle. These are filling up and it would seem that the Hercules Garden, begun by the second Duke and revived by the tenth, will again amaze and delight visitors and be, as Sir Robert Menzies described it in a letter in 1760, 'the garden of gardens' for the twenty-first century.

Andrew Hay of Craignethan wrote in his diary on 10 November 1659: 'Cam to Mellerstane, wher we met with Jerviswood,

The herbaceous border in the Hercules garden at Blair.

The re-created Chinoiserie bridge.

Jane and John Haddington, the present Earl and Countess.

who took us in and we took a drink with him. It is ane old melancholick hous that has had great buildings about it.'

Nothing now remains of this 'melancholick' house bought by the first George Baillie of Jerviswood in 1643. His grandson married Grisell Hume and a fascinating picture of their life can be gleaned from Lady Grisell's account books that cover the years 1692–1733 and record much building, including entries for a new kitchen and a bath house costing £65.4s. 4d. Her entries for the 'gardine' show her buying limes, yews, thorns, planes, elms, geans, firs, chestnuts, walnuts and fruit trees and there is one that reads: 'For young trees bought by John Hope which was a perfit cheat £2, 10s.' Vines are 'nailed up' for 1s. 8d. and seed is purchased for vegetables while flowers purchased include anemones, ranunculus, jonquils and tulips. A bowling green was laid out in 1710 and a peacock also acquired. Spades, hoes, forks, rakes, 'shuffels', a watering can, scythes, a 'roling ston' and

a '34 foot glass for hote beds' are listed, as are the wages of 'men to work with the garner at 5sh. per day'. In 1715, 300 lime trees and '90 frute trees' were shipped from 'Grenwich' in London to Berwick for a cost of 7 shillings. From Lady Grisell's 'Bill's of Fair' we learn that 'sallarly, spinach, peas, sparagrasse, bottoms of Raeteechocks and (presumably the same) Hartichokes' were on the menu. These would have come from the 'gardine' as did all manner of fruits and nuts that are mentioned.

Mellerstain passed via the marriage of Lady Grisell's second daughter to the Earls of Haddington, who still live there today. The old tower, much repaired according to Lady Grisell's accounts, was replaced, although the wings were retained when the present building was begun by

The grand sweep of lawn linking the terrace and the ornamental loch at Mellerstain.

William Adam in 1725 and completed by his son Robert a few years later.

If you want a lesson in grand landscape design, Mellerstain House is a good place to start. The strength and simplicity of the layout, started in the eighteenth century by Adam *père et fils* and consolidated by Reginald Blomfield at the beginning of the twentieth century, is testimony to 'good bones' being the basis of everything (forget about the plants – they can be replaced).

As houses go, they don't come much larger or more classical than this, but landscaping around such a powerful building must have been a challenge even to experienced landscape designers like the Adams. They laid out the parks with wide rides and designed a sloping three acres of grass down to a Dutch-inspired canal with raised grass walks and classical statues. As your eye is drawn down the valley and across the lake, you see the distant Cheviot hills via a folly halfway up the opposite hillside.

In 1909 Sir Reginald Blomfield was commissioned to create this lake[15] from the canal with terraces linking it to the house via a swooping six hundred yards of lawn. This was to be his grandest commission. He triumphed; the shape and area perfectly reflect the proportions of the house while anchoring it in the landscape.

As you come out of the south side of the house, the upper terrace is composed of lawn and clipped yew surrounded by balustrades. Descending via a divided staircase over the roof of a pillared loggia, you reach a second and larger terrace which is laid out as a parterre with gravel paths and box hedges containing roses – Bonica, Little White Pet, Cardinal Hume and Rose de Rescht – and catmint (*Nepeta mussini*). Stone butresses divide up a mixed herbaceous and shrub border. This planting scheme was done by the present Earl and Countess of Haddington to replace the vivid red and yellow hybrid tea roses planted by the previous (twelfth) Countess. They retained her planting at the front of the house in the border running along it, containing old-fashioned roses: centifolias, gallicas, musks, damasks and bourbons.

The cultivated areas, the terraces, private garden, tea house garden and rhododendron walk are looked after by gardener Gordon Low and the remaining thirty acres of lawns by groundsman Alec Johnstone. The rhododendron walk was about twenty-five years old when Ian Johnstone (now retired) came as an apprentice gardener to Mellerstain in 1945. The entrance to this long walk is via an elegant pair of wrought iron gates and at the far end is a fine stone figure to lead the eye. Other attractions include a thatched miniature tower folly where the ladies of the house took tea on their walks. Nowadays visitors to Mellerstain can take tea in the stables and purchase plants in the courtyard.

The last three gardens in this chapter were all designed and made within a period of fifteen years but they are very different, reflecting the different life styles of the families who commissioned them. They bring 'grand designs' up to the start of the First World War, which was a seminal turning point in garden history: so many gardeners were killed in the war and wealthy families no longer could keep up the conspicuous lifestyle that culminated in the opulent gardens of the Victorian[16] and Edwardian eras, aided by cheap labour and fuel.

The garden at Manderston, near Duns in Berwickshire, is not as well known as the unique silver-plated staircase inside the house; the stairs take three weeks to clean and they were both made at the same time. The story of the re-building of Manderston for Sir James Miller (the maternal great-great-great grandfather of Adrian, the fourth Lord Palmer) is part of a good rags-to-riches, turn-of-the-century, tale.

Miller, son of a self-made herring merchant from Leith, wanted a fitting home for his bride Eveline Curzon, whose brother was Lord Curzon, later Viceroy of India. When architect John Kinross enquired how much he could spend on the building he was told 'it simply doesn't matter' … which sounds a bit like what the architects of our new Scottish Parliament building wished they'd heard, but I digress. The designs were based on Kedleston Hall in Derbyshire, where Eveline grew up, and during construction between 1903 and 1905 there were never less than 400 people working on site at any one time. It was to be one of the last, great Edwardian country houses built in Scotland for the lavish lifestyle of that era. The gardens were laid out and the many whimsical buildings in it were designed at the same time: the walled croquet lawn, the marble dairy, the classical stables and the mini fortified tower house

The current owner of Manderston, Adrian, the fourth Lord Palmer.

built for the head gardener, a Swiss chalet and various summer houses.

In contrast, when Lord Palmer brought his bride to live here in 1977, it had not been lived in for a generation, the furnishings were covered in dustsheets and the inside walls of the great neo-classical house were white with mildew. The armies of servants had long departed – with the exception of two gardeners, retained by Lord Palmer's parents (who never lived there) to keep up the fifty-six acres of gardens and woodlands. It was a daunting prospect.

There can be very few walled gardens left in Britain that are still maintained with the planting as originally planned prior to the First World War. Then it was quite common to devote a whole walled garden just to the ornamental, a cutting garden to provide

The sunken rose garden, Manderston.

exotic plants for the house. Ornate gates and a terrace take you down to the series of small gardens containing elaborate bedding out, borders of roses and dahlias, fountains, statues, arbours and – at the back – a neat row of greenhouses for cut flowers and pot plants. Lord Palmer used to come to stay with his grandfather at Manderston during the school holidays. He remembers watching the butler crossing the lawn bearing a large silver tray to whichever summer house they chose for tea.

Below the south face of the house is a sunken rose garden laid out as a parterre with clipped yew and box dotted with fountains and statues. A border runs along the upper wall that shelters shrubs and climbers such as camellias, wistaria, *Hydrangea aspera* and actinidia. Across from here is an earlier, man-made, lake where a two-storey boathouse modelled on a Swiss chalet was built for Eveline, complete with a fireplace. At the far end, where the water cascades into the lake, an oriental garden is planted with deciduous azaleas, which annually don their autumn coat of many colours. The scent from them in May and June is quite overwhelming. Lord Palmer, a descendant of the other half of the biscuit firm of Huntly and Palmer, was one of the few peers to survive the Blair 'Lords' Clearances', remaining as one of twenty-nine elected members who sit on the cross benches, speaking on agriculture, arts and heritage.

His favourite is the woodland garden, the creation of his maternal grandfather Major Bailie, son-in-law of Sir James Miller. Bailie was a keen gardener and collector of plants with a passion for moving things around until he got exactly the effect he was after. He once provoked an exasperated gardener to exclaim, 'Ach, Major, why don't you plant the blessed things in a wheelbarrow?' Certainly the planting is impressive, with imaginative combinations and variations of shapes and textures. It contains beautiful mature specimens of ericaceous shrubs and trees, including eucryphias, the handkerchief tree, *Magnolia wilsonii*, plus many species of acer, rhododendrons and azaleas.

The apple store decorated with monkeys, Earlshall.

The castle of Earlshall in Fife was built during the 1540s. As an early 'Renaissance château', it marked the beginning of an era when gardens were planned and laid out at the same time as the buildings. It pre-dated another Fife castle, Kellie (1573), where the famous architect and designer Sir Robert Lorimer grew up in the late nineteenth century. No book about Scottish gardens would be complete without paying tribute to the work of Lorimer, who wrote about the ideal of a 'Scotch country gentleman's home', where

the 'great parquetted, sparsely furnished room of many windows' looks out on to a garden that is quite in tune with the house, a garden that has quite a different sort of charm from the park outside, a garden that is an intentional and deliberate piece of careful design, a place that is garnished

The carved stone gateway at the end of the topiary lawn, Earlshall.

and nurtured with the tenderest care, but that becomes less trim as it gets farther from the house and then naturally marries with the demesne that lies beyond.[17]

Set against the prevailing fashions of the time, the great garden debate raged between the William Robinson school, championing wild and picturesque gardening, and Sir Reginald Blomfield, who demanded an architectural style. Most others stuck to ubiquitous Victorian carpet bedding. Lorimer was at the start of his career when working on Earlshall. He was to Scottish gardening a one-man version of the English Gertrude Jekyll and Sir Edwin Lutyens partnership – combining the skills of both architecture and horticulture into a homogenous whole. He wrote:

To say that the architect should design the ground that lies immediately round his house has now become a platitude. But how the division of labour should be arrived at between architect and nurseryman is not so well understood. Many people seem to think that they must necessarily and instantly get by the ears. The one wants to build a wall; the other to plant a gooseberry bush; and so the ding-dong begins.

Robert Lorimer's 1901 Gatehouse at Earlshall.

It is a tribute to Lorimer's landscaping skills that his nineteenth-century garden layouts at Earlshall still exist in the twenty-first century and are instantly recognisable as his work. As at Kellie, Balmanno, Balkaskie, and Formakin, he indulged his fondness for sitting-places where discussion could be comfortably pursued. Lorimer loved garden houses and decorated them with his favourite motifs: hearts and monkeys. At Earlshall he incorporated a summer house, apple store and dairy, potting shed and dower house into the walled garden. Never intruding on the overall design but instead complementing it, Lorimer's attention to detail is everywhere. The ventilation grilles in the wooden doors of the apple store are carved hearts; a stone monkey holding an apple sits on top of its roof. Dates with hearts are carved on the garden steps, while homilies are carved above doorways: 'He who loves his garden still keeps his Eden' and 'Here shall you see no enemy but winter and rough weather'[18] – carved in the stone gateway at the end of the topiary lawn.

Earlshall has a long history dating back to the fifteenth century when James IV granted to Alexander Bruce a charter to the lands of 'Erlishall'. There may have been a building at this time but the present castle was started in 1546 and, like many, it was added to over the centuries. By the time Lorimer was called in to restore Earlshall it had become home to a family of agricultural workers. Fifty years of zero maintenance had left the building in a derelict state. The gardens had been ploughed up to grow potatoes, although the original walls were still intact. Robert Mackenzie, a bleach merchant from Perth, bought the castle in 1890 and commissioned the young Lorimer to restore both the house and the garden. Mackenzie did not want to follow the fashionable 'Scottish Baronial' style much in vogue at the time, instead wishing to retain the purity of the building just as Lorimer's father had done at nearby Kellie Castle. The Arts and Crafts movement believed in celebrating natural materials – stone and wood (which accounts for the harling not being put back on the walls) – and idealised the craftsman.

Earlshall Castle framed by the yew topiary.

Paul Veenhuijzen, the present owner with gardener Nicky MacKintyre.

Lorimer's inspiration for the garden had its roots in the early-Renaissance-style gardens like the one at Edzell. From the first courtyard, entered through Lorimer's 1901 gatehouse, the countryside appears to come up to the house separated only by a ha-ha.

The natural park comes up to the walls of the house on the one side, on the other you stroll out into the garden enclosed. That is all – a house and a garden enclosed; but what a paradise can such a place be made! Such surprises – little gardens within the garden, the 'month's' garden, the herb garden, the yew alley. The kitchen garden, too, – and this nothing to be ashamed of, to be smothered away far from the house, but made delightful by its laying out. Great intersecting walks of shaven grass, on either side borders of brightest flowers backed by low espaliers hanging with shining apples, and within theses espaliers again the gardener has his kingdom …

Today the old gardener, Henry Colliar, remembers the pony who pulled the mower living in the stable off the potting shed. The kitchen garden is in use and the clipped topiary yews, much fuller now, echo the fantastic form of the building. Against the walls yew (instead of stone) buttresses create sheltered areas for planting. It is much as it was when H. Inigo Triggs visited when the work was newly done. He drew up a plan of it for his book of 1902 (*Formal Gardens of England and Scotland*). The present owners, Paul and Josine Veenhuijzen, who bought Earlshall in 1999, have used Trigg's plan extensively to restore the garden. They found

Ros Weaver, Greywalls.

the remains of old box hedging dumped in the wood and have reinstated the box edgings. They have put back the orchard that had disappeared and are planning an ambitious trimming of the yew hedges and topiary. They have collected some of the Wemyss ware pottery, made in 1914, painted with rooks roosting in the tall elm trees outside the garden. Best of all, they have re-created Lorimer's curved wooden slatted seat in a stone arbour where they sit of an evening, listening to the cooing of doves and the cackling of rooks.

For many, the ideal place to play golf is East Lothian. Forget St Andrews, which is windy and cold; forget Loch Lomond and the West Coast courses, which are damp and full of midges. The famous microclimate of this stretch of East Scotland is the driest and sunniest of all. Generations of Stuart kings came to play here. Prime Minister Lord Balfour, an East Lothian loon, used to holiday here in the 1890s and was instrumental in extending the railway from Drem to North Berwick for the benefit of his golfing cronies. Sir John Lavery painted and golfed locally. Lord Asquith rented nearby Archerfield House and it is held that Churchill was appointed First Lord of the Admiralty under its roof in 1908. In the 1890s Muirfield Golf Links became home to the 'Honorable Company of Golfers', the world's oldest golf club, started in 1744 in Leith. The original thirteen rules of golf drawn up by the Honorable Company can still be seen hanging in the clubhouse.

So it is hardly surprising that when, in 1901, the Hon. Alfred Lyttelton, a keen golfer, decided to build a house, it was placed 'within a mashie niblick shot of the eighteenth green at Muirfield'. This was Greywalls. It is generally believed that the architect Sir Edwin Lutyens employed his gardening partner Gertrude Jekyll to plan the planting schemes within the walled enclosures that he made. No plans exist, but the current planting is very Jekyllesque.

Ros Weaver remembers trudging around the garden at Greywalls in the rain in the mid-1990s and thinking,

'God, what am I going to do with this?' Since the late 1970s, she and her husband Giles had found that running the country-house hotel had taken up all their resources, leaving little time or money to spend outside. The house had been turned into a hotel after the Second World War but it was not until about ten years ago that it became commercially viable.

Ros Weaver had taken over the running of the six-acre garden in the late 1970s, when James Walker, head gardener at Greywalls since 1920, had retired. Without his continuous care the important layouts designed by Sir Edwin Lutyens might have disappeared, particularly during the Second World War. The fact that half of the garden was laid down to vegetables probably prevented it from being completely dug up to aid the war effort, when people were urged to 'dig for victory'.

Roz Weaver spent time studying Jekyll's planting at West Dean Park in Sussex and employed designer Laura

Greywalls House and the old rose garden now replanted in the style of Gertrude Jeykll.

Garden seat at Greywalls.

McKenzie to re-plant the garden in the same style. Together they banished the hybrid teas and floribundas so beloved of the 1950s and '60s, with the approval of Jane Brown, the garden writer and an expert on Jekyll. Now the planting is soft and voluptuous, reminiscent of the swagged and draped elegance of an Edwardian lady's dress. You are reminded of parasols and feathered hats, while the faded pinks and apricots of the climbing roses drape themselves over the walls like reclining beauties on a chaise longue.

The lovely Mrs Willy James, wife of the second owner, used to entertain her lover Edward VII here before the First World War. The house was not large enough for the James' parties and they commissioned Sir Robert Lorimer to build a 'nursery' wing in 1911, having already added a fine entrance courtyard and lodges to house the staff in 1908. The house was described by Sir Laurence Weaver in his book *Houses and Gardens by Sir Edwin Lutyens* as 'a small, albeit dignified, holiday home'. So Greywalls is not only the sole surviving Lutyens house in Scotland today, it is also the only one where Sir Robert Lorimer was also employed.

If the enduring image of an Edwardian garden is of a place to promenade, of secluded seating areas where assignations can take place and of tea, cucumber sandwiches and lemonade served on the lawn on a warm summer's afternoon, then Greywalls is the quintessential example. Sitting on the seat that lets you look through a 'fish eye' in the wall, you see none of the harsh edges so often found in Scottish gardens. The gentle countryside drifts into the distance, echoed by the curving sky. The clatter of a lawn mower in the distance and the cooing of wood pigeons gives it a very English and very timeless feel.

One of the best things about the garden at Greywalls is the walls, although why the house's original name High Walls was changed to Greywalls remains a mystery. The walls are not even grey, but a mellow mix of yellow, cinnamon and pink brick, with pantiled copes of grey slate. The arched doorways in the walls have beautiful detailing using these grey slates in an Art Deco design. There are straight walls and curved walls cunningly laid out to create rooms

and vistas; radiating paths link entrances and exits through the doors, beckoning you through. It is the perfect place to wander. You can almost hear the swish of oyster-coloured satin skirts and smell the scent of rose and lavender water. The straight lines are softened by the curves of the walls and the proportions are totally satisfying, being neither too large nor too small but just right. Everywhere there are places to sit, in sun and in shade, in solitary contemplation, or in companionable conversation.

Because of the microclimate, the envy of other, colder East Coast areas, there is rarely a frost at Greywalls. The soil may be sandy but behind the greenhouses there are huge compost heaps, lovingly tended, to alleviate the problem. The excellent drainage meant that the grass tennis courts could be re-instated in 1999 and, like the golf courses, can be used all year round. Today, sixty-five per cent of the guests come for the golf, while the rest are able to summon refreshments while they sit and look out over the golf course towards the Firth of Forth. Heaven indeed.

Santolina and lilies surround teepees of sweet peas in front of the greenhouse at Greywalls.

Notes

1. The kitchen garden and orchard would have been separate gardens probably leading off the walled privy garden. Today the planting, imposed in the 1930s when the garden was restored, is mostly composed of inappropriate bedding plants and roses that would not have been available at that time. These are incorporated in box hedging clipped to spell out the Lindsay family motto.

2. Ochterlony of Guynd describes his visit to Edzell in the seventeenth century in *Notes on Forfarshire.*

3. *The Renaissance Garden in England.*

4. *The Scottish Château: The Country House of Renaissance Scotland.*

5. Made for James V by his illegitimate cousin Sir James Hamilton of Finnart.

6. For example, 'rouser' = watering can (Fr. *arrosoir*); 'yardis' = yards (Fr. *jardin*); 'grape' = fork (Fr. *grapper* = to dig); dyke = wall (Fr. *digue*); ' beetrave' = beetroot (Fr. *bettrave*).

7. At that period 'curious' would have meant made with care, or artistic – *OED.*

8. Originally a water works in the grounds of York House in 1675, the company was incorporated in 1691. Legislation in 1719 allowed purchasers of the forfeited estates to grant annuities on the value of their shares and the York Building Company was bought by a consortium to exploit this opportunity, becoming the largest landowner in Scotland with Sir Archibald Grant of Monimusk as one of its leading manipulators and beneficiaries. But 'in spite of furious energy, progressive ideas and inspired dishonesty', it failed, finally collapsing after the South Sea Bubble disaster in 1720. Initially the company let out many of the gardens and Macky tells us that these were in good order (he is one of the few travellers who comments on each and every garden of all the 'seats' that he visits). However, the creditors continued the destruction of the properties, stripping out anything that could be sold or re-used including standing timber.

9. Macky, *Journey Through Scotland*, vol. III (1723).

10. It borrowed heavily on John Evelyn's translation of the book published in 1651 by Frenchman Nicholas de Bonnefons, but it addressed the climate of Scotland.

11. Daniel Defoe, *A Tour Through the Whole Island of Great Britain* (1724–6).

12. Inspired by Sir William Chambers, a Scottish landscape architect, who designed the Chinese buildings at Kew Garden and later (in 1772) published his book *A Dissertation of Oriental Gardening.*

13. Anon., *The Curiosities Natural & Artificial of the Island of Great Britain* (c. 1780). The same anonymous writer describes 'the seat of the Duke of Athol' as 'very noble; the gardens formed by nature. You have here variety of mounts and flats adorned with statues, and a neat green-house; as also an handsome stove, with many curious plants in it, such as pineapples, torch thistles, oranges, lemons, &c. and several curious coffee-trees, which thrive very well.'

14. Robert Heron, *Observations made in a Journey through the Western Counties of Scotland; in the Autumn of 1793*, 2 vols. Of Blair Atholl he writes: 'The garden, properly so called is large and well laid out, although perhaps not so very well kept, as might be wished. In the middle is an artificial piece of water which has no disagreeable effect. I thought is rather disfigured however, by some figures of hay makers and other rustics which have been awkwardly set up in it.' Further he walked in the woods with 'the gardener for my guide' and saw a 'grotto, in front of which poured a cataract. Within this grotto was a mossy seat; and the situation on the river, is one to which a heathen poet might well suppose the river nymphs likely at times to retire from the waters.' Later 'my conductor surprised me with a tale and an object, the latter of which I was sorry to see in such a situation … He and other men at work in the gardens had been, that morning, frightened from their work by the sudden appearance of some madman who had levelled a gun at them … We went on, till upon turning the corner of a walk, he suddenly started back, and seemingly in the utmost terror and astonishment, fled with precipitation … 'There he is!' I turned my eye to where he directed, and might, indeed, have been surprised, had I not recognised a brother of those stucco figures which I have already mentioned, as having very impertinently intruded themselves into the garden. It was the figure of a fowler, in the act of levelling his gun so as to point against whoever should approach … My guide … boasted to me, that, he had seldom failed to surprise and terrify strangers by means of it … The trick and the tales are extremely childish.'

15. It has recently been dredged and restored.

16. Walled and Victorian gardens of the period are specifically addressed in another chapter.

17. Christopher Hussey, *The Work of Sir Robert Lorimer* (1931).

18. From Shakespeare, *As You Like It.*

CHAPTER THREE

Castles and Walled Gardens

View of the maze from the roof of Cawdor Castle.

CASTLES AND WALLED GARDENS

'A garden is a sort of sanctuary, "a chamber roofed by heaven". Wherever intrusion is possible, and any movement other than that of birds is heard, we have no garden in the fullest, sweetest sense of the word . . . The garden is a little pleasaunce of the soul, by whose wicket the world can be shut out from us . . .'

SIR ROBERT LORIMER [2]

Gardens evolved and changed as the social climate changed and for the most part they were walled.[2] Scottish walled gardens are not only more numerous but intrinsically different from their English cousins. Our weather is harsher, we have more rabbits and deer and in the old days we had more poor and starving citizens who needed to be kept out of the larder. Scottish lairds were also poorer than their English counterparts and this was reflected in the whimsical vernacular style of many walls and of buildings within the walls. These spaces provided a microclimate for fruit, vegetables and flowers as well as a safe environment which, built up over the years, produced a priceless resource of deep loam.

There is something about the atmosphere of a walled garden; the surprise as you enter, the rush of warmer air inside, the intimacy, the contrasts in textures of stone, plants and often water. The scents are stronger for being contained by the walls and there is a peaceful feel engendered by the enclosure – the Chinese would explain it perfectly by the Feng Shui theory – all the spirits being contained within and not escaping. Thus they are a place for all the senses, soothing the soul and satisfying one's curiosity as they gradually reveal themselves.

A need for privacy and enclosure we think of as a peculiarly British thing, but since Roman times and before, growing spaces have been enclosed with whatever materials came to hand. Spiked sticks and ditches, crude stone walls and hedges were gradually replaced in the sixteenth century by 'hewn and polished' stone set into harled walls topped with coping stones. By the eighteenth century, garden walls, up to twenty feet high, were lined with bricks that absorbed more heat; different methods of heating the walls were devised and by the late twentieth century concrete, gabions and even steel were being used.

Since the First World War there had been a steady decline in the resources needed to keep up large gardens in terms of labour and money. Cheap imports of fruit and vegetables from all over the world meant that it was actually more expensive to grow your own than to buy them from the supermarket, shrinkwrapped, freeze dried, sanitised and sprayed with chemicals to keep them fresh on their long journey from Israel or Africa.

After the Second World War, the generation that had custody of many walled gardens lacked resources, energy, imagination and money. More, the social revolution that had taken place left all but the very wealthy stranded in their large houses without the staff to maintain their erstwhile lifestyles. There was almost a refusal to believe that things could or should change, but even so, terrible damage was inflicted on historic houses and gardens. Houses were blown up and gardens bulldozed. Everything was about 'labour saving' and that in turn destroyed much valuable history. So the decline accelerated – the high taxation imposed by the government in the 1950s drove many owners to plant their gardens with hideous, but tax-effective, sitka spruce plantations. Some walls fell down, some were pulled down, property developers started to target them as potential building sites. They were turned into housing or industrial estates, visitor centres, scrapyards and car parks – at worst. At best into nurseries, mazes, training centres for horticultural colleges, orchards and sculpture parks. Of course there also remain the loved and cared-for ones, growing fruit and vegetables or as ornamental gardens. Some now are just a grassed space.

It was not until the next generation that hope resurfaced and in the 1980s and '90s, new ideas and uses were found for these gardens and they lurched forward into a more fruitful era. By the twenty-first century the situation was seriously on the turn for the better. Today some are highly viable in terms of visitor figures, some are lovingly tended by their owners with or without help and with varying success. Some have had the glasshouse or another building converted into a sympathetic dwelling for the owner to live in and enjoy the enclosed garden.

Cawdor is one of the oldest castles continuously inhabited, by the same family, in Scotland. Traces of the medieval walls in the two walled gardens adjacent to the castle would suggest that there were *jardins clos* here from the earliest time of the central tower in the mid-fifteenth century, and certainly from the time that the wings were added in the sixteenth century, forming a classic courtyard block with separate buildings within it to house the dining hall, kitchen, stores and guests. It would seem that the gardens were placed to give good views of them from the castle windows and in particular from the roof, as was the fashion of the time. Thomas Pennant, on his tour of Scotland in 1769, describes his

The Paradise Garden at Cawdor.

visit to 'Calder' (as it was then known): 'The ancient part is a great square tower; but there is a large and more modern building annexed, with a drawbridge.' Riding into the surrounding policies, he describes the fine trees and the waterfalls.

They must have been enlarged by Sir Archibald Campbell, son of the fifteenth Thane of Cawdor, who wrote in 1725 that he had 'levelled a considerable piece of ground, a part thereof was a deep morass and the rest a hill, of which he [sic] has made a handsome garden where all sorts of fruit grow that are in Scotland'. This is now the flower garden that was replanted by the first Earl of Cawdor's wife in 1850 and continues along much the same lines today. The kitchen garden is the older, dating from the late sixteenth century. Lists of seeds bought in the seventeenth century include French sorrel, lamb's lettuce, Savoy kale, endive,

Cawdor flower garden seen from the roof.

Angelika, Dowager Countess Cawdor.

Derek Hosie, the head gardener at Cawdor.

Indian cress, Spanish thistle, Turkish parsley, various herbs and double hollyhocks.

In 1981 the late sixth Earl, who had a great interest in classical history, turned part of the walled kitchen garden into a maze. Together with his wife Angelika, now Dowager Countess Cawdor, the gardens were revitalised and opened, along with the castle, to the public. It is one of the most successful private visitor attractions in the north of Scotland.

The design for the maze was based on a mosaic floor pattern in the ruined Roman villa of Conimbriga in Portugal, depicting the Minotaur's labyrinth at Knossos in Crete. Labyrinth means 'double axe' in Greek and relates to the building called The Double Axe which was the sacred symbol of the Minoans in the Bronze Age. When myth became linked with archaeology the labyrinth, home of the Minotaur, took on a different identity and, from its association with a place that was hard to enter, down the ages the word has come to mean a garden puzzle.

In medieval times a knot or 'mase' was a standard part of any garden, usually low growing and composed of herbs. The mystical element in the designs gradually lessened after the Renaissance but until the seventeenth century the hedges were kept low at three to four feet. Later, higher hedges provided more sport as mazes were planted for fun. The maze at the Villa Garzoni in Tuscany had a grotto at the centre with a tap that activated water-spouts all around the maze – the first person to get to the centre could soak

The laburnum arch at Cawdor.

The present head gardener at Cawdor Castle, Derek Hosie, arrived to take up his post during the creation of the maze and remembers spending his first day planting holly hedge plants. The magnificent yew hedges and sweet-smelling fat box hedges have also mostly been planted during Hosie's time and are beautifully kept. Some are ingeniously clipped to match in with the ancient walls of the gardens, their sloping 'copes' leading seamlessly into the copes of the walls. Some of the yew and box are clipped into topiary shapes and there is an interesting example of a mixed yew and beech hedge.

The holly maze covers about a third of an acre in part of what was the sixteenth-century walled kitchen garden, although, as mentioned, parts of the walls are medieval. It appears to be square but is in fact a trapezium. A field maple hedge (*Acer campestre*) has been planted against the outside walls and was chosen for its low maintenance and autumn colour. Next to this, a double arch of laburnum (*L. x watereri* 'vossii') runs around all four sides and is a stunning walkway when it flowers in early summer. Honeysuckles are planted at irregular intervals up the laburnum to provide extended flowering.

Hosie will dispel any doubts about planting a holly hedge to grow to maturity in your lifetime. His complaint is that they grow 'far too much' rather than far too little and in a wet year the holly hedges that make up the maze put on upwards of eight to fifteen inches. They are of course growing outwards too so when the paths have narrowed to around two and a half feet, a major clipping takes place to take one foot off each side, but this has be done over two years – one side at a time.

Perhaps the reason that new mazes are not so common is that they are very labour intensive: the Cawdor maze can take three people two and a half weeks to clip – and you can run into other problems. Fifteen years after it was made, the maze had to be closed as it was found that the sheer weight of the visitors' feet, tramping the paths to the centre, was compressing the soil onto the shallow rooted plants and literally suffocating them. Lack of light at the

the others. Le Nôtre designed an elaborate labyrinth for the gardens at Versailles. It had an unusual, non-geometric shape with wandering paths and the object was to find all forty lead statues, with fountains, depicting Aesop's fables. This labyrinth/maze was built in a bosquet[3] with paths bordered by green latticework, backed by high hornbeam hedges.

roots can cause die-back as the maturing plants spread outwards.

The outer holly hedge is the lovely male form *Ilex hodginsii*, which has large, shiny, dark green, oval leaves. This is clipped to three feet in height and is the most difficult for the clippers. The next nine rows are graded in height and are all of the common holly (*Ilex aquifolium*) so that by the time you get to the centre you cannot be seen – the last two rows are clipped to seven feet.

Before the 'English Landscape Movement' became the rage in the eighteenth century, walled gardens were attached to houses and castles, but in the main these were swept away and re-created at a distance from the house. One who disapproved of this fashion was John MacCulloch, who wrote of his travels through Scotland from 1811 to 1821 in the form of letters to his friend, Sir Walter Scott: 'All is vanished together, and the house is now a cold, dry specimen of architecture, placed on a cold, dry, shaven, and polished lawn, where not even a daisy is suffered to raise its head.' [4] He rails against the 'Capability-men' who banished the gardens to a distant place and describes the fruit and vegetables in loving detail, stating: 'It can never take from their ornament, that they are useful.'

It was not just about how much was needed to be grown for the house and estate. The size of the area enclosed and the type of wall surrounding it also served as a yardstick for the family's importance, much as today a person's car can tell you about their monetary standing. In towns, plans show long narrow walled strips behind the houses. These would have contained a privy, a drying green (often low hedges were grown so that sheets could be draped over them), possibly a patch for vegetables and sometimes a stable. The average well-to-do farmhouse or manse boasted a walled garden of a half to one and a half acres, while the great landowners cultivated areas from three to fifteen acres.

Some had two or more walled gardens, but few of these immense gardens survive now.

Inheriting a garden from keen gardening parents is not always easy, but Ronald Munro Ferguson relishes his guardianship of a space that has been in the family for many generations. He does not feel constrained by more than 240 years of history and enjoys planning and improving the garden. Novar is a classical 1760 house, unusually built around an oblong courtyard that is entered through a tunnel. Coming into the courtyard is quite a shock and gives you a feeling of being in the North of Italy rather than just off the A9 between Inverness and Wick. An elegant oval stone pond with a peaceful arching water jet is surrounded by restrained plantings of *Vitis cognitiae*, old-fashioned climbing roses and box, with classical urns, pots and statues. These show up well against the Mediterranean-yellow lime-washed walls that have been returned to their original eighteenth-century colour.

Ronald Munro Ferguson of Novar.

The water garden at Novar.

Novar has long been an important garden, in fact several important gardens, that are now being lovingly and painstakingly reorganised. These gardens are about enclosed spaces and water. The inner courtyard has been replanted and the outer courtyard emptied of the garages and lean-to stores that crept in after the Second World War. Simplicity has been returned and the centre of this car-parking area now contains a raised bed planted with a tapestry of thymes.

The double walled garden, covering five acres, also dates from 1760 and is surrounded by eighteen-foot-high brick and stone walls topped by sandstone copes, intersected with massive buttresses, added 100 years ago. It is divided by a further wall down the centre, which contains archways leading to and from both halves. One half now is used for vegetables, soft fruit and orchards divided by grass walks that lead you past interesting and unusual trees. These were planted at the turn of the century by the present owner's great-great uncle, Lord Novar, and include narrow-leafed variegated hollies and junipers, a huge and beautiful

A stone archway linking two gardens at Novar.

The gardener's house at Novar set into the walls of the garden.

Novar, a classical 1760 house.

cercidiphyllum and, it is claimed, the most northerly gingko tree in Britain.

In the other half of the walled garden a large formal pond has been made with a commissioned fountain. One thousand fish, a mixture of red and golden koi carp, pink, blue and gold orfes and grass carp, swim in the pond. There is a house let into the side wall which traditionally would have been for the head gardener to keep an eye on the garden. The room overlooking the garden has now been turned into potting sheds. Formal parterres in intricate designs have been made with box hedging, grown from cuttings.

Ronald Munro Ferguson's father (who inherited Novar in 1942) was responsible for the water garden with its two spectacular waterfalls and dramatic planting. Most people would plant one or two clumps of gunnera, but here there are huge swathes creating high drama, which together with the drifts of rodgersias produce a simplicity of planting that is stunning. It was in the early 1960s that he started creating this garden from a burn that flowed through the old slaughterhouse yard, and also provided the flushing system for the stone privy with its two seats. The existing acers and azaleas have been added to and are complemented by ferns, mixed shrubs and a fine strawberry tree. A new wall has been built to enclose one end of the water garden. He adored water and neighbours would say to Ronald, 'Your father used to think he could make water run uphill' – obviously the love of water is inherited.

The best shape and aspect of a wall had been debated for centuries, curved, zigzag, serpentine or straight. Gardens could be round, oval, hexagonal, square, rectangular or just irregular shaped, with six or seven sides. At Pitcullo in Fife, Sir Angus Grossart is very concerned with the walls that remain in the grounds of the tower house that he has spent the last twenty-five years restoring. Any time left over from running his merchant bank, numerous other directorships, interests in the art world, and a Georgian house in Edinburgh's New Town, is spent overseeing the works at his country house. Palladio, when writing the introduction to his four books of domestic architecture in the fifteenth century, would have instantly recognised this preoccupation:

The city houses are certainly of great splendour and convenience to a gentleman who is to reside in them all the time he shall require for the administration of the republick, or for the

directing of his affairs. But perhaps he will not reap much less utility and consolation from the country house: where the remaining part of the time will be passed in seeing and adorning his own possessions and by industry, and the art of agriculture improving his estate.

Dating from the twelfth century, Pitcullo sits on a mound with a commanding view of distant St Andrews and the sea. Sir Angus bought the ruined tower house in 1977 and has been working on it ever since. But in the last ten years, he has also turned his attentions to the policies and farm buildings that he bought in 1995. He doesn't grow flowers, apart from spring bulbs in the grass. Maybe growing bulbs is not so different from growing money. You can start with just a few, but if you dig them up and divide them each year and let them self-seed, you can end up with carpets of them.

But Sir Angus's gardening is more a voyage of discovery that is about restoring the different periods of landscape around his castle in meticulous detail. After a massive 'clear-up' operation, moving mountains of rubbish that had been dumped for years amongst the overgrown trees and shrubs on his new land, he could suddenly see the geometric shapes and vistas of earlier landscaping emerging. Two years were spent 'restoring a hill'. Next he set about saving the ancient hollies that had survived the munching of generations of cows. There is no instant gardening here: everything takes as long as is necessary. One holly hedge next to the house took twenty years to 'get back', while the walls in the Victorian walled garden took a year to re-point.

Sir Angus Grossart of Pitcullo.

One of the first things he tackled was the ruined doocot.[5] Twelve hundred nesting boxes have been accurately restored in slate and sandstone, a new/old oak door closed with an antique box lock has also been added. Around the doocot is a fence to stop any four-legged invaders and the traditional ring of trees is being re-planted to allow the doos to settle before they enter. The stringcourse to stop rats climbing aboard has also been re-instated.

But by far the biggest ongoing project are the three walled gardens of different periods that reflect the social and economic changes that have taken place at Pitcullo over the centuries. The earliest one is probably contemporary with the fifteenth-century part of the castle and it is certainly shown on a map of 1774 hanging in the castle. It is a small enclosure adjacent to the castle that was

Earliest small enclosure surrounded by holly adjacent to the castle at Pitcullo.

Pitcullo's bronze of Sir Isaac Newton as 'Master of the Universe' by Eduardo Paolozzi.

The seventeenth-century walled garden at Pitcullo.

walled with holly.[6] Where there are gaps, the holly is being replanted and a double row of trees leads up to a folly.

Below the castle are the remains of a seventeenth-century walled garden, also shown on the map. The ruined walls on three sides have been repaired and rebuilt. In the middle of this flat, mown space is a ten-foot high bronze sculpture by Eduardo Paolozzi of Sir Isaac Newton as 'Master of the Universe'. The geometric figure sits powerfully silhouetted against the surrounding countryside and seems very much at home in this ancient setting. When the garden was originally made there would most probably have been a parterre of some kind here with statues that could have been looked down upon from the house.

But times changed, and by the Victorian era, the castle had become a ruined

folly and a mansion house[7] was built between it and the seventeenth-century walled garden. A new kitchen garden was made further away from the house and this has also been getting the Grossart treatment.

The gardener's bothy, set into one wall, has been restored and contains the garden office. The potting shed is similarly undergoing rehabilitation. Inside where once would have been rows of vegetables it is now a mown green sward. As a believer in the Ruskin philosophy of 'never seek to finish, always leave something for the imagination', Sir Angus is in no hurry; there is lots left here for the imagination.

In a warm dry part of the East Coast of Scotland nestles an unusual walled fruit garden, which the owner does not wish to be identified. To visit the garden you go from the old house, with its immaculate manicured lawns and sunken rose garden, through a farm gate into a dark pinewood. At the other side of the wood stands an ancient yew at the top of a double avenue of gean[8] trees, that runs away at right angles along a high stone wall. Dappled sunlight breaks through their leaves, lighting up the shiny green leaves of the *Vinca minor* growing around their feet. Down to the left are groups of ferns and the stone façade of an ice-house. If you clamber down for a closer look there is a spring and a green cool pond for the production of ice, and now, because you are aware of the high walls, you gain a clue that it also provides water to nurture what lies behind the walls. At the end of the gean walk, you may see a shadowy figure moving about, and under a large sycamore a timeless, ancient sight: the bee man, complete with veil and smoker, is tending his old wooden hives. As you get closer you can hear the buzzing of the bees and see the puffs of smoke.

Beside a wooden door in the wall is stacked a neat pile of old-fashioned square straw bales. The surprise on opening the wooden door is wonderful. You emerge out of the dark shade of the wood into the vivid sunlight and the warmth, which hits you with a rush. The fifteen-foot high walls are lined on the inside with warm faded stones, which are covered with beautifully trained fruit trees. A wall can raise the temperature by seven fahrenheit degrees. The aspect of a wall will also affect the temperature so that the same soft fruit bushes and fruit trees trained on walls facing north, south, east or west will ripen at different times. Wall-trained fruit produces a larger crop than free-standing trees; whether grown as cordons, fans or espaliers, there is a great art to the training and tying them in to the walls.

So in this garden, by having a second walled garden set like a diamond inside a square, many different microclimates are produced. This second garden is entered through a wooden gate set in another wall, a lower wall this time with a deep pantiled coping. These walls are about eight feet high; the entrance is on a sharply angled corner and two walls run away from you in a perfect V. Between these walls and the outer walls are beds, neatly edged with clipped box, containing every sort of soft fruit you can think of. Growing in regimented rows like a parade ground of well-trained soldiers are strawberries, raspberries, gooseberries and redcurrants, whitecurrants and blackcurrants. There are sections containing old apple and pear trees, deeply mulched with straw; wooden beehives sit amongst them. Neat rolls of netting lie ready to cover the ripening fruit. From the overhanging pantile roof there are iron hooks from which to hang nets over the wall-trained currants, the pear, apple and cherry trees.

Through the next wooden door and you are in a six-sided, diamond-shaped garden and the climate changes again; it is noticeably warmer and here there are peaches, greengages and nectarines, even figs, which ripen trained

A wall-trained fruit tree in the walled garden.

A walled garden within a walled garden creating different microclimates.

against the walls. Some of these have wooden boards behind them to help 'bake' the fruit. Artichokes and asparagus fill up the box-edged beds and more strawberries planted to ripen earlier. A central circle is filled with herbs, lavender and sweet geranium, to tempt the bees. Another bed is filled with blowsy, scented paeony-roses. All around you are the sights, smells, sounds and tastes of contentment; even the sense of touch is gratified when you stroke a furry peach, or run your hands along the warm rough stones.

This garden was built at the beginning of the nineteenth century, by Napoleonic prisoners-of-war who were bought over to Scotland, and it would seem that the garden has changed little since it was first laid out. The pantiles would have come from the Low Countries as ballast on ships, returning after delivering their cargoes of Scottish coal and timber. With its box hedges, ash paths, huge heavy wooden ladders propped up against the walls,

hand-wrought hooks and proper nets made of string, you half expect to see a gardener dressed in an apron and collarless shirt.

Although walls had been used for growing fruit trees since the medieval period, it was in the kitchen gardens of the nineteenth century that garden walls attained their highest degree of sophistication. Many that remain in gardens today are handsome and mellow with age but the scientific thought that went into their construction has been forgotton in most instances. It was the great walled kitchen gardens of the Victorians that embodied the guiding principles of that era. These feats of engineering were run like mini-empires or food factories. Each person and plant had an exact position and place and expected behavioural pattern.

The class system controlled the first and scientific principles guided the second. There were rules that dictated the clothes worn by, and living quarters allotted to, the gardeners.[9] The exact angle of the apprentice gardener's cap was measured as meticulously as the angle of the glass in the peach house to catch the sun's rays, and even the spacing of the fruit trees and the right height and materials for the walls were laid down. In the potting shed would be a large pair of brass dividers so that the head gardener could measure to see if the correct space between the bedded-out plants had been achieved. This was an age of rigid rule and regulation. Fruit, flowers and vegetables had to be available on demand, all year around so temperature control was essential. Forcing houses and pits heated by fresh manure to grow exotic fruit and vegetables and to extend the growing season were surplanted by ranges of glass houses heated by huge coal-fired boilers with complicated water-heated systems.

In Edinburgh, the hot-house and garden designer Walter Nichol had written a book, *The Gardener's Kalender*, that was in its second edition by 1812. With true Presbyterian dourness he states that:

> *The cultivation of culinary vegetables is certainly the most important branch of gardening. It occupies the attention of a large proportion of the community, of the fruits of whose labours all daily partake. To the palace, and the humble shepherd's cot, the kitchen-garden is a necessary appendage … The labours of the industrious man yield peace; of the scientifically industrious man, wealth. But the garden of the sluggard is a reproach to him, and to the public a certain loss.*

The Protestant work ethic personified. In 1853 another Scottish gardener, Charles M'Intosh dedicated his two-volume *Book of the Garden* to his employer, the Queen of the Belgians. His chapters on walled gardens, and on walls in particular, list: Aspect of ..., Foundations of ..., Materials for ..., Copings for ..., Trellised ..., Height of ..., Arranged ... to suit various situations, Colour of ... and Construction of ..., Garden Walls. With a further five hundred pages on glasshouses, heating, pits, cold frames, angles of glass for different fruits and their requirements under glass and against walls, the reader is left breathless. The chapter on Miscellaneous Garden Structures contains his thoughts on the head gardener's house that was normally set into the walled garden so that he could keep an eye on things at all times.

— ❧ —

Blairquhan in Ayrshire, as its late owner, Jamie Hunter Blair, would say, 'is a very grown-up house'. Driving down the 'long approach' to Blairquhan Castle, you get tantalising glimpses of the house and think how comfortably it sits in the landscape. This is no accident of nature. Instead, it was carefully designed, two hundred years ago, to create an impression of grandeur and harmony. You cannot fail to be impressed, not just by the handsome gothic appearance of the house, but also by the person who chose to place it exactly in this particular spot – it is just right. Jamie said

The late Jamie Hunter Blair of Blairquhan.

that originally the site was like the place where Eeyore's house was built: 'A dark and gloomy place'.[10]

In front of the house is no small carriage sweep; nearly an acre of gravel gives room for a whole ballroom-full of cars and often there were, when the castle was full of guests. The thing about Jamie was that he did everything with enormous dash, style and enthusiasm and on a big scale. On closer examination this appears to be a trait that he had inherited. It was Jamie's great-great grandfather, Sir David Hunter Blair who started landscaping the surrounding countryside. Sir David came into the estate, which had been bought, on his behalf, in 1798 and in 1821 he commissioned architect William Burn to design the new mansion on the site of the derelict castle which had started as a tower in 1346. Both men were in their twenties and through their shared energy and enthusiasm for the project, they became firm friends.

Sir David was a gifted amateur landscaper with great vision. There were very few wooded areas on his arrival and his mother wrote that the estate was 'much in need of improvement'. Improve he did. He diverted the river Girvan to enhance the view from the library and altered the existing public roads by moving them away from the castle. He then set about making new lodges, drives and pathways including the three-mile 'long approach' which runs from William Burn's Bridge to the castle. He set about creating gardens and an arboretum. In the policies he planted nearly 1,000,000 trees including over 600,000 larch, numerous Scots pine, oak, ash, beech and rowans. Two ornamental lakes were added with walks to and from them. He named one for his wife and the other for his daughter Maria.

Successive generations of Hunter Blairs have all been interested in trees and have added to Sir David's plantations and woodlands. Sir Edward, the fourth baronet, started planting the pinetum on the site of the old orchard in the second half of the nineteenth century. Jamie's father, Sir James the seventh baronet, was a forestry graduate who worked for many years for the Forestry Commission before settling down at Blairquhan where he increased the

forestry to around a thousand acres. Over the last three decades, Jamie, who was a past president of the Royal Scottish Forestry Society, undertook a massive restoration programme which included creating a tree trail. He also restored the approach loch to its 1800 dimensions and converted some seven estate cottages and the old potting sheds into holiday lets.

In the walled garden, built in 1820, the glasshouses sit on one hill facing another hill that acts as the fourth wall – a most unusual design by John Tweedie who was responsible for the layout. The walls (the bricks were made on the estate) rise to eighteen feet and run round three sides rising and falling with the contours. As in many gardens of this period, the walls have flues in them so that they could be heated and thus protect the fruit trees from frost. Heated walls had begun to be built in the eighteenth century, but normally it was only the south wall that would incorporate a fire place on the north side, with flues running inside the walls to keep early frosts off the fruit blossom.[11] They would have required a garden boy to attend to the fire all through the night. Gradually after the Second World War, the garden started to decline in a way so common to walled gardens, as money and labour became scarce.

Ten years ago Jamie decided that it was time to reverse this decline and, having studied his favourite gardens, he chose a classical design planted in an ornamental fashion so that not only could he enjoy it, but his guests

and the tenants in the seven holiday cottages could as well. The tatties and the Christmas trees that had taken over the garden were banished and an ambitious restoration programme was launched. Garden designer Laura Mackenzie was engaged to advise and design the sweeping borders, walks and plantings around the restored glasshouses. One lawn is large enough for a marquee and people can hold weddings and events there. Jamie, who was pretty good at events, held a 'laburnum party' every year on the fourth of June, at which the guests had to wear yellow and all the food was yellow, while the drinks were yellow champagne and yellow chartreuse. This event was held to coincide with the flowering of the laburnum arched walk.

This maybe gives an indication of the character of the man who lived at Blairquhan until his death in December 2004. He loved it and shared it with the guests who came in droves to stay. Since opening the house and grounds to the public, Jamie did not change the way he lived in the house; he lived in it all. There was a feeling of continuity from another era and he succeeded in recharging the great house with life and activity while surrounding it with cared-for policies and a very loyal garden.

‘Bigger and Better’ could be the motto and with cheap labour, copious amounts of coal to fire up the boilers, huge walled gardens with acres of glasshouses and miles of fruit, trained against scientifically engineered and often heated walls, exotic flowers, fruit and vegetables could be supplied to the groaning Victorian dining table. Both Nichol and Loudon discuss at length the siting and disguising of these gardens behind shrubberies and wooded areas that were not just for shelter but to hide them from sight. The aesthetics of these working gardens did not accord with the Victorian sensibilities and entry by the south wall was recommended, indeed commanded, so that the 'baser parts rendered conspicuous from the North' can be avoided. These baser parts consisted of potting and tool sheds, forcing pits, manure heaps, boiler houses (stoves), storerooms and living quarters for the garden boys and journeymen. Loudon also is concerned 'to create a favourable first impression by showing 'the highest and best walls' on entry when the family came to visit the kitchen garden with their friends. Loudon discusses the size for the average family at length, ranging from one to twelve acres, although one anfd a half to five acres 'with abundance of manure, is capable of supplying a respectable establishment'.

The one-and-a-half-acre walled garden at Ballindalloch in Banffshire is not probably quite as big as Loudon would have liked for the size of the castle. Ballindalloch is a very grand pile. I use the word 'pile' because it is so many buildings piled upon each other over centuries with the Victorian baronial additions triumphing over all. Begun as a simple Z-plan tower in the sixteenth century, it had two wings added in 1770 by General Grant who fought in the American War of Independence and later became governor of Florida. In the 1850s Sir John Macpherson-Grant commissioned architect Thomas Mackenzie to re-model and 'baronialise' the building. The present walled garden was made at the same time and is a good brisk walk away from the house.

Sir Walter Scott also shared his friend John MacCulloch's dislike of the landscape fashion and wrote about the cruel banishment of the kitchen garden:

It were indeed high time that some one should interfere. The garden, artificial in its structure, its shelter, its climate and its soil, which every consideration of taste, beauty, and convenience recommended to be kept near to the mansion, and maintained, as its appendage, in the highest state of ornamental decoration which could be used with reference to the character of the house itself, has, by a strange and sweeping sentence of exile, been condemned to wear the coarsest and most humbling form. Reduced to a clumsy oblong, inclosed within four rough-built walls, and sequestered in some distant corner where it may be best concealed from the eye to which it has been rendered a nuisance, the modern garden resembles nothing so much as a convict in his gaol apparel, banished, by his very appearance, from all decent society. If the peculiarity of

Clare Macpherson-Grant Russell, laird of Ballindalloch.

the proprietor's taste inclines him to worship of Flora or Pomona, he must attend their rites in distance and secrecy, as if he were practising some abhorred mysteries, instead of rendering an homage which is so peculiarly united with that of the household gods.

The present laird of Ballindalloch is Clare Macpherson-Grant Russell who has lived here with her family since 1978. Together with husband Oliver Russell, she spruced up the house and turned it into a thriving corporate entertaining venue, where foreign royalty and wealthy businessmen were pampered guests (often arriving by helicopter on the huge front lawn or being chauffeured in after landing their private jets at RAF Lossiemouth further north). In the 1990s it was decided to open the house and gardens to the public and at this point upgrade the gardens as well. I was asked to help and together Clare and I mulled over plans that I made for the walled garden.

It was in a sorry state of decline, with some fruit cages sitting where the range of glasshouses had been. In the nineteenth century they had included vineries, peach and melon houses as well as areas for exotic pot plants and flowers for the house. Outside, the double herbaceous borders that ran down the centre had been grassed over and the vegetable beds had long gone. Some fruit trees grew in a stranded fashion dotted around the grass. In the working area behind the north wall, the head gardener's house remained with a couple of new greenhouses and some cold frames.

The plan was to make a visitor-friendly rose garden, but one that could be maintained by one man, three days a week, excluding mowing. There was no question of having anything labour intensive such as trained fruit trees against the walls, or of having borders running around under them. Instead, lines of flowering cherries were planted all the way around in grass at a distance of fifteen feet from the walls.[12] In the spring the grass is a mass of bulbs. Wide shrub-rose borders were made fifteen feet inside these, fifteen feet wide. A simple cross plan of wide grass paths led to a circular stone-paved area in the middle of which was placed a large circular Haddenstone pond and fountain. Wooden pergolas made by the estate carpenters from Ballindalloch wood were erected for the climbing roses. In the centre of each of the four square lawns were statues of the four seasons surrounded by pools of lavender. Originally each of the four corners were colour themed, but as the years went on there were some roses that did well and a few that disliked the growing conditions that had to be replaced with tougher varieties. The garden was opened in 1996 to coincide with the 450th anniversary of Ballindalloch as the Macpherson-Grants' family home.

Further north in Aberdeenshire is another walled garden a long way from its house, Hatton Castle. There has been a building on this site since the 1300s, but the present

One of the 'Four Seasons' statues surrounding Haddenstone.

Haddenstone pond, seat and statue at Ballindalloch.

house was remodelled in 1810 by the Duff family who had made their fortune by usury. Whatever had been here in terms of gardens disappeared when the Duffs embraced the fashionable 'landscape movement'. The family was powerful throughout Banffshire and Aberdeenshire, where various branches owned the estates of Craigston, Drummuir, Carnousie and Mayen. David James Duff inherited Hatton from his Duff aunt in 1970. He knew it well, having spent his school holidays there from the age of eight with his aunt who was a keen gardener and had put together a vast collection of daffodils. When he married his wife Jayne in 1987 he was adding a valuable asset. Jayne James Duff not only runs the large house, catering for the endless stream of

paying visitors who come to shoot and enjoy the estate and gardens, but took to gardening herself like a duck to water.

Daffodils and design were an early preoccupation for Jayne. The banks of the woodland garden are carpeted with the sweet-smelling *Narcissus pseudo narcissi* that have naturalised here. Mixed in are many rare cultivars of the type that send a frisson down the spine of daffodil fanciers. These have been transplanted from the nursery rows where they were growing in the two-acre walled garden. The other half of the garden was full of vegetables laid out in orderly patterns.

The collection occupied the top half of the garden, in the sloping area running down to the burn, but with only

Jayne James Duff,
Hatton Castle.

one gardener and herself to tend the area and keep the beds weed-free it was impossible. Jayne had as many of the cultivars identified as possible – some date from 1917 – and then began planting them in the woodlands that grow on the steep slopes covering the two hundred yards between the walled garden and the house.

Built of harled red sandstone, this impressive building sits gauntly surveying the rolling wooded countryside, surrounded by huge lawns and a gravel sweep. Given the climate and the four-legged predators, it would be difficult to cultivate the immediate policies; often deer graze on the front lawn. Instead she has concentrated her efforts in the walled garden where her eye for plant combinations, colour and design are shown off well.[13]

As a result of her labours the walled garden now combines a pleasure garden with a productive vegetable area, through

which you can wander the paths and allées. There are seats on which to sit and admire the gentle colours and sniff the heady scent of the hundreds of old-fashioned roses. The central allée, leading to a massive yew house, is planted with laburnum trees that arch over a mixture of shrubs and herbaceous plants in creamy custard yellows, blues and whites. There is also clever mixture of textures here. The strap-shaped leaves of yellow iris and the furry foliage of the startling blue meconopsis, the small ferny-leafed 'old yellow scotch' roses, sweet-scented ponticum azalea, potentilla, hosta and alchemilla spill over the paved path and are thrown into relief against the dark green of the yew hedges.

The fruit trees each stand in a pool of flowers: around one, aquilegias, epimediums and martagon lilies form a flowery skirt. The toffee apple tree, cercidiphyllum, plays host to rose 'Rambling Rector' surrounded by stately cardoons. Clematis and honeysuckle fill up gaps and scramble through the larger shrub borders at the top end.

In the remaining vegetable section a half-acre of fishing net protects the immaculate rows from the pheasants who are reared in the surrounding woods and would strip the soft fruit and grow fat on the asparagus, salads, root and green vegetables if allowed to. The old walls are covered with espaliered fruit trees, red currants and gooseberries. Borders of cutting flowers for the house are edged with low-growing pink and white astilbe that makes a perfect hedge.[14] In late summer the mood changes as flame red *Tropaeolum speciosum* engulfs

Rows of orderly vegetables at Hatton Castle are protected from marauding pheasants by half an acre of fishing net.

Astilbes form low hedges on either side of the path that runs along the fruit section of the walled garden at Hatton Castle.

the yew house. The James Duffs' two young sons now climb up inside it, just as their father did at their age: it is perfect for hide and seek.

The newest walled garden to be mentioned in this chapter is ironically the one that pays most attention to the original date of the house in its planning. As you arrive at Spedlins Tower near Lockerbie, a notice on the gate announces: 'You are entering a rabbit free zone, please keep the gate shut.' Before moving here, Nick and Amanda Gray used to come

up for weekends to find that the rabbits had just wiped out everything that they had planted the weekend before. It was disheartening and very expensive, as any gardener with rabbits will tell you, so eventually they conceded defeat and rabbit-fenced the whole two acres.

Nick, an architect, and Amanda, a designer, used to live in a glass house in Yorkshire that they designed and built so that they were living 'in the garden'. Sixteen years ago when their children had grown up, they came to Scotland looking for a site on which to build another modern house. Instead they ended up living in a tower house that dates from the early fifteenth century – because 'we just knew the moment we saw it that we had to live here'. When they retired from the design business they had run together in London and Yorkshire for thirty years, they came to live full time at Spedlins. It is not everyone's idea of an ideal retirement home; the kitchen is on the third floor up a steep stone wheel stair, the bedrooms are on the floor above, and their studies, where they collaborate and draw the designs for the gardens and follies, are on the fifth floor.

Although the tower had been restored by a previous owner, it was pretty basic, with no central heating, sitting starkly in an open field with a cart track up to the only door. The Grays now have a drive coming around the tower that enters an enclosed car park area surrounded with low, rough harled walls and a raised hedge of robinia trees. These are proving a bit brittle for the climate but the ivy planted all along the walls is thriving. In each corner of the entrance court, there are follies with conical slate roofs; one is the log store, the other is called 'Mrs G's tea house' and both are smothered with climbing roses and honeysuckle. Another project that echoes the sixteenth century is a parterre on the other side of the tower which has been laid out adjacent to a stone terrace. Surrounded by a high yew hedge on two sides, the third side is made up of an allée of holm oaks planted in a raised stone bed edged with box. At the far end of this allée is an entrance pavilion containing stone seats below a doocot in the roof for their Birmingham Roller doves. The matching pavilion on the other side is

The Tea House at Spedlin's Castle.

Nick and Amanda Gray in one of the garden pavilions at Spedlins Castle.

whimsically known as 'The Banqueting Hall'. Lit by candles and small electric stars in the midnight blue ceiling, it just has room for six to dine 'under the stars'. The parterre itself is a stylised design of circles and crosses edged with box and filled in with contrasting pink and white gravel[15] that glows eerily at night in the moonlight when viewed from the top of the tower.

Further afield, the next project was started in the boggy area beyond the cottage where the Grays' daughter and her family live. A pond is emerging and they are planning a studio on the edge that will be linked to wooden walkways around and across the pond. Originally they brought in a dowser who found the spring that feeds the pond, but as Nick says, 'a pond should not be undertaken lightly', as they

are now having to dig it deeper to support the wildlife and keep the weeds at bay. It is positioned in such a way as to reflect the tower in the water.

When Nick worked in London he used to come up to Spedlins, mow the lawn and go straight back down again. His is still the main physical input while Amanda chooses the plants and nurtures them. The sheer amount of physical work they both do makes me think that this 'retirement' is a bit of a myth.

So in this twenty-first-century garden the walls have returned to the castle garden after their banishment during the nineteenth century. Elizabeth Grant of Rothiemurchus[16] writes of her family's return to the Doune from London in 1812, after a period of four years and the disappearance of 'the dear old formal kitchen garden' next to the house:

We found the Doune all changed again, more of the backwater, more of the hill, and all the garden, gone. This last had been removed to its present situation in the series of pretty hollows in the birch wood between the Drum and the Miltown moor; a fashion of the day, to remove the fruit and vegetables to an inconvenient distance from the Cook, the kitchen department of the garden being considered the reverse of ornamental. The new situation of ours, and the way it was laid out, was the admiration of every body, and there could not well have been any thing of the sort more striking to the eye, with the nicely managed entrance among the trees, and the gardener's cottage so picturesquely placed; but I always regretted the removal. I like to be able to lounge in among the cabbages, to say little of the gooseberries; and a walk of above a quarter of a mile on a hot summer's day before reaching the refreshment of fruit

is almost as tormenting to the drawing room division of the family as is the sudden want of a bit of thyme, or sage or parsley to those in authority in the offices, and no one beyond the swing door idle enough to have an hour to spare for fetching some.

The doocot glimpsed through the allée of Holm oaks and yew at Spedlins.

The parterre at Spedlins viewed from the top of the castle.

Notes

1. Architect and designer, born 1864, died 1929.
2. The geographic spread of the gardens in this chapter is incidental. They are chosen principally because they illustrate various types in the evolution of the walled garden moving on from the gardens discussed in the previous chapter.
3. 'Bosquet' = a thicket or wood.
4. *The Highlands and Western Isles of Scotland* by John MacCulloch MD FRS LS GS &c. &c. &c., vol. I (1824).
5. Dovecot, i.e. nesting-place for 'doos', or doves (or pigeons).
6. Holly was adopted by the Christians from the pagans who believed that it had significant magical powers of protection, particularly against poison and lightning, thus explaining its planting next to old dwellings.
7. Since demolished.
8. Wild cherry, *Prunus avium*.
9. These are described in Chapter 7.
10. As described by A.A. Milne in *The House at Pooh Corner* (1928): 'Eeyore's Gloomy Place, which was where he lived'.
11. These hot walls were difficult to regulate and too hot a fire could scorch as well as warm, so that in the nineteenth century they tended more to be used to ripen the wood of the fruit trees in the late summer and early autumn. The chimney tops would sometimes be disguised with decorative features like Grecian urns. Wall protectors were much used and these could be made of nets, straw or canvas hung from special hooks. Sometimes glass panes fitted onto brackets, set into the walls, were used also to protect the blossom from frost. Later hot water pipes running through all four walls of the garden proved a more efficient method by distributing heat evenly. These would be connected to the coal-fired boilers that produced the required and very differing temperatures for the vineries, the fruit and flower houses.
12. Ten years on, the trees were pollarded to restrict their size and climbing roses planted to grow up them so now they have cloaks of roses.
13. Jayne James Duff has developed her horticultural interest a stage further, studying at Rosemary Alexander's school of garden design at the Chelsea Physic Garden in London. She has set up her own design business so that she can use her experience to help others who want to make gardens in this tricky climate.
14. These are trimmed with a strimmer after flowering to keep them compact.
15. Gravel was first shipped by boat to Scotland for the Earl of Mar's garden in the early eighteenth century.
16. *Memoirs of a Highland Lady.*

CHAPTER FOUR

Plants and Collectors

Snow on birches growing at Scone Palace.

PLANTS AND COLLECTORS

HERE LIES MASTER DAVID DOUGLAS, BORN IN SCOTLAND AD 1799. AN INDEFATIGABLE TRAVELLER, HE WAS SENT OUT BY THE ROYAL HORTICULTURAL SOCIETY OF LONDON AND GAVE HIS LIFE FOR SCIENCE IN THE WILDS OF HAWAII, JULY 12, 1834.

So reads the inscription on David Douglas's gravestone.[1] Speculation continues as to whether Douglas was pushed or fell into a cattle pit that had already trapped a wild bull. His dog Billy[2] was found sitting faithfully guarding his master's bundle left on the ground beside the pit. Dropping dead in the shrubbery rather than being gored to death by a wild bull is the end that most gardeners would imagine for themselves after a lifetime at this normally peaceful pursuit. But David Douglas was no ordinary gardener and in his short life of 35 years he managed to leave his mark on almost every garden in Britain via his plant introductions. Most famous for sending back seeds of the Douglas fir, his travels produced douglasia from the primulaceae family and if you grow mahonia, flowering currant, mimulus, garrya, clarkia, limnanthes, lupins, sunflowers or cammassia, these will have descended from plants or seeds collected by Douglas.

Born in 1799, the son of a stonemason employed at Scone Palace in Perthshire, Douglas started as an apprentice gardener there at the age of ten. He moved on to work at the Firth of Forth estates for Sir Robert Preston, who encouraged him to use his extensive library to educate himself; two years later he was invited to join the staff of the Glasgow Botanical Gardens. The Regius Professor at the time was the celebrated W.J. Hooker,[3] who became his mentor, and together they went off plant-hunting in the Highlands and Islands of Scotland. Later Douglas began the first of many trips to the North American continent to collect specimens and seeds for the Royal Horticultural Society, which was founded in 1804.

He survived many hair-raising adventures in both Canada and America involving native Indians, atrocious storms, near starvation and life-threatening encounters with bears. His diaries and the letters he wrote home give graphic descriptions of his travels and of the dramatic scenery of the 'Grand Rapids' and the Rockies. But it was the great soaring pines that he had only heard about and never seen that captured his imagination. In 1827 he introduced the sugar pine, *Pinus lambertiana,* and in the same year the Douglas fir,[4] *Pseudotsuga menziesii,* seeds of which have grown to a height of almost 200 feet in Britain. Even non-conifer lovers should be converted by this tree – it has wonderful tactile bark which is immensely craggy and rutted and foliage that hangs in great soft swags of dense dark green bearing handsome egg-shaped cones. Most of Douglas's other introductions will be quite familiar: the noble fir, *Abies procera*; the grand fir, *A. grandis*; sitka spruce, *Picea sitchensis* and the Monterey pine, *Pinus radiata,* all of which are used extensively in commercial forestry today. Douglas would be pleased to see the thriving commercial forestry at his birthplace, Scone, where his trees are grown from stock propagated in their own nursery.

There are two pineta at Scone, the old one planted in 1848 containing 68 different species and the new one planted in 1972 containing 60 species. There are fine mature examples of many of Douglas's conifers growing here on the site of the ancient city of Scone that was moved stone by stone in 1800 to improve the vistas on the estate. I wonder what Douglas's stonemason father, who must have helped shift the houses, would have thought had he known how his infant son would be remembered here 200 years later.

There are many famous Scottish plant collectors who risked life and limb to discover horticultural treasures that can be found in our gardens today. From the mid-eighteenth to the twentieth century, they sailed to the four corners of

The Gothic Chapel at Scone.

The two pineta at Scone in winter.

Lord and Lady Mansfield.

the earth. Robert Fortune, from Berwickshire, was in China in the late eighteenth century, supplying us with Japanese anemones, forsythia and winter jasmine. George Forrest, from Kilmarnock, had some death-defying adventures in western China and Tibet, searching out thousands of species of primulas, rhododendrons, camellias and magnolias at the turn of the nineteenth century. Euan and Peter Cox[5] from Perthshire hunted extensively during the twentieth century in the Himalayas and China.

There were other less well-known Scottish travellers from the early eighteenth century onwards, variously described as naturalists, botanists, collectors, gardeners, artists, writers and surgeons, or as a combination of two or more. Amongst them were Thomas Coulter from Dundalk, who worked as a doctor in Mexico and travelled in California sending back large collections of cacti and later 50,000 botanical specimens. Hugh Falconer from Morayshire spent years in India and is known for his involvement in the first production of Indian tea. Robert Brown, a botanist from Angus, searched in Australia, sending back 4,000 plants. Also from Angus, George Don set off to collect orchids in the Gold and Ivory coasts of Africa, while William Kerr of Roxburghshire sent back peonies and the double *Kerria japonica* from his travels in China, Java and the Philippines. Edinburgh minister's son Sir John Kirk accompanied Dr Livingstone on his epic voyage through Africa as 'surgeon naturalist', leaving us over a hundred plants that commemorate his name. These are just a handful of the intrepid Scottish explorers.[6]

Another surgeon/plant collector, Archibald Menzies, is typical of these men, many of whom came from quite humble beginnings and dedicated their lives to plants. Born in 1754 in Aberfeldy in Perthshire and educated at the local church school, the young Menzies studied at the Royal Botanic Garden in Edinburgh under the tutelage of one of the founder members, Dr John Hope. Aged twenty-four, he made a botanical tour through the Highlands and Hebrides before joining the navy a few years later as assistant surgeon aboard the *Nonsuch*. At the same time as fighting the French in Canada and off the Cape, he continued his botanical studies, sending back plants and seeds collected on his voyages to Sir Joseph Banks[7] of Kew Gardens.

Menzies later sailed on the *Discovery* – as surgeon-botanist to Captain George Vancouver – on which 'not one man died from ill-health between that date [1790] and the expedition's return in 1795'. At one point he was arrested by Vancouver for protesting about the loss of his plants, but he did succeed in bringing back a number to Britain, most famously *Araucaria araucana*, the monkey puzzle tree so beloved of the Victorians. He had grown the seeds in a cold frame on the deck of the *Discovery* and five had rooted by the time the ship docked in Britain. One grew at Kew for nearly a century. Menzies became president of the Linnean Society[8] in the year before he died. He left his collection of grasses, sedges and cryptogams to the Edinburgh Botanic Garden.

View through the woodland garden at Ardkinglas to Loch Fyne.

The River Kinglas.

The Campbells of Ardkinglas, in Argyll, began planting trees there after the 1745 uprising, but the pinetum was really started by their Callender descendants in the nineteenth century. Using many species introduced by David Douglas, it was continuously planted right through to the twentieth century. In the early 1930s, much new planting took place under the supervision of Sir Michael Noble MP, brother of the owner. He was a dedicated gardener and a friend of the Aberconways at Bodnant,[9] who supplied him with a large and interesting collection of rhododendrons and azaleas

Champion tree, Abies alba, *at Ardkinglas.*

that they had grown from seeds collected on trips to China and the Himalayas. These were incorporated into the pinetum and it flourished until he became too ill to continue.

When the late John Noble inherited the estate it was run down and crippled with death duties, so he had to find ways to bring in some income[10] in order to restore it. The days of seven gardeners and a productive walled garden producing vegetables for the big house were long gone, so this was grassed over, but he had plans to use it in future as a nursery for the seedlings and cuttings propagated from the woodland garden. The pinetum had become a forest of sycamores and scrub knitted together with brambles and weeds. The trees and shrubs were in a bad way, with no air and no light, and it was not until the employment of David Gray, a knowledgeable gardener who arrived in the 1990s, that the long task of renovation began. Gray has singlehandedly brought back the fifteen acres and undertaken a vast amount of replanting in the newly cleaned garden.

Occupying a swooping hillside around which runs the handsome river Kinglas, you can see five 'champion' trees.[11] One of these is the Alerce or Patagonian cypress, *Fitzroya cupressoides*,[12] with the widest girth in the British Isles of 252 centimetres. This seventy-foot species has become rare due to over-felling in its native habitat of Chile and Argentina. It is an exceptionally long-lived and slow-growing tree much prized for the durable quality of its timber. It is a highly prized tree here, too, as it is rare to find large mature specimens in the British Isles. It is thought that all the existing mature specimens originated from a single introduction but there are no records to show how this tree arrived at Ardkinglas, where it was planted in 1870. The growing conditions are perfect: high rainfall (around 110 inches per annum), free-draining fertile sandy loam and relative shelter at sea level making frosts rare; in fact, they are so good that specimens from the Royal Botanic Garden in Edinburgh are sent here to be nurtured.

The house at Ardkinglas[13] is one of architect Robert Lorimer's greatest creations. Given a free hand and a virtually blank cheque, this stunning, Arts and Crafts-inspired, neo-baronial holiday mansion was built for the equivalent in today's money of five million pounds. As well as using the spectacular views, Lorimer utilised the earlier gardens that dated from around 1745, when the first trees were planted. In the 1860s two eccentric Callender bachelors created the idiosyncratic 'Caspian Sea', a kidney-shaped ornamental loch that can be seen from the windows of the house to the west. Apart from the loch, another amusement that the brothers made for themselves was a miniature steam train that ran along Loch Fyne. On the 'Caspian' they created a fleet of six-foot-long gunboats modelled on Nelson's ships; each had small iron cannons mounted on the decks that fired real bullets. 'Battleships' was their favourite pastime and various wrecks have been retrieved from the bottom of the 'Caspian' together with some of the cannons, all of which are lovingly displayed at Ardkinglas. Today Lorimer's terraces and the Callenders' loch are planted with masses of the deciduous common yellow azalea, magnolias, camellias and ornamental trees that are a dramatic sight in early summer.

Further down the road are the gardens of Crarae, described by Roy Lancaster[14] as 'the best example of Himalayan Gorge gardening'. The present inhabitants of Crarae house are Sir Ilay and Lady Campbell, who inherited it in 1967. The fifty-acre garden was started by Sir Ilay's grandmother, Grace, in the early twentieth century. Initially she cultivated the area around the house but it was her son, Sir George, who created the majority of what you see today by gradually clearing the native trees in the glen from 1925 onwards.

Grace's nephew was the famous plant collector and writer Reginald Farrer and his influence and plant introductions can be seen all over the garden. Today there are species from New Zealand, Chile, Tasmania, China, Japan, the United States and the Himalayas. Trees were Sir George's great love and they provide the canopy for over four hundred species of rhododendrons and azaleas as well as countless other acid-loving shrubs.

Sir Ilay Campbell, Crarae.

The spectacular gorge planting in autumn at Crarae.

Eucalyptus trees surround a bonfire of turning leaves at Crarae.

Sir George was more of a gardener and less of a collector, which accounts for the very robust feel of the plants; they are all entirely happy where they are. Many he grew from seeds given to him by plant-hunting friends. Of these, rowans, maples, tulip trees, prunus, cotoneaster and berberis are some that contribute to the drifts of autumn colour. He did, however, collect some species and there are fine mature examples of eight species and hybrids of eucryphia, some twenty of eucalyptus, several magnolias and nine different northofagus. Other gifts came from gardens across Scotland: Arduaine, Inverewe, Dawyck, the Islands of Colonsay and Gigha and the Royal Botanic Garden in Edinburgh.

Crarae Gardens are indisputably one of the finest examples of woodland gardening in Scotland. Autumn is the climax and, in my view, the best time to visit it. The incredible range of blooms in the spring and early summer, overhanging the steep gorge with its fast-flowing burn, take your breath away but in autumn the turning leaves of deciduous azalea, witchhazel, birch, katsura and fothergillas create a spectacular horicultural bonfire of colour. Sir George was not just a knowledgeable plantsman: he had a good eye for grouping and colour, too.

Sir Ilay was closely involved with the garden towards the end of Sir George's life and he and Lady Campbell have always worked in the garden. Maintaining existing gardens depends on the contents and the manpower needed to look after and replace those contents and their surroundings. Gardens are not static works of art. They are, like humans, prone to illness and death and so the promise of eternal life is an illusion. There is no quick fix and it will not wait for a better time; now is always the best time for looking after them. The mild, moist climate that Crarae enjoys on the shores of Loch Fyne, with its fertile acid soil, produces as many problems as advantages. The jungle-like growth occurs not just in the thousands of trees and shrubs that thrive here but also in self-seeded trees and weeds that grow rapaciously and need stern treatment if they are not to engulf the former.

But in spite of Sir Ilay forming the garden into a charitable trust in 1978 and opening full-time to the public, visitor numbers plummeted. In spite, too, of his forming a 'Friends of Crarae' organisation with members paying an annual subscription, and in spite of getting help from the European Regional Development Fund and the Countryside Commission, Crarae was handed over to the National Trust for Scotland (NTS) in 2001 so that it could be saved for the nation. It is interesting to speculate on how the NTS will go about increasing the visitor figures, as it is not just about the decline in tourism to the Highlands. People want more than just one attraction when they visit anything, now. I couldn't help noticing the contrast a few miles down the road where the Loch Fyne Oyster Bar, restaurant, food shop, tree nursery and snack bar were doing a roaring trade on the wet October day of my visit, while the car park at Crarae was empty.

View of Loch Fyne from the hillside at Crarae.

Loch Awe from the garden at Upper Sonochan.

Sir Eddie McGrigor and his wife, Mary, Upper Sonochan.

On the west coast of Scotland you are constantly reminded of the weather. There are days in the winter when you can drive through miles and miles of nothing but boiling waterfalls, hills, sheep and rain, but it is precisely these conditions that provide the ideal habitat for the plants that grow in Sir Eddie and Lady McGrigor's garden at Upper Sonochan in Argyll on the east shore of Loch Awe. Upper Sonochan House originally sat divided from the loch by a hayfield and trees but, since the great storm in 1968 that bought down many of the trees, the McGrigors have planted over five thousand shrubs and trees over the five acres.

The main emphasis is on rhododendrons, azaleas in large swathes, shrub roses and acid-loving species of amenity

trees. With no early-morning sun to burn them, lots of tender plants such as agapanthus thrive and in the damp climate meconopsis and primulas self-seed beside the burn. The quantities of ferny lichen on the branches of the shrubs and trees give testimony to the purity of the air here, while the loamy soil has a good depth and is free draining. Grass paths meander amongst the generous plantings through which you catch views of the loch, as you follow them around. On a wet day, rushing peaty brown burns intersect the paths and mist swirls up from the loch, adding to the drama. The names of the rare rhododendrons and azaleas roll off Eddie

McGrigor's lips, many of which were 'occasionally slipped me by Dr McKenna of Tarbet' (a well-known specialist). Lovely mature specimens of swamp cypress, eucryphia, enkianthus, parrotia, sorbus, fothergilla, camelias, acers, escallonia, cornus and magnolias are just a few trees and shrubs that I recognised. With something for every season, the shelter-belts of *Viburnum tomentosum* Lanarth form a beautiful froth of lace in spring. The first week of May is the best time for colour, but there are rhododendrons in flower here from February until August and the autumn colour is spectacular.

Lush planting of shrubs and perennials at Upper Sonochan.

Wallace Fyfe, Ascog Hall, Bute.

The roof of the sunken fernery, Ascog Hall.

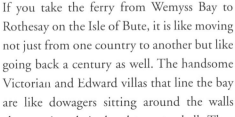

If you take the ferry from Wemyss Bay to Rothesay on the Isle of Bute, it is like moving not just from one country to another but like going back a century as well. The handsome Victorian and Edward villas that line the bay are like dowagers sitting around the walls chaperoning their daughters at a ball. They have the same stately respectable air and ample proportions, their filigree ironwork like lace fichues around their shoulders.

Ascog Hall, just outside town, is one of these villas, a turreted Scottish baronial piece of conceit built by the Rev. James Montieth. A Free Church of Scotland minister, he found an outlet for his romanticism in this choice of architectural style. The house dates from 1843, but it was the next owner, a rich merchant from Glasgow, Robertson

Buchanan Stewart, who adorned his summer home with the ornate sunken fernery in 1870. Fern collecting was a very Victorian obsession, with over ten thousand species to choose from – ranging from extremely hardy to the very tender specimens that could be ideally displayed under glass.

Wallace and Katherine Fyfe bought the property just over a hundred years later, in 1986. It was in a ruinous state and they have painstakingly renovated the house and restored the fernery over the last twenty years. The roof was rebuilt using the original design with the help of a grant from Historic Scotland, while both advice and plants were given by the Royal Botanic Garden, Edinburgh (RBGE). In 2000, Ascog won the Scottish prize given by the Historic Gardens Foundation to 'reward restoration of architectural features in parks and gardens'.

The Fyfes' work was aided by an article in the *Gardeners Chronicle* dated 1879, written by B.S. Williams about his visit to Ascog as a guest of the Stewarts in October of that year. In it he describes:

A span-roofed house with rounded ends, the roof rests on stone walls, and is composed of an iron framework. It is well built and altogether has a very neat and good appearance. It is situated in a well-selected spot on one side of the garden where it is well backed up with trees. The shrubs occupy a rising bank in front so that one only sees the roof above the wall, the bank and trees form a great protection in keeping the house sheltered from cold weather.

Williams goes on to describe the grotto-like entrance which is planted with hardy ferns. Once you are inside, his delight and

The restored interior of the fernery at Ascog.

obvious knowledge of the specimens originating from Southeast Asia, China, Japan, Europe, the Atlantic Islands, Australasia, New Zealand and South America give a clue as to the diversity of the collection which, re-created from his lists, now numbers 120 different species.

The RBGE's involvement has been crucial and in return for long-term access to the collection for study and conservation purposes, they have provided a range of ferns, tree ferns and temperate conifers to go into the fernery. Out of what was just a very dilapidated and ruinous building full of mud and broken glass, only one fern had survived – *Todea barbara* – which Williams claimed in his article to be a thousand years old. When the red Bute sandstone walls were uncovered, they revealed shelves and crannies for planting the mosses and ferns. The original pebble floor emerged from under the debris and is a warm sand colour

Adiantum capillus-veneris (Maidenhair fern).

Wendy and John Mattingley, Cluny Garden.

made with stones from the beach. It wanders around the fernery, criss-crossing the water that gurgles in at one end, flows through ponds and streams and exits underground at the other end.

In the absence of flowers, the wide range of greens creates an intensely peaceful feel, causing the visitor to slow down and examine the intricate textures and patterns of the fronds and stems of the ferns and mosses. Water drips and runs down the walls and the humidity, a crucial element in growing sub-tropical and temperate ferns, creates a Tolkienesque atmosphere where you could almost imagine Gollum from *The Hobbit* lisping 'Precious, precious …' as he flaps his way around and sloshes onto the small islands

in the water. On hot days the Fyfes have to water the house several times to keep the humidity at the correct level, but the mild Gulf Stream that flows past the island keeps the temperature warm enough in winter.

To the central Highlands and a visit to Cluny House, Perthshire, on the steeply sloping north bank of the River Tay. In early autumn there is no shortage of colour, vivid red *Tropaeolum speciosum*, the Scottish flame flower,[15] scrambles and climbs through, up and over shrubs and conifers cascading down to greet you around corners. The

brilliant yellow leaves of *Acer shirasawanum* 'aureum' stands sentinel at the entrance to the garden, a pool of light echoed by another golden acer at the far end of the lawn.

The part of the garden nearest to the house is quite modest in size, the main interest being the self-seeded plants growing in the gravel. Here, tall white *Anemone japonica*, Jacob's ladder, aquilegia and hellebore are amongst the plants that thrive. Wendy and John Mattingley took over the garden when they moved into Cluny in 1987 and they allow the plants here to run around and riot as they please, only thinning where necessary. Next to the gravel garden is a lawn surrounded by large shrubs and trees that screen the paths plunging downwards to the woodland gardens. The aspect, climate and soil in this part of Perthshire replicates conditions in the Himalayas and is ideal for growing plants from that part of the world, in particular primulas, meconopsis, trilliums, lilies, rhododendrons and azaleas, as well as acid-loving trees and shrubs. Wendy's

Acers and conifers surround the lawn at Cluny House, Strathtay.

The countryside glimpsed through the trees from Cluny garden.

late parents, Bobby and Betty Masterton, began planting the six-acre garden in 1950, growing many of the plants from seeds collected on the Ludlow–Sheriff expedition to Bhutan in 1948.[16] There are also two giant sequoias, one of which is a member of the 'Big Tree' club of Britain having a girth of eleven metres and a height of forty metres. Planted in 1860, it has tactile reddish bark and is home to tree-creepers and mistle thrushes, while up at the top buzzards and jackdaws roost. The sequoia sits in a clearing in a wood that is used for plant propagation. Rows of neatly potted-up seedlings and cuttings are surrounded by

huge bins of leaf mould and compost that when deserted, looks like an elves' workshop. Red squirrels shoot past, startled away from their feeding boxes as you approach. In the distance you can hear the soughing of the wind in the high branches and the sound of wood pigeons cooing, punctuated by the occasional screech of a pheasant.

Marked by arrows, the paths snake up and down the hillside and around corners, producing surprises. As you come out of the shade into the light, the turning leaves of a *Rhus typhinus* are lit up, while around another, a view is suddenly revealed where the sun highlights a

Autumn colour at Cluny.

field of stubble dotted with bales of golden straw. There is drama in a planting pocket punctuated by ten-foot stems of the giant lily cardiocrinum pushing up through ferns, hostas and the woolly leaves of *Meconopsis nepaulensis*. Further on, a boggy pond in a shady area contains skunk cabbage and drifts of primulas. The garden is home to the National Collection of Asiatic Primulas, but many others can be seen in the garden. From March through to June, varieties like *P. edgeworthii*, *whiteii* and *sonchifolia* are followed by *griffithii*, *tanneri*, *strumosa* and *americanum* before the candelabra get going.

Throughout the area grow large woodland specimens of oak, chestnut, rowan, birch, beech and yew and many varieties of pine. Some have jackets of ivy; others have cloaks of tropaeolum or clematis. The arching stems of shrub roses, enkianthus, dogwood, euonymus, viburnum and cotoneaster jostle for attention on either side of the path, their stems, berries and leaves in full autumn fig. Around their feet grow ground-cover plants, geraniums, cyclamen and wild strawberries. Clumps of *Actea alba* with curious blood-red stems and white berries stand out against the carpets of leaves and needles, which come in a wonderful array of colours and textures.

This is one of the 'cleanest' gardens I have seen, with not a weed in sight. The Mattingleys and their four part-time helpers pull every weed by hand and then mulch with their own leaf mould and compost. As a result, a pot full of Cluny soil containing a plant purchased from the plant stand will most probably reward the new owner with quite a few random seedlings of other plants. The spindle bush that I brought home had

Snowdrops carpet the ground at Cambo, near St Andrews.

Hordeum jubatum (Foxtail barley) at Cambo.

no less than eight other treats growing in the pot, including primula, Jacob's ladder, viola, aquilegia and forget-me-knot – a nice reminder to go back again.

———— ❧ ————

On the eastern side of Scotland, Cambo House, near St Andrews in Fife, is surrounded by gardens and woodland that run down to the sea just above the entrance to the Firth of Forth. Fortunately for Catherine Erskine, she was already a keen gardener when, aged twenty-two, she married Peter

Catherine Erskine, Cambo.

Erskine and left Surrey to live at Cambo. There was lots to do and in the intervening years she has tackled the acres of garden and policies, put into action a complete restoration of the two-and-a-half-acre walled garden, organised the letting of the flats in the main house and the holiday cottages, catered for the paying guests[17] and functions, brought up five children and created a mail-order business dealing in snowdrops.[18]

To get to Cambo, it is necessary to drive through miles of woodland carpeted with snowdrops. There are millions and millions and over the last twenty years Catherine has built up a thriving business selling these single snowdrops 'in the green'. A cold spring is a bonus for her business as it prolongs the season for digging up the

A burn runs through the walled garden at Cambo.

bulbs, which have finished flowering. It is important that the bulbs do not dry out and that they are planted with their stalks and leaves still green which then die back into the bulb to produce vigorous flowers the following year. Catherine has also built up a collection of some 138 out of the 400 named cultivars of snowdrops and now has enough stock to be able to sell some of these too. They include doubles and singles as well as a collection bred to remember the children of the shooting tragedy in Dunblane: one with a pale yellow lining to the flower is called 'Sophie North'.

The walk from the house passes through curving borders that in mid-April are filled with early primula and a collection of hellebores. Drifts of scillas and chionodoxa run under the shrubs and pools of erythronium nod their pagoda-like heads in shades of yellow, white and pink. A large-scale eradication of sycamores and snowberry bushes further down has opened up this area and revealed clumps of the Autumn crocus, which are lifted and divided annually, some going into pots for sale at the plant stall.

The ornamental potager at Cambo.

Around four thousand visitors a year come to see the gardens and in particular the unusual walled garden. It is built up the sides of a U-shaped area with a fast-flowing burn running through the bottom. This flows under the wall at one side and is channelled in a stone-lined culvert criss-crossed with ornamental bridges. It disappears out under the opposite wall and rushes on down through the woodlands to the beach and the sea below. The walls, which are twenty feet high in places, are for the most part brick-lined. Two of the original greenhouses have been restored out of the eight that used to be there in the garden's heyday at the end of the nineteenth century. The Erskine children have made a goldfish pond in the foundations of one of them and others have been made into ornamental beds.

To make the garden more attractive visually, while still using it as a larder for the house, a potager is laid out in a symmetrical design. The beds are planted with a mixture of vegetables, herbs and flowers with box edging. Gooseberries are grown as cordons lining the path leading through to a huge double herbaceous border that swoops up to the top wall. To the right is a mature lilac walk comprising twenty varieties of this much-neglected shrub; Catherine's favourite is the Persian lilac. On down the other side are fruit trees underplanted with paeonies lining an old-fashioned shrub-rose border. Across from this on the other side of the burn is a cutting garden growing fresh flowers for the arrangements that are put into every room of the house. With seemingly no spare time, Catherine is fortunate that her recreation is gardening.

So from the humble snowdrop to heather, which seems to have become almost as much of a national plant in Scotland as the national emblem, the thistle. Heather is indigenous to our country and the best place to see it is on hillsides in August, but for the cultivated variety, there is no better place to view it than at Tillypronie in Aberdeenshire.

When Queen Victoria used to dine with her neighbours at Tillypronie her faithful servant, John Brown, would accompany her. Brown, too grand to eat with the servants but not grand enough to eat with the Queen, took his meals in splendid isolation in a special wooden hut in the garden. The present owner of the house, The Hon. Phillip Astor, has not met his neighbour, Billy Connolly, who played John Brown in the award-winning film *Mrs Brown*, but if he did, he would sadly not be able to show him the hut, for it has disappeared.

There are stories in abundance at Tillypronie, which was bought in 1951 by Astor's father, the late Lord Astor of Hevor.[19] Philip Astor's happiest times were spent here during his school holidays, roaming the 15,000 acres with the many friends and relations who filled the rambling house, and leaving for school was always a wrench.

The house's royal connections began with its purchase by Sir James Clark, physician and close personal friend to Queen Victoria, and are still maintained during the Royal Family's annual migration to neighbouring Balmoral today. Clark was the son of the Earl of Findlater's butler at Cullen house and his meteoric rise from 'Banffshire loon' to Royal confidant is a tale in itself. He is credited with introducing Victoria and Albert to Balmoral in 1848. Four years later they bought the estate and completed building the castle in 1856. Clark and his wife always stayed at Birkhall while attending the Royal

Nasturtiums on the terrace above the heather garden at Tillypronie, planted after Royden's plan.

Pools of heather below Tillypronie.

family and, although he bought Tillypronie in 1855, it was his son Sir John Clark who built the present house in 1867. The lintel, laid by Queen Victoria, is above the front door and at the same time she planted an *Abies magnifica* across the gravel sweep, opposite the front door. This tree blew down in the great gale of 1953; in 1960 the present Queen planted a copper beech on the same spot.

Commemorative trees are a big feature at Tillypronie. The pair of giant Californian redwoods planted by the front gates in 1867 are now a hundred feet high. The Roydens (owners of the house from 1925 to 1951) planted another two for the silver jubilee of George V in 1935 and Gavin Astor continued the tradition on the centenary of the house. Other luminaries who have planted trees in the

gardens include Sir Harold Macmillan in 1958. A wander around the pinetum reading the plaques on the trees provides a horticultural visitor's book of past guests staying at Tillypronie as well as memories of past and present members of the Astor family. The pinetum was planted in 1958 and contains 300 different named varieties of conifers laid out in an ordered pattern. On his travels, Lord Astor would pick up pine cones and bring them home in his sponge bag. The trees raised from these were planted in the gardens, adding memories of his travels.

Lord Astor and his wife Irene spent as much time as possible here. They were a 'gardening team' and added considerably to the 1920s layout of the previous owner, Sir Thomas Royden. Royden had laid out the rock gardens

Mike Rattray, the gardener at Tillypronie, Aberdeenshire.

Plaque commemorating a tree planting at Tillypronie by Sir Harold Macmillan.

below the house, built the water garden and had plans drawn up for the heather beds, but never made them. It was left to the Astors to interpret these plans and they planted great pools of heathers, using forty different varieties, in the shape of clouds, complemented by over 150 species of dwarf conifers. I have always had a bit of a problem with heather gardens, being of the opinion that heather looks better on hills in all its purple glory in August, so I was pleasantly surprised by the heather garden at Tillypronie. No dinky little beds here, but huge undulations the size of tennis courts. This is a grown-up heather garden that is at its best in late August. The house and gardens are 1,125 feet above sea level, so the conditions for growing heather are perfect.

What we call heather in fact comes from two separate genera – Erica and Calluna. *C. vulgaris* is the Scottish heather that in times gone by was an indispensable part of daily life. It was used for insulation in walls, for thatching and for making slate-pegs. It made beds to lie on that were praised for their softness and their restorative powers on weary nerve endings after a fragrant night's rest. Dyes for tweed and tartan are made with the juices and intoxicating liquors brewed from fermented flowers or teas for the tee-totals. Heather was used to make brooms, colanders, chimney brushes, floor mats, baskets and besoms for scrubbing out whisky containers. Widely used by herbalists to treat a range of ills from consumption to coughs, it is a truly useful plant.

Notes

1. Ann Lindsay Mitchell and Syd House, *David Douglas* (1999).

2. Billy, a scotch terrier, had been bought by Douglas on his last visit home to Scotland in 1829. He accompanied Douglas everywhere during his last five years. After Douglas' death in Hawaii, Billy was sent back to Britain where he was cared for by friends.

3. Father of Sir Joseph Hooker of Kew Gardens.

4. Described as a 'first-grade construction timber' a mature tree can command a price of £1,000 for 1,000 cubic feet. To grow large Douglas firs requires a moist climate and acid soil so they do better on the west coast of Scotland than the east. They mature at about 60 years old and the normal life span is around 120 years but, being shallow rooted, they are susceptible to wind blow.

5. See Chapter 6.

6. Sir Joseph Banks, president of the Royal Society in London from 1778 to 1820, specifically sought out Scots explorers, sending Francis Masson from Kew on the first plant hunting trip to S. Africa in 1772 and Thomas Blaikie from Corstorphine, Edinburgh, to Switzerland in 1775. Banks maintained that 'So well does the Seriousness of a Scotch Education fit the mind of a Scotsman to the habits of the industry, attention and frugality that they rarely abandon them at any time of life and I may say never while they are young.'

7. He had been introduced to Banks by Dr Hope.

8. The Linnean Society, formed in 1753, followed the binomial system of plant names as recommended by Carl Linnaeus, where plants had a one-word generic name and a single specific epithet.

9. Laura McLaren, the first Lady Aberconway,

started the gardens at Bodnant in 1894. The family supported many plant-collecting expeditions and planted many of the seeds at Bodnant – breeding from them after 1918. The gardens are open via the National Trust, but the house is still occupied by the Aberconways.

10. The Loch Fyne Oyster Bar was started by John Noble and marine biologist Andrew Lane in 1977; at the time Andrew Lane was running the salmon hatchery and suggested that they re-introduce oysters into Loch Fyne, where they had flourished in centuries gone by. (In 1771 the Duke of Argyll had threatened 'banishment' to any one caught lifting oysters from the shore.) In the middle of the nineteenth century oysters were widely consumed by rich and poor alike, but pollution and over-fishing had caused them to die away and the few left became very expensive. At Ardkinglas over one million oysters are harvested annually.

11. A 'champion' tree is deemed to be either the tallest or the broadest example within the British Isles.

12. *Fitzroya* is named after the Captain Robert Fitzroy, a British Naval officer who commanded the famous five-year voyage of the *Beagle*, which included the naturalist Charles Darwin amongst its passengers during the mid-nineteenth century. The introduction of the tree is credited to Cornishman William Lobb in 1849. Lobb, along with Ernest Wilson, was employed by the Scottish nurserymen, the Veitch family, who, over three generations, ran the largest nursery of its kind in Europe (see Chapter 6). Many plants that they sold were 'discovered to order' by their in-house explorers. Other discoveries include *Tropaeolum speciosum*,

Embothrium coccineum and *Crinodendron hookerianum*, all of which thrive in the same environmental conditions as provided at Ardkinglas and are West Coast favourites.

13. The house was commissioned by Sir Andrew Noble. The family had made a fortune with the Tyneside armaments factory Armstrong. Completing it in 1907, Lorimer designed all the fittings and fixtures inside, as well as the large terraces upon which it sits, commanding picture-postcard views of Loch Fyne and the surrounding mountains. The house incorporated every 'mod con' and was completed in an astonishing eighteen months.

14. Writer, plant collector and gardener.

15. This plant is of Chilean origin and has nothing to do with Scotland – it just happens to thrive here. It is also known as 'the de'il's guts' for its tenacious climbing abilities.

16. Lanarkshire-born George Sheriff (1898–1967) joined forces with Londoner Frank Ludlow (1885–1972) after the First World War, plant hunting in Bhutan and southeast Tibet.

17. The house can sleep thiry-eight comfortably and often it does when events like the Open Golf Tournament at St Andrews are happening and the family play host to visitors.

18. Snowdrops – *Galanthus nivalis*. Gerard the herbalist, in common with other early botanists, called the snowdrop 'the bulbous violet' and spoke of it as an introduction to Britain, not as a native. The generic name *Galanthus* is Greek for milkflower, while *nivalis* is Latin and relates to snow. There are nineteen species of this bulbous perennial, mostly found in upland woodlands from Europe to western Asia, but in particular

Italy, Switzerland and Austria. In places to their liking they will naturalise freely. They flower in late winter to early spring. Many doubles and trebles have been bred and most have a delicate scent, which is more apparent when they are brought into a warm room. These incredibly hardy bulbs can be grown from seed in containers in an open frame but need to be shaded in summer. Species hybridise readily, so if you grow several varieties they will not come true from seed.

19. Chairman of *The Times* and (from 1967) Life President of Times Newspapers.

CHAPTER FIVE

Specialists

Plants growing hydroponically at Achiltibuie.

SPECIALISTS

'It is pointless to battle against the elements, better to persuade and discuss with them instead.' PROFESSOR GEOFFREY DUTTON

Scotland has a long and honourable tradition of producing botanists; they went hand in hand with the medical profession. There were other sorts of botanists too, gardeners who became plant collectors and curators of botanical and horticultural organisations in places as far away as Australia, India and America; closer to home the Scots invaded England, becoming founder members of the Royal Horticultural Society, directors of Kew Gardens and the Chelsea Physic Garden as well as nurserymen and garden designers to royalty and the aristocracy from the eighteenth century onwards. Some wrote books and others illustrated them. They were appointed to the Linnean Society, knighted for their work and occasionally died on the job in some far-flung outpost.

Pete Brownless is involved in giving plants their correct names, a practice known as nomenclature, and he is Garden Supervisor for the plant nursery at the Royal Botanic Garden in Edinburgh. When I asked for directions on how to find his house on Stoneyhill Road in Musselburgh, I was told to look for the only house in this 'strictly-green-lawns-and-bedding-plants-land' that did not have either. When at last I had sorted out the Stoneyhill Crescents and Avenues from the Places and the Drives, I knew I was in the 'Road' when I spotted interesting-looking plants around the front porch of a modest semi. Crammed into this front patch of around 18 square feet and the back garden of around 240 square feet, are 2,000 plants, and this with over fifty per cent of the back area devoted to water – if your maths is good you can work out the ratio of plants to earth. The planting method is simple: three plants that flower at different times go in together, so there is always something out. When they are not flowering, they have interesting leaves. Pruning and

shaping have to be ruthless and everything has to 'perform'. Needless to say there was not a weed in sight.

In the tiny, back, south-facing garden I wondered why someone so passionate about plants chose to live here instead of somewhere more rural. The answer is simple; it is the warmest, driest, sunniest place in Scotland. At fifty feet above sea level there is no risk of flooding but

Pete Brownless, Stoneyhill Road.

at the same time it is near enough the sea to benefit from the warming effects and far enough away not to get salt-laden winds. Pete is a practical man and realised that, unlike most newly built houses, the garden had soil and not builder's rubble and that the house was small enough inside – and the garden outside – to be easily managed on his own, after a hard day at work. In his words, 'one person, one day do-able'.

Pete trained at the Writtle Horticultural College in Essex before going to work at the University of Wales, growing horticultural material for students to study. Twelve years ago he combined a trip to the Edinburgh Festival with an interview at Edinburgh's Botanic Garden and since then he has worked as their Garden Supervisor in charge of the nurseries. This involves plant- and seed-collecting trips to places including Chile, China and Europe as well as the naming of plants. As chief propagator, he also lectures and answers numerous letters of enquiry about identifying plants and their problems. He says that using the Latin names is easier than using the English ones as Latin serves as a universal language and he can communicate with plant experts in China and Russia, for instance, who do not speak English. The reason plant names keep changing is that, as botanical experts get better at recognising subtle nuances that differentiate one plant from another, they alter the names to facilitate identification. He assures me that they do not keep changing them to be difficult – it is more a matter of 'fine tuning' of the Latin descriptions. Latin names trip off Pete's tongue in a steady flow and when I weakly enquire after the common name of the exotic-looking *Berberidopsis corallina* climbing up the fence, I am told that it has over fifty common names in its native Chile. As all of them are in Spanish, he suggests that I can call it the 'climbing Chilean coral plant'.

Dominating the garden is a long, narrow, raised fishpond teeming with fish:[1] goldfish, tench, rudd, golden Chinas, datas and rosy red minnows. Ten varieties of dwarf water lilies are growing in there, all neatly planted in washing-up bowls

The back garden at Stoneyhill Road.

filled with compost and covered with gravel. Just coming into flower, the white South African aquatic perennial *Aponogeton distachyus* nestles up beside the giant Himalayan mare's tail rush. Flat paving stones on top of the raised sides provide the perfect seating area to sit and sip an evening glass of something refreshing and spot any weed that has the temerity or the tenacity to find a space. The variety of unusual[2] and tender plants growing there would take pages to enumerate, but a few give the flavour of the place, these are such as the yellow *Fremontodendron californicum*, *Aristolochia durior* (Dutchman's pipe), the Greek *Dracunculus vulgaris* (dragon arum lily) and the spiky crucifixion plant *Colletia armata* (which looks like a climbing cactus and should not be tangled with in the dark).

———— ✤ ————

Bee's – 'seeds that grow' – were the first packets of seeds that botanist Gordon Smith bought, aged five, with his pocket money at Woolworth's. He would plant packets of godetia, clarkia and sweet william in patterns in his plot at his childhood home in Strathtay. Most children would try radishes and carrots, but in the belief that 'real Scotsmen don't eat vegetables', he still eschews vegetable-growing in his garden: 'you can get those in Safeway,' he says. Until my visit to this Upper Deeside garden, I had never seen someone scarifying the front lawn and using a vacuum cleaner to hoover up the moss. Gordon Smith is no conventional gardener.

As a taxonomic[3] botanist with a degree from Aberdeen University, Gordon Smith spent twenty years teaching botany in Kuala Lumpur. He is fascinated with the variability of plants and likes to have 'lots and lots' of different kinds in his garden. If he gets interested in a family or genus he will 'worry it to death'. In illustration of this, he points out the ten species of epimedium growing around the garden. His knowledge is daunting and he does remember all the names. This is just as well because, when not lecturing part-time at Aberdeen University, he travels the world gathering

information and slides for his lectures on natural history, rainforests and gardens.

I first met Gordon Smith when he swooped off a large bus shepherding a group of plantspeople around my previous garden in Aberdeenshire. Needless to say he knew much more about what I was growing than I did. At that time he was Hon. Secretary of the Friends of the Cruikshank Botanical Garden in Aberdeen, a member of the National Trust Gardens Committee and an enthusiastic conductor of tours around Scottish gardens. These commitments have been given up to free up time for travelling.

I could not help smiling when I looked into his greenhouse, as it contained beds – not for plants, but for his

Gordon Smith, Ballater.

two cats, Mac and Tavish. His tomatoes were always a disaster, because of his travelling, so this seems a better use. 'Pussies rule OK' is his motto and on hot days Mac rules, curled up in the birdbath under a tree. The central bed in the back garden he calls his 'set-aside', as currently it contains a bonfire in the middle while he saves up for the gothic octagonal urn that he wants to buy. When the garden is open, occasionally he puts a notice on top of the bonfire that reads '*mons flagrans*'. Currently he is planting the alpine alchemilla around the edge as *A. mollis* proved too much of a thug. He intends to use this quadrant for annuals. 'Redevelopment is more interesting than care and maintenance,' he says, 'but it becomes that if you don't do it.' His other 'set-aside' is his rockery, but the days of the willow herb are numbered, as his plant collection needs more space.

The rose border has been planted like a rainforest with an over-canopy of larger shrubs such as his beloved lilacs; *Syringa vulgaris* Mme Lemoine and the small leaf *S. velutina* and a lower layer of things like herbaceous geraniums, *Epimedium sulphureum* and *E. pubigerum*. In the adjacent bed he grows *Paeonia veitchii var, woodwardii* with single pink flowers and delicate leaves. Smith strokes the fat buds of pale yellow *P. whitmania* and looks forward to the 'two days of flowering so I don't go away while it is out'.

There are so many interesting plants growing in this relatively small area; *Hylomecon japonicum* the Greek poppy, *Lonicera korolkowii* with tiny leaves and flowers which plays host to roses, 'Duchesse de Montebello' and Smith's other duchess, 'd'Angoulême', which needs support. He has a collection of

A rich mixture of plants at Ballater.

Herbaceous perennials in front of the greenhouse at Ballater.

trollius and some *Lathyrus vernus*, the spring flowering pea, in startling purple and blue together with a pale pink form. Other unusual plants that caught my eye included *Anemone sulphurea*, which is also known as *Pulsatilla alpina*, the thistle *Silybum marianum* and a ranunculus with creamy apricot bells.

The soil here is 'glacial till moraine' as it was originally the bed of the Dee; unless you improve it, you can't grow anything, as it is too free-draining. Apart from the unusual, there are some very healthy-looking ordinary plants too. *Salix helvetica* is a must, he says, as is the double white gean tree and cercidiphyllum. In the herbaceous border he likes the old-fashioned plants, macleya, thalictrum, aconitum and aquilegia. Rose 'Félicité et Perpétue' grows up a purple prunus and 'Betty Sherriff' (grown from the original seed from Bhutan) up an oak tree. In spite of his wanderlust, Gordon Smith believes that 'Britain has the best gardens in the world'.

There is something faintly surreal about looking at a palm tree laden with ripening bananas silhouetted against a heaving Atlantic sea whipped up by a mixture of driving sleet, hail and snow, in Scotland, in January. Nick Clooney, the manager of the Achiltibuie Hydroponicum on the windswept northwest coast of Scotland, explains that his boss, Viscount Gough, bought the property because 'he was fascinated by the idea of growing fruit and vegetables in a daft place'. On the day of my visit I could see why. On this salt-drenched, soilless rocky outcrop facing the Summer Isles, anyone fool enough to try to grow things would be rewarded with

Chimney pots are used as planters in Gordon Smith's garden.

Nick Clooney the manager of the Hydroponicum, Achiltibuie.

The Hydroponicum at Achiltibuie looking out towards the Summer Isles.

a blasted heath. One can only speculate about the effect this might have had on history if, at the time of the Highland Clearances, this form of horticulture had been available. Starvation played as large a part as wicked lairds did in driving the crofters from the land. With the ability to grow a huge range of food that includes basil, salads and spinach, courgettes, aubergines and peppers, bananas, pineapples and tomatoes with very little heat and no soil, who knows how many people could still be living in remote areas of the Highlands? In the tiny crofting township of Achiltibuie, two hours northwest of Inverness, the Hydroponicum supports fourteen families, attracts around 8,000 visitors a year and grows all the fresh produce for the Summer Isles Hotel and the café, with surplus for sale.

It all started when the previous owner, Robert Irvine, decided to grow fresh fruit and vegetables for his Summer Isles hotel on the land surrounding his croft. It saved him driving the thirty miles of one-track road to get onto the main road and fifty-five more miles to Inverness; it prolonged the growing season; it made him impervious to the atrocious weather conditions and it provided his guests with delicious food. If you have eaten a tomato grown in Holland, you can

Herbs and vegetables growing on the tilted staging at Achiltibuie Hydroponicum.

be pretty certain that it was grown in a hydroponic nursery. Yet few people have heard of this form of gardening that is increasingly being used to produce commercial crops all over the world and is becoming the preferred way of growing greenhouse produce. It is perfectly adaptable to domestic greenhouse and window-sill gardening as well.

Man has always had to adapt his methods of growing food to his environment. The Aztecs grew crops in raised beds surrounded by water in their parched environment high up in the Andes and irrigation to aid growth has been in existence in China, India and Africa for thousands of years. Hydroponics, a technique which grows plants without soil, was mainly developed in the 1930s and 1940s by the Americans as a method of providing their troops with fresh food when stationed on dry, inhospitable atolls in far-flung Pacific outposts.

In spite of growing in a soilless medium (a mixture of vermiculite and perlite) and being fed on water containing nutrients, very little water is required compared with conventional growing methods. As the root systems do not have to spread over wide areas to find food, large trees and shrubs can be grown in tiny six- to nine-inch pots, thus saving space. It is also low-maintenance, as all that is required is a daily check by one person, with a 'conductivity meter', into the tank of water. That person then adds nutrients to the correct formula, depending on the range of plants served by that tank, and in half an hour thousands of plants can be fed and watered.

Plants are composed of 95 per cent water, almost 5 per cent carbohydrates and a small quantity of trace elements. It is by mixing these elements with the water that continuously flows around the base of the pots (where it is absorbed by a

Banana palms at Achiltibuie Hydroponicum.

wick) that the fertiliser is made 100 per cent available to the plant. The water is pumped up onto the tilted staging and then flows back down into the tank underneath to be re-circulated. When you are growing plants in soil, the whole mass has to be filled with fertiliser but only a small percentage of food is available to the plant at any one time. If the ground is too acid or alkaline, too wet or too dry, the roots cannot absorb all the elements needed to make them grow properly.

At Achiltibuie there are three different temperature zones inside vast poly-greenhouses. The coolest is equivalent to the south of England and this is where the majority of the vegetables, soft fruits and herbs are grown. The second zone emulates the south of France and contains early strawberry crops from April, tender herbs including basil, olives, melons, peppers, capsicums and aubergines and Mediterranean flowers. In the third zone, which is kept at a minimum 10°C in winter, you could be in the Canary Islands. Growing in here are bananas, oranges and lemons, tamerillos (tree tomatoes), strelitzias, figs, the parrot plant and passion fruit, to name but a few. Flowers are mixed in with the edibles in each house and in the downstairs café the tables are placed around a huge lily pond that also contains aquatic bamboos and flowers. Mail-order kits are sold for those who want to experiment back home.

———— ✦ ————

When English teacher Stella Rankin and her scientist husband Professor David Rankin came to view their present house in

Looking out over the hillside garden at Kevock.

Lasswade, near Edinburgh, they saw the camellias growing in the garden and 'lost their hearts'. There were not just camellias, but magnolias, a magnificent metasequoia, *Acer griseum*, stranvaesia and eucryphia were a few of the mature specimens growing in the one-acre garden. The thoroughly 1960s modern house is built on the edge of a precipitous slope with a commanding aspect of a glen dominated by Mavisbank House. This, with the view of the River South Esk and the ornamental lake, is the reason this cantilevered house was built here. The Rankins bought it from the creator of the garden Sir John Randall (who invented 'cyclotron' for radar in the Second World War). They have speculated as to the extraordinary agility of the late Sir John, as he had no proper paths to walk around and tend the garden, just little tracks. In parts it would be useful to have abseiling skills, but the Rankins 'formed a strategy' for weeding. Eventually the garden became too much for Randall, as he was crippled with

Stella Rankin, Kevock House

The steep south facing slope below Kevock House.

angina. Fifteen years ago it passed to the new owners and the exciting task of discovering exactly what Randall had planted only truly emerged once they had ripped away masses of choking brambles and dug out plantations of nettles that he could no longer control.

Today you can walk around the garden on the paths constructed by the Rankins and it is apparent that this is an incredibly 'loved' garden. The scientist's precision (he studies the structure of molecules at Edinburgh University) and the English teacher's love of flowers and plants marry well. He provides the horticultural expertise and she the love of arrangement, but both decide on combinations and colours. Holidays are trips to mountainous areas to climb and look at plants in the wild. As members of

an official seed-collecting organisation, they have grown many of the plants in the garden from seed and others from cuttings. China is a great inspiration for the Rankins and many of the plants originate there. Stella Rankin is currently learning Mandarin and they plan further trips to this rich plant source.

Gardening on such an incline does of course provide ideal conditions for a range of plants. As it is south-facing and very free-draining, quite tender plants survive, such as the pretty pale-blue abutilon and yellow fremontodendron. The narrow strip of flat land adjacent to the house is home to a collection of alpines in 'stone' troughs. These they make using cardboard boxes as moulds filled with a mixture of peat, sand and cement which is aged with manure and soot. The top

half of the hill is dry and the Rankins have constructed rockeries where they grow more alpines in gravelly screes. In winter, tender treasures are lovingly protected with sloping glass panes to keep off the wet. As the ground flattens out, there is a 'spring line' and this has been cleverly harnessed by drainage systems to feed into two ponds where bog-loving plants (including gunnera) can be grown. Another water supply, via a ditch from the adjoining field, flows gurgling along narrow rills and winds around the bottom half of the garden, splashing into small ponds and marshy bits. This is where their collections of candelabra primulas thrive and self-seed. They include: *P. rosea*, *P. florindae* and *P. sonchifolia*, which grow with *Iris delavayi*, dactylorhiza (marsh orchids) and early snowflakes.

The mature trees and shrubs planted by Randall are constantly being thinned and replaced as they fall prey to old age or storms, providing places for the ever-expanding collections of a huge variety of species. Another advantage of the steep slope is that you can look down on things that you would normally only see from underneath, you find yourself at 'nose' level with a sweet-scented daphne or witch hazel and can stroke the furry buds of *Magnolia kobus*. Under-planting is essential to cut down on the weeding, so ground-cover plants such as geraniums and rubrus are used extensively on the steepest parts. Great use is made of climbing plants over and through trees and shrubs: codonopsis scrambles up a silver blue fir; *Hydrangea petiolaris* runs up a larch tree which shades a favourite seat by the pond; Kiftsgate rose engulfs a huge holly tree in summer. *Tropaeolum speciosum* loves being here so much that it has become a weed.

David Rankin's current passion is arisaemas with their curious 'tails'. Stella Rankin is particularly proud of the two large specimens of the tactile pine *Sciadopitys verticillata* that are rarely seen this size. Her hobby has turned into a full-time job, now that she has retired from teaching to concentrate on the garden. Near the house sit immaculate ranges of cold frames and a greenhouse where thousands of seedlings grow in pots. As the garden attracts increasing numbers of plant lovers and fellow members of the Scottish Rock Garden Club, Stella sells off the surplus lilies, fritillaries, trilliums, meconopsis, primulas and narcissi to visitors.

A grassy walk winds its way under tall conifers.

On the other side of Edinburgh, Tanfield House sits in the valley made by the Water of Leith and from the roof there are dramatic views north over the treetops of the Royal Botanic Garden and south, looking up Dundas Street, to Edinburgh Castle. The roof is also the site of the largest roof garden in Europe.

When Allan Black of the Michael Laird partnership was given the design brief for a new office block for Standard Life, it had to fit into the landscape and not be obtrusive. Although a tall building would have space around it for a garden, they decided instead on a low building covering a much greater area and put the garden on the roof. Grazyna Portal, a landscape architect, was brought in and the dreams became a reality.

It being 'an occupiable space', there are building regulations, but more specifically the total weight of the garden requires a floor loading capacity of three times the normal requirement for an office floor. Rather like an iceberg, the weight of the growth above the soil is less that the weight of the roots below and these are getting bigger all the time. Add the weight of two feet of planting material spread over the one and a half acres of roof space to incorporate fourteen thousand plants together with the hard landscaping materials and then add the weight of the water needed for the plants.

After all the concrete and structural slabs, the asphalt and insulation layers, the drainage and root resistant membranes had been laid, the builders flooded the area to test for leaks. Satisfied, they then placed polystyrene (for less weight) instead of stones at the bottom of the planting layer, then a mixture of compost, forest bark, hydroscopic rockwool (for structure) and 70 per cent soil. Through this runs a high-tech system of dripo-meters and irrigation pipes for watering.

Part of the one-and-a-half acre roof garden at Tanfield House, Edinburgh.

The garden runs around the staff restaurant in the middle of the roof and the three stunning atria that run up from the ground floor of the building, through the two floors of vast open-plan offices. It provides a terrific layer of insulation to the building, rather like a huge undulating duvet, in a textured chequerboard pattern, which snakes over the roof and encloses small concrete or grass areas for sitting out. Interestingly, the curves are all created by the spaces, as in paths, grass, stone and the atria domes, rather than by the plants themselves. The planting is very restrained and only seventy varieties of plants have been used; these are mainly evergreens planted in clipped blocks to create a solid architectural feel. I was amused by the consternation caused to the designer by a lax, arching, rambling rose that had arrived via some bird's stomach – not a welcome visitor. There were a few other intruders who had found their way up onto the roof, including an ash tree seedling, the aforementioned rambler, *Rubrus discolor*, cotoneaster and some nesting ducks from the Water of Leith. These provide great entertainment – and some anxiety – when their young occasionally fall off the roof or get stuck in the drain holes.

Apart from the cold drying winds that can burn plants and dry out the soil incredibly quickly, one of the main problems comes from hot air. With a huge number of warm human bodies inside the building, there is a constant cooling exercise going on pumping this hot air out. Interestingly there seems to have been more die-back from the hot air hitting the plants near the exit pipe, than from the arctic Edinburgh winds.

The Mediterranean-type plants such as lavenders, rosemary, santolinas, oleavia, ceonothus and genistas all seemed very happy. Seaside plants such as hebe and sennecio thrive, as do some grasses and species of bamboo. I particularly liked the bamboo *Sasa veitchii*, with its dramatic dappled leaves. There is a great variety of conifers, from prostrate ground-huggers such as *Picea abies* 'reflexa', the horizontal spruce, to a lovely whorley-needled pine, *Chamaecyparis obtusa* 'nana gracilis', and the blue *Picea pugans glauca*. There was wind-scorch visible on some, but

the main wake was for the phormiums who, unlike the yuccas, had passed away from altitude sickness.

It is always good to see a design concept that is working and this one really does. As you look out from the restaurant over the woolly cushions of plants, your eye is led onto the trees beyond. It is a lovely, almost pastoral, view.

From a rooftop to a hilltop, where the conditions in the garden of medical scientist and poet Professor Geoffrey Dutton could not be more different. He has seen around forty springtimes come and go in his nine-acre hillside garden situated in the Perthshire uplands. The rocky terrain

Professor Geoffrey Dutton, Perthshire.

One of Geoffrey Dutton's garden rooms.

rises from 700 to 900 feet and, together with the climate, would be too daunting for most gardeners. Professor Dutton, however, sees things differently, maintaining that 'poor soil is a gift of nature – you can always enrich soil but it is difficult to impoverish it'. The stress-tolerant plants that he grows flourish in these conditions. Of the elements, he has discovered that 'it is pointless to battle against them, better to persuade and discuss with them instead'. On the day of my visit he was bemoaning the mild winters of recent years that cause some shrubs to 'flush' early, leaving them susceptible to late frosts – the resulting splits in their branches have to be carefully taped to help them to knit back together.

We climbed up hill and down glen. The snow was still lying on the ground, as it does until the end of April, but spring bulbs could be seen thrusting through in places where it had thawed. Snow-laden eddies whirled past us and the heavy black skies were broken with shafts of sunlight illuminating the purple stems of the silver birches and throwing the clipped rounded clumps of beech, juniper and cypress into relief against patches of an intensely blue sky. Greeny-grey swags of lichen hung from the old indigenous rowans and willows, attesting to the sharp clear air. What the professor has created single-handedly in this ancient landscape is a magical place, filled with mystery and romance.

As in most areas of life, gardening has its fair share of control freaks – not least amongst plant breeders (not to mention the genetically modified food gang). Most people's approach to gardening is to 'guide' their piece of land, but Dutton's theory is to let the landscape and the environment 'guide' you instead. The tendency of trying to change the environment in order to grow the plants that we want to grow is instantly apparent if you examine the contents of an average trolley at the garden centre checkout. The mind boggles as to how many different garden conditions that person will need in their garden. The natural way is to grow things that will thrive in the environment that is already there and be in harmony with the surrounding landscape. While there is no such thing as a 'natural' planting, because by definition the moment man has a hand in the arrangement nature is suborned, the movement towards working with nature has grown, particularly over the last twenty years.

Geoffrey Dutton describes his marginal garden as a 'formal' one and considers he is 'adorning the geomorphic elements' and gardening within these. The gorges, the shape of the hillside and the lie of the land dictate everything. Separate garden rooms, 'floored with moss, grass or heather and walled by rocks or the branchwork of trees and bushes', are planted with imported varieties to emphasise their natural shapes. Paths and alleyways lead you from one to another of the thirty-six different areas that are individually named. From small intimate spaces carpeted with wood anemones and bluebells to dramatically planted steep banks that plunge downwards to the boiling brown waters rushing through the gorge in the centre, this unique garden is probably the best example of natural planting in Scotland. The professor has an artist's eye for colour, texture and shape. His two books, *Harvesting the Edge* and *Some Branch Against the Sky* make inspiring reading, particularly if you find yourself with a high, cold and windy piece of land. He explains how to work with a marginal environment and take advantage of the positive aspects, rather than fighting against them. The plants he grows 'must derive from a similar ecosystem to that of the site if they are to thrive as "natives" there'. Above all they must look natural. For instance, he grows masses of the common yellow azalea *Rhododendron luteum*, which is a really hard-working, decorative and hardy shrub: 'Ghent

The gorge in the centre of Geoffrey Dutton's marginal garden.

hybrids inherit its tough grace, but modern Exbury types look sadly out of place.'

The rules, though, are strict. First, a rabbit and deer fence must be rigorously maintained and the area inside kept vermin-free. Geoffrey Dutton keeps outdoor cats that live in a 'cat tenement' on the back verandah of the house and, judging by the amount of feline pawprints in the snow, they are on constant patrol. Second, after the peripheral windbreaks are planted, it is essential to create inner pockets of shelter in which to grow things and it is in this area that Dutton is at his most ingenious. It is vital to identify the different soil conditions – the acidity, neutrality or alkaline content. The direction and control of the wind is important too. He showed me where he had cut a hole in the trees at the top of one hillside to allow the wind in to move the frost (stagnant air creates a frost pocket). The main damage, though, comes from violent wind during storms and from 'snow break' and certain plants simply cannot stand up to these two. With temperatures plunging to -24°C in winter, with early and late frosts and drought conditions at some stage in most summers, (he pointed out the pipes dug in throughout the garden for watering) trees and plants have been chosen with care.

These restrictions do not seem to affect the constant procession of variety and colour. The professor showed me a book he has published, with colour pictures of the garden in spring, summer, autumn and winter. Illustrations show snowdrops and hazel catkins, wood anemones, primroses and sorrel, bird cherry and gean, amelanchier, azalea and alpine rhododendrons. These are followed by shrub and rambling single roses, meconopsis, rodgersia, aruncus and foxgloves. Later, catmint and campanula, iris and ligularia, *Hydrangea paniculata* 'praecox' and hebes are the stars. In the more shaded areas are shown ferns growing at the foot of hazel, rowan, ash, red elder, hornbeam and oak. Everywhere are the individual humpy hedges, grown for shelter, clipped into rounded clumps to echo the shapes of the mountains beyond. In autumn the hillside becomes a bonfire of colour as leaves turn and drop, before the garden's long winter sleep under a thick blanket of snow begins.

Maybe this chapter should have been sub-titled 'Growing Conditions'. In visits to the six gardens described, it is the diversity that is the striking element. Here are botanists, professors and horticulturalists gardening in very different terrains, using such diverse methods of culture that the interest is as much in the contrasts as in the situations.

Notes

1. Pete Brownless has no less than three tropical fish tanks inside his house and a large hardy fishpond outside. Nearly half of his small garden shed is given up to a filtration system to keep the water clean for the outside one. This he built himself and he says, 'Fish-keeping is as much sewage-station management as anything.' While most of the oblong-shaped pond is about eighteen inches deep for the lilies, a section in the middle is four feet deep so that the fish can go down to the bottom in cold weather. Feeding the fish is entirely dependent on the temperature. Once a week at 10ºC, twice a week at 13º, every day at 15º and twice a day above 18º. Feeding them indiscriminately can kill them. Brownless' fish share his vegetarian diet, although goldfish are omnivores. He feeds them flake food but as a treat they get an orange cut up into tiny pieces. His indoor tropical fish enjoy courgettes. When buying fish, he advises, look for undamaged ones that are feeding actively and with a low respiratory rate. He tells me that you should never add new fish to an outside tank until the temperature is over 10ºC and then preferably after a period of quarantine. One of the best places to see ornamental fish is in the glasshouses at the Royal Botanic Garden, Edinburgh, where huge specimens teem through the ponds. Outdoors too there are numerous fishponds. Apparently the Botanics never have to buy fish as the citizens of Edinburgh use the gardens as a home for their unwanted pets and are constantly slipping goldfish into the ponds.

2. Anyone looking for unusual things for their garden should think about attending the twice-yearly sale of plants held by the 'Friends of the Botanic Garden' (to raise money for the RBGE). The first takes the form of an auction and the second is a bring-and-buy sale but will also have many unusual and interesting plants provided by the Botanic's own nurseries.

3. Taxonomy is the science of systematic classification, (from the Greek *tassein*, meaning to arrange).

CHAPTER SIX

Nurseries

Binny Plants.

NURSERIES

'To appear more formidable too in quackery, they have published pompous catalogues of they know not what, collected I know not where, and strangely jumbled together no body knows how, of half the plants in the creation, and some that I believe never were in it; but they have forgot to provide even specimens of many of these wonderful productions, and when you go to purchase them, you have the mortification to find that they were sold the preceding week or day.' WILLIAM BOUTCHER [1]

For as long as people have travelled from one place to another, so plants and seeds have travelled also. The early monks were known to have exchanged plants from monastery to monastery and, where they excelled in fruit-growing,[2] would have supplied varieties of trees to the surrounding countryside as well. Physicians going abroad to study at universities in Europe from the twelfth century onwards would have exchanged herbs, seeds and plants. On the large estates of the landowners, careful accounts were kept and most record purchases of seeds, plants and trees, often from Europe and England (as has been discussed in previous chapters). The list of subscribers to Boutcher's book on trees[3] reads like a *Who's Who* of the aristocracy together with the luminaries of the gardening and professional world of the time, from Sir Joseph Banks to William Adam. The eighteenth century was a time of great planting in Scotland and much has been written about the grand schemes on properties belonging to the Dukes of Argyll[4] and Atholl[5] and the Earls of Haddington,[6] Bute[7] and Stair.[8] They would have had their own nursery gardens, run by their gardeners, to propagate both ornamental and fruit trees for their own use, often selling off the surplus. James Sutherland, the Superindendent of the Edinburgh Physic Garden, is recorded as selling trees and shrubs from there, to the Earl of Morton at Aberdour Castle, in 1691.

Loudon writes that tree nurseries were first established during the seventeenth century in England and he lists the first two in Scotland as having been operating in the 1670s. Many more were to start up during the eighteenth century, with William Boutcher being one of the most successful.

He expanded his enterprise to other sites in and around Edinburgh, supplying trees, shrubs, flowers and vegetable seeds as well as garden tools and books. The fig-tree plants sold by Boutcher were recommended by James Justice, the botanist and writer,[9] although his pineapple plants were said by the *Caledonian Mercury* to be selling 'at London prices'. In 1723 Boutcher joined the Honourable Society of Improvers in the Knowledge of Agriculture in Scotland. The group's official seedsman was Archibald Eagle who, like Boutcher, seems to have sold a variety of garden accoutrements as well as plants and seeds. Eagle's nursery by the middle of the nineteenth century was described thus:

About half way between Edinburgh and Leith, on the west side of the [Leith] Walk, is the site of the Gullow-lee, once a rising ground ... This accursed Golgotha, however, has been literally carted away, to convert the fine sand of which it chiefly consisted into mortar for the builders of the New Town; and the forsaken sand-pit now blooms with the rarest exotics and the fresh tints of nursling trees, the whole ground being laid out as the nursery of Messrs Eagle and Henderson.[10]

The first *Statistical Account of Scotland* (1796) talks of nurseries nearer the big cities and market gardens of a more commercial nature, supplying fruit as well, which 'in good fruit seasons, bring the proprietors a plentiful return'. There were nursery gardens from the borders to Highland Perthshire, some employing up to fifty souls cultivating trees, shrubs, flowers and roots as well as 'a great collection of exotic plants ...'

Collecting exotic plants was extremely popular at the end of the eighteenth century and one who was reputed

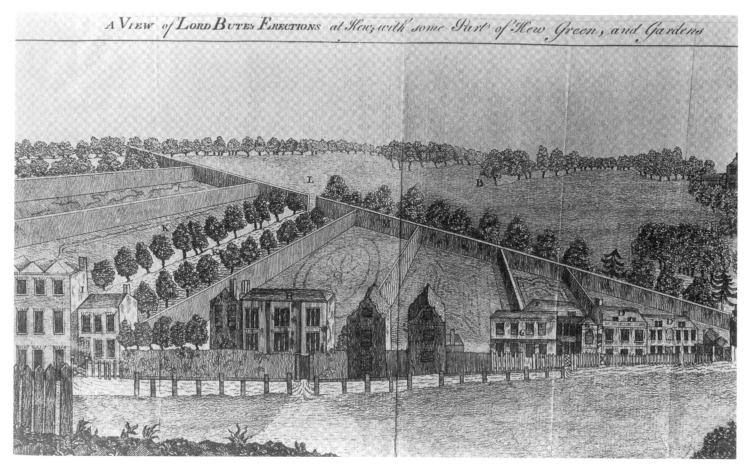

An engraving c. 1780 showing Lord Bute's Erections at Kew.

to have an 'uncontrollable passion' was James Justice,

> who had travelled, on the Continent, and spared no expense in procuring all the best sorts of florists' flowers from Holland, and many curious plants from London. Such was his passion for gardening, that he spent the greater part of his fortune at Crichton, near Edinburgh, where he had the finest garden, and the only pine-stove, in Scotland.

Justice published *The Scots Gardeners Director* (1755), which specifically took account of the climatic conditions when gardening in Scotland. He is also credited with being the first person to grow pineapples in Scotland. The Earl of Bute had already established a flourishing botanic garden on his Island of Bute and towards the end of the century Mr George Don, a well-known botanist, had made a 'sale botanic garden' at Forfar in Angus. Another is recorded at Monkwood, in Ayrshire.

Later nurserymen that deserve a mention are: James Gordon of Fountainbridge, who specialised in flowering shrubs and roses; the Dickson family of Hassendeanburn who in 1729 established Messrs Archibald Dickson & Co. of Edinburgh, which continued under various names until 1825; and Peter Lawson, who founded the Lawson Seed & Nursery Co. of Edinburgh, which lasted from 1770 to 1883.[11]

In London, Scots nurseryman James Gordon of Mile End supplied plants for the doomed Queen of France, Marie Antoinette's garden, The Trianon, while another, John Fraser of Chelsea, sent plants to Russia for Catherine the Great. The most famous

Jacques-Laurent, Agasse
The Flower Seller, *1822.*

Scottish nurseryman, John Veitch, came from Jedburgh. In the early nineteenth century he travelled south and established a nursery dynasty lasting generations, firstly with the 'Exeter' nursery in Devon and latterly the 'Royal Exotic Nurseries' in Chelsea. In its heyday, the Royal Exotic was probably the largest of its kind in Europe with up to fifteen different departments selling everything from ferns, orchids and tropical plants to florists' flowers, seeds, fruit and tree stock. Many plants that they sold were 'discovered to order' by their in-house explorers. The most notable of these explorers were Ernest Wilson and William and Thomas Lobb.[12] The arrival of 'cylinder' glass,[13] the repeal of the Glass Tax in 1845 and the use of cast iron for the glazing bars sparked a wave of greenhouse and conservatory building to house the new 'exotics' that came flooding in from around the world. Via their collectors, Veitch's nurseries reintroduced commercial quantities of the monkey puzzle tree[14] and made the first introduction of that other tree so fashionable after 1854, the wellingtonia.[15]

Today there are so many garden centres that the concept of the hands-on nursery which sows its own seeds and raises plants from divisions and cuttings is becoming quite rare. Growing for wholesale supply to the garden-centre trade is big business, requiring factory conditions, and the competition with the large suppliers in northern Italy and central Europe is fierce. There is two-way traffic, as much of the Scottish-grown stock of conifers is free of disease that is rife in Europe, while the climate in Scotland is ideal for tree nurseries. The extra summer light means longer growing time for the trees and the lengthy winters prolong the lifting season by an average of six weeks a year, with the size of tree being moved only limited by the length of the truck transporting it.

The five gardens[16] in this chapter are all commercial nurseries specialising in certain types of plants that, for the most part, the owners propagate themselves. These are far removed from the supermarket-type chains of garden centres.[17]

Cally Gardens has become a mecca for plant lovers from all over Scotland and beyond, since Michael Wickenden started his unusual nursery here in 1987. Having left school at sixteen, Michael became a gardener at Gravetye Manor in Sussex, the old garden of the pioneer of natural gardening, William Robinson,[18] who so influenced Gertrude Jekyll. Learning by experience and from books, Michael says that the first publication to inspire him was Graham Stuart Thomas' *Perennial Garden Plants*, where he discovered the plants that he would then find in Bloom's catalogue of perennials, his other early inspiration. Later he gained useful knowledge working at the famous gardens of Mount Stewart in Co. Down.

In the 1970s, when self-sufficiency was becoming popular, Michael became increasingly interested in growing organic fruit and vegetables. At that time making a

living from organic gardening was difficult, so he concentrated on collecting unusual plants. He realised that there were few nurseries specialising in the sort of plants he enjoyed, so the quest was on to locate a suitable site and somewhere to keep and propagate his finds.

It took ten years before he found the derelict walled garden near Gatehouse-of-Fleet in Dumfriesshire. His passion is plant hunting and so far he has explored in Chile, East Africa, Tasmania, New Zealand, New Guinea, Slovakia, Japan, China, India and the Russian Far East. The seeds he has gathered in these countries are grown at Cally and there he now has around 3,000 varieties of mainly perennial plants, most of which can be bought in the sales area.

Plant hunting in the twenty-first century is a very different pastime from the previous 300 years. It may be easier to

Michael Wickenden, Cally Gardens.

DO COME IN – an old notice on an entrance to Cally Gardens.

get to many of the places, but it is far more difficult to obtain seeds and plant material. Permission needs to be sought from the country in question and to collect legally you need an official business contract with the country so that any profit arising from collecting has to be shared. Michael is passionately against the business-driven, global patenting of plants that goes by the name of Plant Breeders' Rights (PBR).[19] He believes that the needs of science should take precedence over business, that nature should not be 'owned' and that natural genetic material should be freely available, rather than being bought by whoever appropriates it first. It is now illegal to propagate a plant for sale that has a PBR label as the person who first registers any plant or cultivar can charge a royalty for each new plant, which is enforceable via DNA.[20] At Cally gardens none of the plants have PBRs so buyers are free to propagate away.

Michael's own favourites, out of the bewildering array of exotic flowers and foliage on offer, is for the very large perennials that can grow to ten feet in a season, such as *Sanguisorba tenuifolia 'alba'* (white burnet), *Cimicifuga racemosa* (black snake root), the prickly teasle *Dipsacus inermis* and *Baptisia viridis* (indigo plant). Others that caught my eye were *Anthericum liliago* (St Bernard's lily), with its delicate white starry flowers, and *Dictamnus albus turkestanicus* (burning bush), another white starry gem. He grows other plants for their unusual leaf shapes, interesting grasses and ferns and his special love, species paeonies. These and many others are listed in the mail-order catalogue that he sends out each year.

Cally walled garden and nursery.

The last three years has seen the near completion of the renovation and restoration of the garden's eighteenth-century brick walls. Originally the kitchen garden for nearby Cally House, it must have been one of several judging from 1792 descriptions by the traveller Robert Heron, and the head gardener's report of 1848. The latter writes of six journeymen gardeners and six labourers, all on ten shillings a week with free lodging and fuel, who looked after 2,000 feet of fruit wall, 3 acres of vegetables, 3 acres of orchards, a 100-foot vinery, a 150-foot-long peach house, an orange and camellia house, 100 feet of pineapple pits and several acres of grass and gravel around the house.

Ten years ago there were no drains, no paths and no borders, just a ploughed area growing potatoes. Michael moved into the old head gardener's house set into the walled garden where, in 1990, he was joined by Sally Harrison,

Show borders in the walled garden at Cally.

formerly a gardener with Beth Chatto.[21] Cally is very much a garden as well as a nursery. Thousands of meconopsis have been grown from seed and now grow in drifts in the surrounding woodland area, a spectacular sight in June with the bonus that they are one of the few flowers that are not eaten by deer or rabbits. Protected by the walls, there is a productive fruit and vegetable area at one end, but it is in the main area that inspiration can be gained from wandering around the thirty large borders. Here, horticulture students from abroad are to be seen lifting and dividing plants. In the last fifteen years there have been one hundred and fifty students from ten different countries, who have come to gain experience – the nationality of the workers being as diverse as those of the plants.

Further north, another walled garden is also being used as a specialist nursery. At the entrance to Duncan Ross' herb garden at Poyntzfield, near Cromarty on the Black Isle, he has laid out the Greek symbol for healing.[22] This depicts two snakes intertwined around a rod – it hangs above apothecary shops in Greece, rather as red and white barbers poles do here. Their shapes have been cut into the grass where they intertwine around a staff similarly made and filled with gravel. The eyes of the snakes are smooth round pebbles and at their head is a seventeenth-century sundial that is set to British Standard Time and is accurate to within five minutes. Planted at the far end of this long narrow installation, between two high box hedges, are early purple orchids enjoying the marshy conditions. Other wildflowers have been planted in the lawn which, combined with the smell from the box and the buzzing of the bees on a hot summer's day, creates a dreamy atmosphere as you enter.

Duncan first rented the walled garden at Poyntzfield for fourteen years before buying it in 1990. With a determination not granted to many, he used totally organic methods to clear the overgrown one-and-a-half-acre

Duncan Ross and Yuriko Matsunobu, Poyntzfield Herb Garden.

wilderness of weeds. It took three years to remove one ton of couch grass and two tons of dockens. He then grew crops of brassicas and potatoes to clean up the soil and he reckons it took a further three years to improve the fertility of the soil using green manure crops such as vetch, seaweed from the nearby beaches and home-made compost.

Today, in the most northerly herb garden in Scotland, Duncan grows 450 varieties of herbs, which he sells from the garden and by mail order as far afield as Japan and Thailand, although the bulk of his business is in Europe and the UK. His original stock came mainly from divisions, cuttings

Herb beds in spring with Poyntzfield House behind.

and seeds from friends as well as from other nurseries. He rebuilt the cold greenhouses against the garden wall and with the help of a heated propagator he raises seeds collected on his trips to India, Asia and North America. I am somewhat bemused at the thought of lemon grass, ginger lilies, patchouli, tea tree and ginseng being exported from Scotland to the Far East, but apparently in Thailand they have a pharmacy that researches European herbs, and these are the ones that he sends there.

Outside, Duncan manages to grow the Corsican blue rosemary which survives temperatures of -18ºC, given the right sharp drainage. He says that with most Mediterranean herbs it is the conditions, not the temperature, that is important and many of the Himalayan and North American herbs really enjoy the cold Scottish winters. Duncan has built up a collection of endangered species, such as jatamanisi from the Himalayas that is mentioned in the Bible – it produces the 'nard oil' used by Mary Magdalene to anoint

Christ. Another Indian herb, the neem tree, is used to make an organic pesticide to protect plants. Nearby is the huge shrub of Siberian ginseng that Duncan uses in winter, digging up pieces of root which are chopped up and made into a vanilla-flavoured decoction for an instant 'pick-me-up'. Another herb, elecampane, grown for its roots, cures coughs and colds; it has enormous decorative leaves and clusters of yellow flowers.

Even the more usual herbs like thyme, basil and chives come in endless different

A border of herbs, Poyntzfield.

Herbs for sale on benches with show border behind, Poyntzfield.

Billy Carruthers, Binny Plants.

varieties and colours, but one of the most interesting sections of the garden is where Duncan grows his collection of Scottish native herbs. Some have extraordinarily pungent tastes: rock samphire, native to the West Coast, tastes of the sea, while the oyster plant, with its decorative blue grey leaves and bright blue flowers, tastes of fish. The latter is only found in Scotland and looks wonderful in a herb border. Wild Scots oregano is good in salads and the roots of sea holly from Coll can be candied and used as a sweetmeat. Others in this group include baldmoney from Galloway – used as a substitute for fennel – and Scots lovage, a small celery-like plant. Even the plainest Scottish food must have been livened up with these herbs.

When plantsman Billy Carruthers chose the plants for the border around his head gardener's cottage on the Binny Estate in West Lothian, he thought that they were all rabbit proof. But alas, it seems that nothing is safe from the armour-plated stomachs of the bunnies; they even eat *Euphorbia hyberna,* a plant that Billy says could kill a cow, it is so poisonous. There are over 120 different species of euphorbias in his collection, many of which are grown in a greenhouse as, coming from places such as Madagascar and South Africa, they vary in hardiness.

Billy Carruthers was born in Glasgow and started gardening as a child when the family moved to Kirkcudbrightshire. Being

a sickly child, he was off school a lot and got bored, so to amuse himself he began growing things. When he grew up he moved to London for twenty years, but the dream of having his own garden stayed with him. Moving back to Scotland, he searched for a year before taking over the old vegetable garden and walled garden at Binny.

Around the cottage is where Billy grows his favourite treasures: the pretty yellow *Weigela middendorffiana,* which he says is a magnet for blue tits and finches that love the seedpods. The grass *Miscanthus floridulus (giganteus)* he loves because even the slightest breeze will set it rustling mysteriously. *Viburnum bodnantense,* 'Charles Lamont', he tells me, is the best form of this useful winter-flowering shrub and was a gift, as was the black-leafed

The nursery in the walled garden at Binny.

toadflax *Linaria purpurea* 'Desdemona', given to him by his late gardening friend Brit Marie Crawford from Naughton in Fife. The colour contrasts well with his favourite rose, 'Gertrude Jekyll'.

Moving across the road into what used to be the old vegetable garden for Binny House are terraces, which make ideal nursery beds and spaces for the polytunnels where he propagates young plants with the help of Edith. 'Edie' is an ace propagator. 'You can give her a single hosta plant and go back half an hour later and there will be a dozen neatly potted-up babies.' This area is surrounded by ancient holly

hedges which, when Billy arrived, he had to cut right back to the ground to 'get them back'. Years of neglect had left them tall and leggy, but holly is very obliging in this way and will regenerate if cut hard.

Like most avid collectors, Billy will find all the plants in a genus and then choose a number of them to propagate for the nursery. His approach is quite different from the large garden centres that stick to the safe, known plants. Binny is like a delicatessen for plant buyers. For instance, if you were planning a black and purple border, you would find lots of potential candidates for this, including black-

Grasses for sale at Binny.

leafed linaria, *Geranium pratense* 'purple heron', which has startling dark purple leaves and blue flowers, the grass *Carex pendula* with black catkins, black hellebores, purple scabious and verbascums.

In this garden you can see examples of 'perennial meadow planting' in several areas that have been created using grasses mixed with perennial plants to great effect.[23] One area is quite mature, but for anyone seeking inspiration and help, there are newer ones, where the plants are small and have not yet joined together. These show you how to go about this style of planting using the sort of plants available in the nursery. Grasses and ferns are Binny's speciality and they grow over a hundred grasses, fifty different ferns and many varieties of bamboos and sedges. Billy's choice of plants is very personal but it

Grasses and peonies in Binny nursery.

is the leaf shapes and colours that influence him as much as the flowers. He believes that 'flowers are a bonus'. He shows me some of the twenty varieties of miscanthus grass that range in height from two to twelve feet. The native deschampsia grass that will grow even in a wood of sitka spruce, and the four-foot calamagrostis grass that will stay upright in 80 mph winds – there really is a grass for every situation.

———— ❧ ————

For John and Gunn Borrowman, taking over from the famous Jack Drake at Alpine Nursery, Inshriach near Aviemore, was not just a steep learning curve but also a hard act to follow. The world-famous nursery started by Drake in 1938 (interrupted by the Second World War and re-started in 1945) used to specialise in mail order, sending alpine plants to places as far a field as Japan and the Falkland Islands.

The nursery sits 750 feet up amidst the beautiful wild and hilly region behind Aviemore and could not be more different from today's huge mass-production garden centres. There are no trolleys, no piles of bright blue and turquoise flowerpots, and no checkouts. The rows of tiny neatly ordered plants for sale are displayed within the alpine garden that Drake carved out of a silver birch wood with the aid of two German prisoners-of-war in the 1940s. A silvery burn runs through the garden, providing ideal conditions for the moisture-loving varieties – in particular the many different primulas that are a speciality. Along with blue Himalayan poppies, gentians, lewisias and saxifrages,

John and Gunn Borrowman, Inshriach alpine nursery.

John Lawson of Inshriach.

around 700 different alpines are to be found here; all are grown from seed or propagated in the garden.

Jack Drake did not label his plants, maintaining that any gardener worth his salt would recognise what they had ordered, an old-fashioned attitude that has thankfully become a thing of the past. John Lawson, who worked as Drake's partner and subsequently took over the garden before selling it to the Barrowmans in 1999, lives nearby and together they have labelled everything.

Today they have stopped doing the mail order and instead welcome over 50,000 visitors to the gardens every year. A walk around the different areas is a great inspiration for the buyer who can see the parent plants growing in an ideal habitat. There are rock gardens, screes, boggy areas and wild places. The garden gets no sun from December to February, thus making it ideal for these kinds of plants. It is the rapid thawing of a plant after a frost that does the most damage and in periods of sharp frost the plants remain frozen. Being above the snow line also provides a protective layer of snow, which is most welcome at the coldest times of the year.

John met his Norwegian wife Gunn while he was studying architecture in Oxford. Gunn had grown up in her family's nursery in Norway and the couple went to live and run this after their marriage in the early 1970s. At this time he could just about recognise a rose or a cactus; thirty years later he has learnt not only to recognise, but to propagate and nurture, a large range and is currently adding the alpines at Inshriach to his repertoire. Jack Drake had eight people working at the nursery in times past but now it is down to John, Gunn and their eldest daughter when she is at home.

Inshriach house and garden.

The area is teeming with wildlife – 'dragonflies the size of Messerschmitts', according to John, foot-long slow worms, red squirrels, frogs, toads, pine martens and woodpeckers. To capitalise on this and provide a more varied visitor attraction, the Borrowmans have converted one of the potting sheds into a tearoom with a wildlife viewing area overlooking a Site of Special Scientific Interest[23] below it where they feed the birds and squirrels. Other changes include a children's play area, an interpretive labelling of trees and plants and the restoration of Drake's original wooden potting shed.

Without the time-consuming mail-order side, they can now concentrate on helping visitors with their selection of plants. The cottages built by Drake for his nursery workers have been modernised and are used as holiday lets. Allegedly, early on in his gardening career, the television gardener Alan Titchmarsh applied for a job at Inshriach – but as there was no vacancy at the time they will not be able to erect a blue plaque saying 'Titchmarsh lived here'.

Ericaceous plants in the woodland.

Kenneth and Peter Cox, Glendoick.

Interest in rhododendrons rather passed me by until I started to notice species with wonderful bark and interesting leaves. The place to find out more about these and hundreds of other varieties is in the extensive gardens around Glendoick House[24] in Perthshire. This is where three generations of the Cox family have collected and bred rhododendrons for the best part of a century.

Begun by Euan Cox in the 1920s, the gardens stretch up the hillside above the 1749 house and contain one of the most comprehensive collections of rhododendrons and azaleas, outside the Royal Botanic Garden, Edinburgh, in the British Isles. Euan, whose father Alfred had purchased Glendoick in 1895 with money made from hemp and jute in Dundee, was a friend of Reginald Farrer, the great plant hunter. They had been together on a plant-hunting

expedition in Burma in 1919 when Farrer died, leaving Euan with the task of distributing the collected seeds to the sponsors of the expedition. Plants grown from these seeds formed much of the original planting at Glendoick.

Euan's son Peter carried on with the work and today the collections have invaded every nook and cranny available: even the ruined mill at the top of the hill is used to house tender species within the walls. The old walled garden is host to species trials; beds around the house show off the dwarf varieties bred by Peter and the 'foliage' collection developed by his son Kenneth. A tour of the garden confirms the many varied leaf shapes and colours, that come in red, purple, silver and variegated leaves in shapes that range from round to long, thin and pointed, in every size from tiny to huge and hairy.

Plant hunting has continued to be an obsession amongst the Cox family, with extensive trips to China,

Mature rhododendrons growing at Glendoick.

Turkey, Nepal and Tibet from 1962 until the present time. They have written twenty books on the subject as well as conducting ongoing breeding programmes. Not confining themselves to rhododendrons, Peter Cox has brought back species of gentian, hypericum, deutzia, holly and meconopsis, together with examples of many ericaceous plants such as magnolias, camellias, and also numerous Asiatic primulas, and lilies that can be seen growing in the garden.

It is by no means a certainty that the next generation will follow the interests of the previous ones. Kenneth says that as a child of three he could recognise wild flowers, but he used to resent having to work in the garden to earn his pocket money. Ironically, it was not until he went to work in the USA during his gap year that he really started to learn about his father's and grandfather's work. He had gone to work on the west coast of America for a rhododendron nursery, where it was assumed that he was an expert because of his name. So he consulted the library there, which was full of books by grandfather Cox and father Cox, and got the bug.

That day I learned some useful facts about rhododendron growing. You do not need peat to grow rhododendrons successfully. Plants have not been grown on ponticum rootstock since the 1950s, as suckers take over and can colonise huge areas (as they have done in the west Highlands). If you buy a 'forced' azalea plant it can take up to three years to recover and flower again and when planting out from pots these plants can refuse to put their roots down, quite often dying as a result. If you want to go for the big-leaf varieties you will need a canopy of trees to shade and protect them. It is vital to study the conditions that the plants originally enjoyed and replicate these if they are to thrive. Sympathetic weeds should be planted as ground cover such as brunnera and ragged robin and you should choose companion plants such as meconopsis, trilliums and bloodroot that enjoy the same habitat.

Not to be outdone by the males, Peter's wife Patricia started up the Glendoick Nursery, selling plants, below their home in 1973. I remember buying my first meconopsis plants here in the mid-1970s. Today is has become an enormous garden centre selling everything imaginable for the garden, but it still retains a section that specialises in Glendoick plants raised in their own nursery. Over lunch in the café, Kenneth waxes lyrical over his plant-hunting trips and his latest book. On his wife Jane's knee sits their son Jamie. Will he too be clambering about the gorges of the Himalayas in years to come dressed in a donkey jacket and sturdy boots? His father says that, as yet, he shows no interest.

Nursery rows of rhododendrons in the walled garden at Glendoick.

Notes

1. Boutcher, 'Nursery-man, at Comely-Garden, Edinburgh' writing on the catalogues of his fellow nurserymen in 1775.

2. Thomas Newte, in *Tour in England and Scotland* (1791), describes the fruit trees at Pluscarden Abbey (founded in 1230) in Morayshire where they followed the ancient tradition of planting them on top of flat paving stones to encourage horizontal root growth.

3. William Boutcher, *A Treatise on Forest Trees* (1775).

4. Archibald Campbell, third Duke of Argyll (1682–1761), landscape gardener and arboriculturist. Raised and planted trees extensively both at his house in Middlesex and on his Scottish estates. Also famous for the citrus trees he grew in his stove house.

5. James Murray, second Duke of Atholl (1690–1764), created the Hercules Garden at Blair Castle around 1750 (see Chapter 2) and John, fourth Duke – known as the 'Planter Duke' – planted over 10,000 acres with over 14 million larch trees (seeds of some being fired by cannon to the more inaccessible places).

6. Thomas Hamilton, sixth Earl of Haddington, (1680–1735), pioneer forester who, with his wife Helen Hope, laid out woodlands and walks at Tyninghame in East Lothian over 800 acres. Wrote *Some Directions about Raising Forest Trees* in 1761.

7. John Stuart, third Earl of Bute (1713–92), although Prime Minister 1762–3, was more famous as garden advisor to the widowed Princess of Wales – Augusta. He gardened at Kew with two other Scotsmen, gardener William Aiton and architect Sir William Chambers (an expert on Chinoisserie). Bute became the first director of Kew at its inception as a Royal Botanic Garden.

8. John James Hamilton Dalrymple, twelfth Earl of Stair (1879–1961), continued landscaping at Lochinch and Castle Kennedy, Wigtownshire, where his ancestor the second Earl had laid out eighteenth-century Dutch gardens linking the two buildings.

9. James Justice, *The British Gardener's Calendar* (1759).

10. Daniel Wilson, *Memorials of Edinburgh in the Olden Time*, 2 vols (1848).

11. Priscilla Minay, 'Eighteenth and Early Nineteenth Century Edinburgh Seedsmen and Nurserymen', from *The Book of the Old Edinburgh Club*, new series, vol. I (1971).

12. Their discoveries include the Scottish flame flower, *Tropaeolum speciosum*, the Chilean fire bush, *Embothrium coccineum* and the Chilean bellflower *Crinodendron hookerianum* – all of which thrive on the west coast of Scotland.

13. Invented by Lucas Chance in 1832.

14. Named monkey puzzle by a visitor to Pencarrow gardens in Cornwall who observed that its sharp leaves would be a puzzle for any monkey trying to climb it.

15. Although John Matthew from Perthshire had previously brought back small quantities of seed that he distributed amongst his neighbours, without bothering to classify the plant.

16. A list of Scotland's specialist nurseries can be found on the internet (www.scotlands-specialist-nurseries.co.uk) and most do mail order.

17. With the exception of Glendoick, which started off as a specialist nursery but, thirty years on, has mushroomed into a full-blown garden centre while retaining a section devoted to its own home-grown plants.

18. Robinson was so incensed by the Victorian dictum of the time that walled gardens should be square or oblong that he had an oval one built.

19. A British Bio-diversity patent company recently paid £32 million to the South African government to gain the patent on a plant called hoodia. It suppresses the appetite and has been used by the Kalahari bushmen for millennia to aid them in long hunting trips when they have to go without food. In a world obsessed with obesity, this is turning into a very profitable slimming drug.

20. This can affect poor regions; for instance, there are rice varieties in India that can no longer be grown by the locals in their area because a company has come in, 'discovered' the rice and subsequently patented it, and the locals are too poor to pay the royalties.

21. Beth Chatto is one of the outstanding gardeners of the twentieth century. She has a nursery selling plants that she has collected in her large garden in Essex made from a patch of wasteland. Her books include *The Dry Garden*, *The Damp Garden* and *The Green Tapestry*.

22. Called a Caduceus, the rod of Hermes, messenger of the Gods. It was adopted by the BMA as their logo.

23. Billy Carruthers admires the work of James van Sweden in America, Piet Oldorf in Holland and Noel Kingsbury in England. These three gardeners have all written inspiring books on the subject of natural planting. Van Sweden's speciality is creating lakes and ponds, using grasses and bamboos with dramatic effect on a large scale. They look as good in the winter as in summer when the colours turn and the seed heads of the grasses and the leaves of the bamboos are edged with frost, producing unforgettable contrasts of colour and texture. Oldorf is acknowledged as the pioneer of the 'new European garden style' and has been designing parks and gardens for over twenty-five years all over Europe. He and his wife Anja have a nursery near Arnhem in Holland selling the kinds of plants that he uses in the huge swathes of planting for which he is famous. Kingsbury is a designer and writer who espouses the natural style of planting he calls 'the new perennial way', in which he echoes nature using garden plants in a loose structure that blends them together rather than in tight groups. His book on the subject is full of ideas in different styles to suit various soil and climatic conditions.

24. The house where the photographer for this book, Ray Cox, was brought up.

CHAPTER SEVEN

Gardeners

Dogtooth violets, bluebells and narcissi in the woodland garden at Wemyss Castle.

GARDENERS

'A gardener is Scotch as a French teacher is Parisian.'

GEORGE ELIOT

By the eighteenth century Scotland had become 'remarkable for producing great numbers of professional gardeners; more perhaps than any other country of Europe'. Patrick Neill[1] puts this down to the excellence of the parochial schools that had been established where children learned Greek, Latin, mathematics and rigid Presbyterian discipline, from an early age. A French traveller, naturalist Faujas de Saint Fond, confirms Neill's view when he waxes lyrical on the food served by the Duke of Argyll at Inveraray in 1784:[2]

If the poultry be not so juicy as in Paris, one eats here in compensation hazel-hens, and above all moorfowl, delicious fish, and vegetables, the quality of which maintains the reputation of the Scottish gardeners who grow them … I was surprised, however, to see on the same table, in so cold a climate, and the middle of the month of September, beautiful peaches, very good grapes, apricots, prunes, figs, cherries, and raspberries, though the figs could hardly be called juicy by a person born in the south of France. It is probable, however, that the greater part of these fruits were produced with much care and expense in hot-houses.[3]

Praise indeed from a Frenchman. Loudon, as usual, was verbose on the subject, stating that:

Scottish gardeners especially excelled in the culture and general management of the kitchen garden which was kept in much better order and at less expense than were the gardens of the same kind and rank in England.

His reasoning was that, particularly in the case of head gardeners, they were 'more accustomed to frugality and labour, stubborn soil and inclement weather … and having an inherent dogged nature'.

In the preface of his book (published in 1775),[4] William Boucher brings up an age-old problem in the recruitment of gardeners, that of money:

I must lay it down as a principle, that some small degree of learning at least is necessary to make a good gardener; and what sensible man will bestow that on his son, to qualify him for an employment, that, to all appearance, will never gain him more than fifteen or twenty pounds a year? Or what boy of spirit and genius will study a profession, from which he can only receive so poor a return … A great man bestows from fifty to a hundred pounds a year on a French cook; for a British gardener, seldom more than from twenty to forty. I despise all national reflections, and esteem an honest Frenchman of any profession, but in particular manner a French cook; yet I can by no means think him intitled to so great an advantage above the other. Every body knows the best cook cannot furnish out a handsome table without the assistance of a good gardener; and perhaps there is as much judgment required in raising materials of the best quality, as in dressing them well … Notwithstanding which, I esteem the various labours of an able gardener, to be of a nobler nature, and of more solid importance to every person, from a Prince to a private man, than all the dishes invented from the birth of Cleopatra to the present date.

Maybe one of the reasons that drove gardeners south was the difficulty of getting even their meagre wages out of an employer who was rarely at home. Between 1731 and 1757 the head gardener at Castle Kennedy, Thomas McAlla, wrote regular letters to his employer the Earl of Stair, who was both a Field Marshal and a diplomat (serving as Ambassador in Paris). In January 1733 he wrote that the factor Mr Ross refused to give him money to pay the 'forten men at days uages and they ar all strangers cam at Mertimes [Martinmas] and hes goten no subsistanc as yet. They threten me every day to get them mit [meat] without it they cannot liue.'

These men were expected to work eleven hours a day from March to September. Another year he is repairing the garden walls and writes:

Your lordshep desires me to giue som money to the masons hir, but I ashour your lordshep I haue not a peny to my self. Your lordshep ordered Mr. Roos to giue me tuenty pound of my by gon uages [past wages], but uold not giue me on farthen. I am uery sor straitned for som money I am deu to som pipell hir causes me nou to aplay to your lordshep for reliff. Mr. Rooss uill not giue me my liuery meall [5] till he got neu orders from your lordshep.

The letter ends: 'I thank God I haue your lordshep to aply to; I see hou it ould be with me uer it otheruays.'

It is hardly surprising that so many of them set off for the softer climes of southern England. In the eighteenth century some, such as James Lee from Selkirk, walked the whole way to London in search of work. He had a successful career working for Phillip Miller at the Chelsea Physic Garden and for the Duke of Argyll at Whitton Place before setting up the Vineyard Nursery with fellow Scot W. Lewis Kennedy.[6] Lee translated the writings of Carl Linnaeus[7] into English and prospered with the introduction of exotic plants that he obtained from collectors and sold in his nursery, in particular the first fuschias. They had many continental clients[8] and were instrumental in introducing William Blaikie from Edinburgh into French high society.

Blaikie, whose family had a market garden in Costorphine near Edinburgh, worked in pre-revolution Paris as a landscape architect and was involved at the gardens of Bagatelle, Monceau, le Petit Trianon and Malmaison. An avid plant collector, he sent back many specimens from Switzerland and the French Alps and these are recorded in his diary of the time.[9] His writing contains acute observations of French life, the French Revolution and the difficulty of getting his clients to pay his fees (sometimes because they had met their end via the guillotine).

Nichol, in his book,[10] in the chapter on miscellaneous garden structures, shows plans and elevations for the ideal gardener's accommodation according to the status of the garden and the gardener in the nineteenth century:

A fashion of very questionable propriety appears to exist very generally in Britain, of placing the dwelling of all domestics in the most out of the way places imaginable; and if circumstances force the site into view, the building is immediately surrounded with plantations, or covered with scandent [climbing] growing plants, as if unworthy of being seen.

The head gardener's house in the more average (but still large by today's standards) garden was set into the walls or had a front window looking into the garden. Nichol urges employers to provide up-to-date gardening books and 'corresponding minor conveniencies' of indoor plumbing, heating and hot water. As for the assistant gardeners, they too should be accommodated within the garden, as 'the master has a right to expect constant attendance to duty night and day'. He lays down the necessary furnishings, urges that there should be no more than two to a bedroom and that 'an elderly female' should attend to the cooking, bedmaking, washing etc. Even Sunday had rules and, apart from the prohibition of 'all Sunday visiting', if they were not required in the garden to do necessary work, they were 'recommended to attend some place of worship at least once a-day'. It was a grinding life that entailed starting as an apprentice in early teens – this to last three years or more 'until the youth attains the age of manhood'. The next stage of journeyman continued until the age of around twenty-five, with each year spent working in a new job in a different garden to gain maximum experience. In large gardens, foremen supervised groups of journeymen and this was the last step to becoming a master gardener or head gardener.[11]

A whole book could be written about Scottish gardeners who in the past achieved fame and fortune. At one stage so many Scots gardeners were employed in the south that moves were made to bar them from jobs. Around 1760 a charter dating from the reign of James VI and I, granted to the gardening craft but never enforced, was revived and efforts made to limit employment to licensed gardeners in respect of training apprentices. These Scots immigrants, with their 'rough tongues and uncouth manners', were further denigrated by the garden designer Stephen Switzer,[12] who styled them as:

> Northern Lads, which whether they have serv'd any time in their Art, or not, very few of us know anything of; yet by the help of a little Learning, and a great deal of Impudence they invade these Southern Provinces.

But in the end the Scots invasion became unstoppable and out of many who prospered between the middle of the eighteenth century and the end of the nineteenth, a few should be mentioned: Phillip Miller,[13] son of a Scottish market gardener in London; John Abercrombie[14] from East Lothian; William Aiton[15] from Lanarkshire; William Forsyth[16] from Aberdeenshire; Charles M'Intosh;[17] son of a gardener at Abercairney, Perthshire; David Thomson[18] from Mull; and Henry Eckford[19] from Midlothian.

Women had not been able to join the men and train as gardeners, being only employed as 'weeding women'. In Scotland the first women had to wait until 1897 before they were allowed to join the staff at the Royal Botanic Garden in Edinburgh. Even then they had to be called 'boys' and wear the same clothes as the other garden boys, a flannel shirt and knickerbockers with a tie and waistcoat. On their feet they wore men's boots and gaiters and on the way to work they had to cover up their female attire with a huge overcoat. Their hair had to be tucked away under a boy's cap. Needless to say there were some who rebelled, but given the voluminous dresses of the day, it is not surprising that most women had to stand and watch. 'If I could only dig and plant myself!' moaned Elizabeth von Arnim[20] in 1898:

How much easier, besides being so fascinating, to make your own holes exactly where you want them and put in your plants exactly as you choose instead of giving orders that can only be half understood ... I did one warm Sunday in the last year's April during the servants' dinner hour ... slink out with a spade and a rake and feverishly dig a little piece of ground and break it up and sow surreptitious ipomaea and run back very hot and guilty into the house and get into a chair and behind a book and look languid just in time to save my reputation. And why not? It is not graceful, and it makes one hot; but it is a blessed sort of work, and if Eve had had a spade in Paradise and known what to do with it, we should not have had all that sad business of the apple.

Marguerite Ogilvie, House of Pitmuies.

The potting shed in the wall of the garden at Pitmuies.

One who would very definitely have rebelled at being called a 'boy' and who has never been afraid to dig is Marguerite Ogilvie. In 1966 when the Ogilvie family first moved to the House of Pitmuies, in Angus, the garden was full of delphiniums that had been planted in the 1920s by the previous owner, Major Crombie. He spent his summers at Pitmuies and held a *thé-dansant* every Thursday afternoon at the height of the delphinium season. It is typical of Marguerite that she thought she could do better and forty years later she has done more than 'better'; she has created

one of the finest gardens in Scotland. Not just one garden, but nine different gardens, in an area covering twenty-six acres that are visited each year by around eight thousand people.

The first part that the visitor sees is the old walled vegetable garden which contains flowers, fruit, herbs and vegetables for the house. The old apple trees play host to clematis and climbing roses and there is an ornamental parterre of vegetables in raised beds. This garden leads into another that is enclosed by a mixture of walls and

The delphinium border at Pitmuies.

hedges on the south side of the house. One whole border is devoted to a great sea of blue delphiniums, descendants of the Crombie flowers, but despite attempts to introduce new varieties, it is these original strains that predominate. Apparently modern seedlings never last more than four years – they do not seem as robust as the old varieties – so the seed is kept and any surplus is sold, in some years as much as three pounds.

There are two double herbaceous borders.[21] The first is planted as a vista that, when seen from the drawing room window, echoes the colour scheme inside the room, like a fabulous flower arrangement. The unusually narrow grass path running down the middle of the border breaks all the rules, with the planting starting quite high and soaring up to eight feet; it is like walking through a horticultural cornfield.[22] One side is backed by an ancient yew hedge, festooned with *Tropaeolum speciosum*, that protects the garden from the prevailing south-westerly wind. Having surveyed the riot of herbaceous flowers at eye-level, the visitor can rest at the other end on a curved stone seat and look back through the allée of flowers, towards the house. In between there is the rose garden, providing a much more orderly contrast, with blocks of colour arranged around a stone pond with a fountain. At the bottom end, a line of *Prunus serrula* with tactile bronze peeling bark is kept clipped as lollipops; these extend onto a part where the old grass tennis court has been made into a formal area of shrubberies and beds around a lawn.

Double herbaceous border at Pitmuies.

As you enter through an archway of the grey weeping pear, *Pyrus salicifolia*, the second double border is backed on both sides by a red hedge of *Prunus cerasifera* 'pissardii', an unusual choice but one that is a good foil for both this and the delphinium border on the other side. Each winter the red prunus is cut down to a compact low shape, bursting into life in the summer, its vigorous growth keeping pace with the tallest herbaceous plants, reaching a height of ten feet in July, so that the delphiniums mingle with its red leaves.

On the other side of the gate the mood changes; old-fashioned roses run along one side of the old drying green in front of the Gothic wash house. In spring, masses of snowdrops, crocus and daffodils are followed by alpine flowers. From here a bridge, cleverly constructed to deceive the eye as to its width, takes you over a burn that flows through to the Vinny Garden. This area contains a variety of interesting specimen trees and shrubs including monkey puzzles, variegated hollies, a tulip tree and a huge *Acer griseum* – one of the largest paper bark maples I have seen and worth the walk alone. The return route to the house is via a second bridge over a burn, or on to the Black Lake and the woodland garden. Wildlife abounds here and on the way you can admire the trees: hornbeams, Spanish chestnuts, rowans and maples, planted from seed collected by Marguerite in Oregon and Japan.

Christopher Lloyd once said, 'Never plant an ordinary plant if you can plant a more interesting one', and this is what distinguishes the plantings at Pitmuies from other gardens. From plants and seeds collected on her travels and from her many friends, Marguerite has put together an extraordinary collection that has been arranged with a brilliant eye to design and colour. Original associations and bold proportions abound and every view is punctuated with an attention to detail; every vista leads your eye to a point. It all looks very natural but it is an effect that cannot be achieved without hours of careful thought. Some gardens have a sameness about the plants as if the most loved ones get put in wherever there is a gap. At Pitmuies nothing is repeated, although the favoured few are allowed to self-seed, so providing linking plants such as white verbascums, bronze fennels and teasles. This is a perfectionist's garden and the plants seem to sit up to attention when Marguerite walks past; they know that she loves them but they also know that they must not misbehave. And her favourite part of the garden? 'The bit that makes me tremble at the time.' Just so.

⁓

Whether or not herbaceous borders make you weak at the knees, the visual impact of the garden created from an old limestone quarry at Carnell in Lanarkshire is dramatic. The gardens were laid out from 1904 by Mrs Georgina Findlay-Hamilton, after she inherited the property, and have been continued by the next two generations. Carnell was originally a sixteenth-century building called Cairn Hill, owned by Wallaces, relations of the heroic Sir William Wallace of Stirling Bridge fame. In 1843 architect William Burn was commissioned to redesign the house, with walled garden being built at the same time. In a fate common to so many, the garden was ploughed up during the Second

World War. It continued to be used as a market garden in the 1950s but has now been largely grassed over and a house built within it. The walls are constructed of rough stones lined with brick, the south wall being lower than the other three, to allow the frost to roll off the garden. Railings, placed on top of this wall, divide the walled garden from the sunken quarry garden and act as a climbing frame for clematis species.

As you enter the quarry from the west, a wide grass strip runs down the middle with, on one side, a sixteen-foot-deep herbaceous border at the foot of the wall, and on the other, a water garden. Continuously maintained

John Findlay and the gardener Hugh Reid at Carnell.

The quarry garden at Carnell.

for a hundred years, the planting has remained much the same. Delphiniums dominate the scheme, providing a link plant throughout the length, complemented with graceful *Veronicastrum virginicum*, *Salvia pratense*, *Artemesia lactiflora*, *Astrantia maxima* and *Spirea gigantea*, together with many old-fashioned favourites such as hollyhock, monkshood, campanula, scabious, lupin, geranium and evening primrose.

The water garden opposite is, in effect, a long pond with islands at intervals down its length running about two thirds of the way along the space. From different angles the water reflects the plants on both sides of the grass, giving a vibrancy and richness to the whole scene. The genius of the planting here is in the texture, colours and height of the plant material. Reflecting the blues of the delphiniums, pale-blue campanulas rise eight feet running riot through the

The water garden at Carnell.

creams and pinks of giant cephalaria, ulmaria (filipendula), aruncus, achillea and astilbe. Contrasting with the feathery flowers of these are leaf shapes, great clumps of hosta and rodgersia and of strap-shaped iris. Looking down on this waving jungle of herbage is a Buddha house complete with ornamental dragons, acquired by the family on their travels in the Far East.

Water also dominates the garden at Wards in Dunbartonshire on the banks of Loch Lomond, not by design but because nature dictates that it does. In winter, when the water level of the loch rises, the flood can run a mile to the very edge of the house turning the lawns into lakes. In the twenty-four years that Sir Raymond and his wife, Sara Johnstone, have lived there, it has never got inside the house. The Johnstones have placed a large bronze fish in one of the many canals that link the ponds around the house and this acts as a flood warning. When the fish disappears under water, then the

Sara Johnstone, Wards.

level is up to the gravelled car-parking area.

It is a gardening challenge that not many would relish and few would be able to cope with, but with great ingenuity the water has been harnessed to create a series of twelve natural ponds around the house that interlink and create garden rooms. A large conservatory attached to the house appears to float on water, surrounded as it is by ponds, giving it a Siberian setting in winter when all the water is frozen. From inside you get a feeling that you are in one of the garden rooms, so seamlessly does the house blend into the garden. Some years ago a devastating fire destroyed a large part of the house but, phoenix-like, it has been rebuilt. With adversity turned into opportunity, the new building is designed to incorporate the views

One of the twelve ponds at Wards.

and vistas through the windows, out over the lawns and pond gardens into the wider landscape of the wild water meadows beyond.

The planting around the house is very lush and colourful and devoted to many bog-loving plants. Skunk cabbage, masses of *Primula japonica*, flag iris, gunnera, ferns and water lilies provide nesting places for the hundreds of ducks that enjoy the ponds. In early summer the deciduous azaleas in pale yellows and apricots light up the dark spaces beneath the huge dogwoods and cercidiphyllums, their flowers following on from the pale yellow witch hazel. Against the walls of the house, where the conditions are drier, grow *Phlomis fruitcosa*, ceonothus, abutilon, delphinium, thalictrum and iceberg roses around paved sitting areas. The blues, whites and yellows give a feeling of lightness and movement.

As you follow the watercourse away from the house, *Meconopsis sheldonii* and blue and white lupins grow. Stately royal ferns and graceful willows take the eye further out to where the flood-plain can only support plants that will survive the ebb and flow of the loch. A series of wonderful huge wooden sculptures sit at the margins. One is a bridge over the watercourse and another is a great tree trunk made into a seat. These are the work of the chainsaw sculptor Nigel Ross who used a fallen oak tree to carve them from. The Johnstones love to go and sit on this seat in the early evening, as it overlooks the nature reserve created by the mile of marsh and fen between them and the loch. Here they can enjoy the birds – waders, herons, black swans and whooper swans – and look out over the rushes and wildflowers that love these conditions. Mown paths meander down to a small jetty where a rowing boat is moored and further on is a wooden bird-watching hut. Nearby, there is a huge weeping lime that spends a third of the year standing in water but seems to thrive. The boat sometimes slips its mooring and arrives on the lawn during floods.

Sara has five sons and twenty-two grandchildren, who all visit this children's paradise where they can horse-ride through the pink, waving, silky grasses in the water meadow, or take the boat and row down the canal to the River Endrick and then out to Loch Lomond for picnics, or make dens in the undergrowth and climb the spiky grey-leafed willow trees. A path runs through a wildflower area that is filled with meadowsweet, buttercup, bull rush, wild mint, forget-me-not, lady's bedstraw, mimulus and vetch, complemented by plantings of *Rosa moyseii* and *Alchemilla mollis*. Masses of trees have been planted around the edges of the garden, including a favourite *Northofagus antarctica*.

At the end of the tour we sat on a seat under a spreading tree and the panting posse of dogs that accompanied us flopped down in the shade amongst the small headstones that are dotted around. This is, after all, the dog cemetery and they seem to be testing out the space in this quiet spot for their eventual celestial rest, after a happy life at Wards.

Another garden that grows on a lochside is Frenich in Highland Perthshire. Loch Tummel was much enlarged when the glen was flooded in the 1950s for one of the massive hydro-electric schemes being set up in the area. The combination of the loch and the surrounding mountains has created one of Scotland's most visited beauty spots. When Colin Hamilton and Kulgin Duval bought the 'two-up-two-down' bothy and old steadings, the garden consisted of a midden and piles of farm detritus dating back decades. Thirty-five years on, it could be said to be one of the most striking gardens in Scotland, not just for its position, but also for the dramatic arrangement of interesting plants that are grown there.

Initially Colin gardened around the house, but became 'bored quite quickly with the shrub rose and Victoria plum style of gardening'; so they were grubbed up, new areas were cleared and the fun began. He started by building a scree garden on the site of the old mill. The planting was inspired by a visit to Beth Chatto's stand at the Chelsea Flower Show, thirty years ago, where he saw her collections of unusual plants, perennials, grasses and bulbs, chosen as much for

Plants invade across the bridge and down the burn at Frenich.

Martagon lilies self-seed in the garden at Frenich.

The wild-flower meadow at Frenich and Loch Tummel.

their foliage as for their flowers. Like Beth Chatto, Colin has an artist's eye for colour and shape which, combined with his love of eccentric leaves and stems, produces striking and bold effects. From the scree garden, a sloping lawn leads you down past exuberant borders into which you plunge, travelling through the shoulder-high jungle of growth down to the wide, fast-flowing burn. In early summer hundreds of purple and carmine tulips push up through a bank of rodgersias with startling effect. When Colin managed to acquire the piece of land on the other side of this churning waterfall, the collection invaded across a bridge, up the opposite bank and swirled around the summer house before running on down beside the burn. Lilies, tall alliums, every kind of thalictrum and poppy riot through rodgersias, rheums and gunneras. There are many varieties of large ferns and of the umbelliferae family, such as hogweed and angelica. *Hydrangea bretschneideri* and mounds of *H. quercifolia* with its draped oak-shaped leaves, grow here together with Colin's collection of the surreal arisaemas that look like a cross between an animal and a bird. *Paris polyphylla,* a graceful spider lily, catches your eye on the way up to the old lime kiln that is encrusted with house leeks.

Martagon lilies are another passion. They grow in the long grass beside the drive and, by scattering their seeds, Colin has established a colony in a gravelled area that surrounds an ash tree, up which grows the rambling rose, Paul's Himalayan Musk. From here the ground slopes down towards the entrance to the wild-flower meadow. After all the theatre and action happening at the back of the house, you come to the front. Suddenly the atmosphere changes and calms as you look out over several acres of gently waving grass and wild flowers towards the loch. This is where Colin says he is getting very excited: having left it as a field for twenty-five years, he is now cultivating it as a wild-flower meadow. So far he has introduced thousands of snake's-head fritillaries, dark purple orchids, camassias, more Martagon lilies, the red dandelion, *Heracleum villosum* and ox-eye daisies that are mixed in with the native clover, vetch, buttercup, lady's mantle, sorrel and plantains. Having introduced the semi-parasitic yellow rattle (that feeds on the roots of grasses, thus reducing their vigour) to create ideal conditions for wild flowers that enjoy the damp conditions, everything is thriving. The meadow gets cut for hay once a year in September, after the seeds have ripened. Escapees from the garden seed themselves here, too, but if their habit is too gardenesque they are removed to the 'waste paper bin' patch at one side. The waste paper basket is an area where 'things get popped in' that are surplus, where they create 'a really vulgar display' in contrast to the rest of the garden.

— ✥ —

Transplanting a flower from the mild South of England to the sometimes inhospitable climate of Fife can be tricky. Transplanting people can also be problematical, but Charlotte Wemyss, who moved to Fife thirty years ago, seems to have found the right garden in which to put her roots down. She started gardening because she was homesick as a young bride. Her husband Michael would disappear off to work in Edinburgh each morning and, because she didn't know a soul, she started to garden rather than mope. Ten

years ago the couple moved in with Michael's grandmother (just before she died, aged 104) at Wemyss Castle. 'Wemyss', which means 'cave', was named for the network of caves on the beaches below. Michael's ancestors have lived there since the castle was first built in 1240, burnt by Edward I and rebuilt in the fourteenth century. John Macky describes his visit there in 1723:

About a Mile from Dyzart, still on the Sea Coast, is the Castle of Weems, the Seat of that ancient Family, that is built upon an Eminence, and with awful Look hath a commanding Prospect of the Firth, in East Louthian, to the South to the Bass [Rock], to the West: Its Gardens and spacious Park run to the North. This Palace is above 200 Foot Front to the South, with a Terrace on the top of the Rock, as at Windsor; and, like it, being of Free-stone and white, is seen at a very great distance. It hath two Wings to the North, and a great

Charlotte Wemyss, Wemyss Castle.

Walled garden at Wemyss.

Charlotte Wemyss describes the awe-inspiring task of flitting into this vast house. She says she was so overcome with trying to fit the contents of their, albeit much smaller, house into an already furnished stately home, that she went off to explore the grounds. After a bit she saw a wooden door set in a high brick wall and opened the door into what turned out to be five and a half acres of walled gardens. Inside there were three geese, a redcurrant patch and some very ancient and mainly dead fruit trees and she thought,

'This is what I will do.' For the last eight years Charlotte has been gradually bringing this secret garden back to life. Everything at Wemyss is on a big scale – for example, the miles of drive down which Michael has planted an avenue of Crimean limes, at the end of which is a dramatic view of the sea through enormous elaborate gates, before you sweep around to the castle entrance. You cannot plant a few of anything here; bulbs have to be planted in thousands if they are to compete with the vast scale of the place. In the woodland garden planted by Michael's grandfather, Charlotte has added to the carpets of erythroniums, narcissi and bluebells, planting rivers of chionodoxas in amongst the many species of holly. Aconites and snowdrops are routinely split and moved around every year and Charlotte personally

Spring bulbs in front of the castle at Wemyss.

planted 5,000 crocus bulbs down the drive. April is when the woodland garden is at its best.

The secret garden is fast maturing and hedges, trees and borders will soon be of a size to compete with the fourteen-foot-high brick walls. Some of the walls have bee boles set in them. Others are 'vented', which would have allowed heat from stoves to be carried to the peaches and nectarines that were grown against their sheltering warmth. In the early nineteenth-century orangery, Charlotte found a tangle of weeds. This has now been transformed into a knot garden planted with clipped dwarf box around a fountain. Its roof went during the Second World War, when the castle was used as a hospital, but the climbing roses she has planted grow up the walls and along overhead wires, providing a scented ceiling in summer. Unusually the walled garden is divided into four sections by more walls with arches and gateways leading from one part to another. In the centre is a pair of magnificent seventeenth-century scrolled iron gates that were bought in Italy by Michael's great-grandfather in 1904.

Charlotte loves to experiment with colour combinations as well as unusual plant associations, believing that if it does not work it should be moved instantly, without waiting for the correct time. Although she refers to her style of gardening as 'romantic mess', this self-deprecation is not justified, as there are some very original planting schemes in the borders and beds that she has created. They are just very full, as she favours the rambling intertwining approach, with no gaps in between. Most of all, Charlotte loves to grow climbers through shrubs and trees, and everywhere I could see arching stems of roses and delicate trails of clematis pouring out of the tops of hollies and the old fruit trees that were retained. Climbers jostle for position up walls and hedges and along chains looped to wooden supports. 'Romantic exuberance' would be a better name.

Another transplanted gardener, this time from the south of Ireland to East Lothian, is Charnisay Gwyn. Her home

is on either side of a camellia house, in the two buildings that used to house the apple store and the garden shed of the walled garden at Tyninghame. These have been cleverly joined up behind to make a good-sized family house by architect/developer Kit Martin who, together with the Edinburgh architects Simpson and Brown, based the plans on a classic Adam pavilion.

The camellia house is used as an extension to the dining room but sitting, reading, eating and growing enviably healthy house plants happens in here as well. Looking out at any time of the year is wonderful, as it is raised up above the garden, giving commanding views out over it.

Charnisay Gwyn, Tyninghame walled garden.

Tyninghame was another 'palace' visited by Macky who talks of the

Castle of Tinninham, a noble old Seat of the Earls of Hadingtoun, with great Additions and Improvements, made by this present Earl. Many Millions of Trees hath he planted in a sandy Down or Links, as they call them here, between his House and the Sea, and they thrive mightily. He hath also laid out several Avenues through his Park, which, when full grown, will be as noble as any in Britain.

Forty years later, in 1763, they would have been looking quite mature when the then Earl of Haddington decided that the glebe land was where he wanted his new walled garden; so he moved the manse and the minister down the road. The eighteen-foot walls were steam-heated with a maze

Allée of yew with classical statues, Tyninghame.

The camellia house at Tyninghame.

of pipes running through the hollow insides. Chimneys are placed at regular intervals, cunningly disguised as urns; these are now home to various birds' nests, but must have looked quite comical with steam emerging from them. The bricks came from Norfolk, arriving as ballast on the returning coal ships; the pantiles from Holland arrived in a similar fashion.

Sadly, no pictorial record exists showing how the garden was laid out in the eighteenth century, but it is believed that there has always been a double yew walk,[23] which forms a handsome wide allée stretching down hill from the camellia house, built in 1840 by the Dunbar Foundry. This was crossed by a rose terrace at right angles and the four squares they contained were cultivated with vegetables. After the war, in the interests of economy, the double herbaceous borders contained within these yew walls were grassed over and the vegetable areas reduced. The late Countess of Haddington had a wonderful eye for colour and design, which still shows in the bones of the planting today. She kept garden notebooks that have been extensively used in

the replanting. One of the squares was planted up at this time as an arboretum, containing many Mediterranean trees and shrubs brought back from holidays on the Iberian peninsula and other Mediterranean resorts. Another square now contains a tennis court. Beyond the arboretum you go through a door in the wall that leads to the Apple Walk, where the trees are trained over arches running the whole length of the wall – a heady sight in blossom time. Before

the war, the Walk ran for 150 yards, but was shortened when the garden was being redesigned.

On coming out of the camellia house, you pass a huge white wisteria in front of a large Judas tree; knots of clipped box on either side contain lavender which sends out delicious wafts of scent on a hot day. Next you pass a high wall at right angles, against which is a classic early lean-to glasshouse which was built specifically to grow pineapples

Old fashioned roses clothe a pergola at Tyninghame.

in, again with the distinctive urn chimneys to let out the smoke from the stove. After this you walk down between the cool greenness of the yew, passing white stone statues of classical figures placed in niches on either side. The central axis contains a small stone pond with a seventeenth-century fountain in the middle. It is all very simple and serene, while retaining a grand feel, and arguably looks better that it did when it contained the double borders that used to be here. There is no shortage of colour and exuberance, though, when you dive off down one of the many intersections. Each one has a different theme, but the strong plantings of old-fashioned shrub roses provide a unity.

One of the intersections that runs across the yew allée is lined with catmint and ornamental vines, leading the eye and the curious visitor to a small garden room built onto the side wall. This has been used as an extra bedroom but is now a flower room. Other intersections are planted with strong leaf and colour contrast, bushes of *Rosa glauca*, deep red poppies and black iris with more catmint as a foil and link plant.

At the far end of the garden, as you turn to come back up the side wall, a huge border of pæony-roses underplants old apple trees. Their shiny green leaves frame the fat buds that were just waiting to burst when I was there, but I would love to see them in the spring, when all the red shoots are emerging and the apple trees are in blossom. One of the greatest luxuries in a garden is to have the space to devote to planting a lot of what you like. With this in mind, further up this side, the present owners are massing *Rosa* Nevada in a new border edged with clipped box. The blowsy cream flowers look really good against the mellow brick of the walls.

Travelling from the mild climate of East Lothian to central Aberdeenshire is like changing continents. It is so windy at Ploughman's Hall that Jean and Tony Gardner take the doors off both ends of the greenhouse in the winter to let the wind through – otherwise it would take off over the hill. Jean says that you get used to the wind and has devised all sorts of cunning devices to protect her borders and beds. One of the most interesting is a vertical 'quilt' made by stuffing straw between two layers of chicken wire and then quilting it in place with tufts of blue farm string, in the tradition of making a bed quilt.

Gardening with your partner, like hanging pictures, is a sure test of compatibility. The garden at Ploughman's, made over the last fifteen years, is a tribute to their teamwork. Tony says modestly that his role is that of

Jean and Tony Gardner, Ploughman's Hall.

Ploughman's Hall from the front garden.

The vegetable garden at Ploughman's Hall.

'hewer of wood and drawer of water' and that he is inspired by Jean's knowledge; Jean says that Tony has 'bright ideas'. Whatever the truth, Tony's lifetime experience as a conservator of forestry, coupled with Jean's degree in botany from Aberdeen University, have stood them in good stead. Jean's mother was the botanical painter and passionate gardener Mary McMurtrie, and Jean says she cannot remember a time when she did not love plants; as a small girl she was even chastised for eating the flowers. She has made a garden in every house she has lived in – twenty years in Kenya, seven years in Mauritius – in climates that could not be more different from the windy hilltop where they now live.

A carved stone plaque on the front of the house announces that it was originally the '*Ploughman's Socys. Hall, founded 1820*'. Later it became an alehouse, but the Gardners bought it as a derelict farm building and after their five children left home they set about turning it into a highly individual home.

Jean confesses to being a 'plantaholic' and everywhere you look there are trays of seedlings and cuttings. Not just in the greenhouse, cold frames and nursery beds, but on every window-sill and table inside the house as well. They get given packets of seeds, which they pop into the fridge before planting them – from lentils to aquilegias, sweet peas and edible peas, small trees and shrubs. No instant gardening goes on here; even the yew hedges have been grown from seed. As they take two years even to germinate, it is the ultimate test of patience. The Gardners' soil is a light loam and, unlike the surrounding granite areas, is composed of blackstone and whinstone. This fertile area is known locally as the 'Girnel of the Garioch', but as the wind dries out the soil very quickly, they have to dig in loads of manure and home-made compost.

Jean explains that, as she likes to grow everything, she has made ten different garden areas to accommodate different types of plants. In the vegetable garden, fruit just blows off any free-standing fruit tree so they grow the apples as 'stepovers' on wires as low edging to the vegetable beds and espalier the pears against the side of the house. The surrounding hedge is composed of sloe and cherry plums and some years Jean makes a hundred pounds of jam from the many varieties of soft fruit. They grow all their own vegetables in neat rows surrounded by lavender hedges, while the herb garden provides not just flavours for cooking, but herbal teas and flowers for drying as well.

In front of the house they have made a flat lawn from the sloping field, which is divided from the house by a terrace. Small alpine troughs are arranged here in front of an immaculate symmetrical row of espaliered apple trees lovingly tended by Tony. These clothe the front of the house, making it look like something from an early sampler. Sweet peas grow up igloo-shaped structures, made from laburnum sticks, flanked by hollyhocks and sunflowers that are all protected by a yew hedge. Below the raised lawn in a long, wavy herbaceous border, Jean explains that, as a concession to their age, to cut down the work she is slowly replacing the perennials with shrubs – *Weigela middendorffiana, Betula utilis* var. *jacquemontii, Viburnum plicatum* 'mariesii' and many others. *Sorbus sargentiana*, with its large sticky buds, has been stooled to create a chunky shrub beside the green snake-bark maple and the red-berried viburnum.

One of the few travellers to explore Aberdeenshire, Banffshire and Moray was Thomas Newte (in 1785) and he remarks on the good soil 'that is favourable to garden and field vegetables' and also to many kinds of trees and soft fruit, which he lists. In Aberdeen he comments on the large gardens around Robert Gordon's School and describes the 'Paradise' garden that was two miles distant from the house at Monimusk [sic], 'distinguished by the beauty of its park or garden, and other traces imprinted on the reluctant soil by the hand of modern cultivation'. He travels on to Duff House in Banff, where he finds the 'plantation and walks about this house … laid out with more taste and elegance, than any I have seen in Scotland'. He admires the ornamental holly trees at Gordon Castle near Fochabers and goes on to visit 'Kilravack-Castle [sic] … about 200 yards from the river of Nairn … on a rock. The verdure and regularity of the gardens intervening between the castle and the river, are strongly contrasted by a black and barren mountain directly facing it, on the other side.' He comments favourably on the castles at Darnaway and Cawdor, both being 'the most pleasing residence of any in this part of the Country' for their prospects, woods and situation. Of Cawdor, he says that 'Nature has been very bountiful to this place'.

Notes

1. Neill was a printer from Edinburgh and founder of the Caledonian Horticultural Society in the nineteenth century.

2. Faujas wrote an account of his stay at Inveraray in his book *Travels in England and Scotland in 1784*.

3. Thomas Newte, in *Tour in England and Scotland* (1791), describes a seven-acre walled garden at Inveraray, with large hot-houses and heated walls for growing fruit, on his visit in 1785.

4. *A Treatise on Forest-Trees.*

5. 'Livery meal' = (literally) living meal; gardeners were paid partly in kind with a 'kist' (= chest) full of meal so they could at least eat.

6. Sir Walter Scott records in his diary on 3 May 1828: 'After breakfast I drove to Lee and Kennedy's and commissioned seeds and flowers for about £10 including some specimens of the Corsican and other pines.'

7. Linnaeus was the first person to realise that plants reproduced sexually and in his writings he arranged plants accordingly. He wrote prodigiously, his best-known books being *Philosophia Botanica* (1751) and *Species Plantarum* (1753).

8. Kennedy was granted free passage between England and France during the American War of Independence (1778–1783) in order to supply plants for the Empress Josephine's garden at Malmaison.

9. *The Diary of a Scotch Gardener at the French Court at the End of the Eighteenth Century* was only published in 1931.

10. *The Gardiners Kalendar* (1812).

11. Often the cook and the head gardener married each other on these estates. Neither of them would have had time to meet anyone else. But with the gardener having to creep into the big house before breakfast took place in the dining-room, to arrange the table decorations and bring the cook the required produce for the day, it would seem a logical outcome.

12. Stephen Switzer (1682–1745) worked for the famous nurserymen London & Wise in London and assisted in laying out the military gardens at Blenheim Palace and also gardens at St James's Palace. He is credited by Loudon with designs for gardens around Edinburgh. Switzer wrote several influential books including *The Nobleman, Gentleman and Gardener's Recreation* (1715) and set up his own nursery at Westminster to supply his aristocratic clients.

13. Phillip Miller (1691–1771) set up as a florist in Pimlico and was appointed curator of the Apothecaries' Garden in Chelsea via Sir Hans Sloane, physician to George I. Published *The Gardener's Dictionary* 1731 and *A Gardener's Kalender* 1732 both definitive works for the next century.

14. John Abercrombie (1726–1806), son of a market gardener, employed as a journeyman at Kew before starting a market garden at Hackney. Wrote *Everyman His Own Gardener*, ostensibly with Tomas Mawe, which ran to twenty-three editions.

15. Willian Aiton (1731–93) trained as a gardener and moved to London to work with Philip Miller, before working for the third Earl of Bute at Princess Augusta's Kew garden and later for George III at Richmond. His son William Townsend Aiton succeeded him at Kew.

16. William Forsyth (1737–1804) also worked for Phillip Miller as well as for the Duke of Northumberland at Syon House before taking over at the Chelsea Physic Garden. Built the first rock garden, worked for George III at Kensington Palace. Forsythia is named after him. Wrote a book, *Treatise on Fruit Trees* (1802).

17. Charles M'Intosh (1794–1864) worked as a gardener at Taymouth Castle, Perthshire. Travelled south to work for Prince Leopold. Returned to Scotland to run the gardens of the Duke of Buccleuch at Dalkeith. Wrote many books, notably *The Practical Gardener* (1828–9: 2 vols).

18. David Thomson (1823–1909), apprentice gardener aged fourteen at Castairs House, Lanarkshire. Worked at the Royal Botanic Gardens in Regent's Park, London. Returned to Scotland to run the gardens first at Archerfield, East Lothian and then for thirty years at Drumlanrig. Editor of *The Scottish Gardener* magazine and prolific author.

19. Henry Eckford (1832–1905), trained at Beaufort Castle (Lord Lovat), worked for James Hogg at Newliston and Sir Peter Murray at Penicuik and the Earl of Stair at Oxenfurd before heading south and ending up hybridising florists' flowers in Gloucester. His 100 sweet pea seedlings were part of 264 exhibited in 1900 that he had bred from the original seeds descended from those sent to Britain by the Sicilian monk Cupani. Ironically it was Silas Cole, a gardener at Althorp, who found one out of Eckford's seedlings that became the Spencer hybrid sweet peas of today.

20. From *Elizabeth and her German Garden* (1898).

21. A true herbaceous border should consist solely of hardy perennials, which are cut down each winter. Previously it was the fashion to incorporate bedding-out plants and bulbs to prolong the flowering season. For maximum effect the best ones are double, long and wide and backed with a high hedge – normally yew – or a stone wall. In garden design terms it is quite challenging to get the proportions, the mixture, the colours and textures and the flowering seasons right. A great British

invention, few really grand double borders get planted now as they are labour-intensive to maintain and expensive to create.

22. Marguerite Ogilvie has pioneered a very effective method of restraining her plants which has now been adopted all over the country and been taken up enthusiastically by the National Trust. When she first devised using netting to support the plants, she had to use orange fishing nets from Peterhead in Aberdeenshire. As time went by, and the idea caught on, the suppliers, Lindsay's, produced a more sympathetic dark brown netting which is invisible once everything grows up. The net is put on in May after an exhaustive week's weeding. This is important, as once it is on and secured to the posts and wires, you cannot get in to weed. For the herbaceous borders the net is started at 18" rising to 3'6" at the back. For the delphinium borders it is put on flat.

23. The present yew hedges were planted in 1900.

CHAPTER EIGHT

Town and Village Gardens

CDs used as bird scarers to protect a vegetable patch.

TOWN AND VILLAGE GARDENS

'The smoke from the houses, the appearances of the villagers, and of their cattle, the trees surrounding their little gardens … I was charmed with the village.'

ROBERT HERON[1]

Looking at James Gordon of Rothiemay's plan of Edinburgh, drawn in 1647, it is possible to see how David I's twelfth-century gardens around Edinburgh Castle were transformed into the seventeenth-century city he depicts. The twelfth-century gardens had stretched along the Grassmarket, but by the seventeenth century, these were covered with houses, although the map still shows the King's Orchard and tilting ground where King's Stables Wynd is now. Houses are drawn with long thin gardens laid out behind them. Later kings had also given pieces of land to knights[2] and favoured subjects.

The houses being built along Edinburgh's High Street had gardens stretching down to the Nor' Loch in what is now Princes Street Gardens[3] and Waverley Station. From the beginning of the fourteenth century, houses were being built on the site of David I's kitchen garden at the Grassmarket and the Exchequer Rolls (prior to 1335) lists the fruit and vegetables that were grown, as well as foreign imports. Flowers, mostly for edible purposes, are mentioned: roses, gillyflowers (wallflower), cinnamon flowers,[4] crocuses (for saffron), violets and primroses. Gardens were important enough that James III passed a law meting out heavy penalties to 'stealers of green wood and destroyers of trees, breakers of orchards, stealers of fruit, and destroyers of cunnigars [rabbit warrens] and doocots'. This law was still in force 200 years later in 1625, when John Rait and Alexander Dean were hanged for stealing 'various herbs, roots and bee-hives' from gardens at Barnton and Pilton.[5]

The Gordon plan reflects the evolution of the city that became the capital of Scotland in the reign of James II in 1449. At this time there were gardens around the religious institutions and churches in Edinburgh. Gordon's map shows the gardens at St Giles' and, also adjacent to the Cowgate, the gardens of the Blackfriars. It was from the gardens of the Church of St Mary-in-the-Fields (Kirk o' Fields) around Infirmary Street that James IV obtained seeds for his new garden beside Stirling Castle. From Perth James imported thorn hedges, herbs and 'nine horse loads of trees'. From Scone he ordered osiers (willows), together with 'wine trees' for his French gardener to nurture at Stirling. In spite of Holyrood being his main palace, he was said to have 'addicted himself much to Stirling Castle', not least because he made it the chief residence of 'his mistress'.

When John Macky was travelling around Scotland in 1723, ostensibly as a tourist but in reality as a spy, he makes detailed reference to the gardens in the towns that he passes through. In Edinburgh he describes Holyrood:

On the North side of this Bass Court is a fine Garden, still well kept, and since the Kings went to live in London, converted into a Physick Garden. On the South side of this Court is another larger Garden, which Duke Hamilton as House-keeper lets out to Gardiners is several Branches. Behind this Palace, the Church or Chapel makes a Wing to the North, and the Laundry another Wing to the South, and between them is a Bowling green wall'd in. St Anne's Yards to the East of the Palace was design'd to be branch'd out into Gravel Walks, adorn'd with Statues; But the Revolution coming on, attended with a long and expensive War, and since that an Union with England, hath put an end to these things.

Travelling along the Canongate, he writes:

The Suburb, which leads from hence in a direct Line to the City Gate, is call'd the Canon Gate, or the Street of the

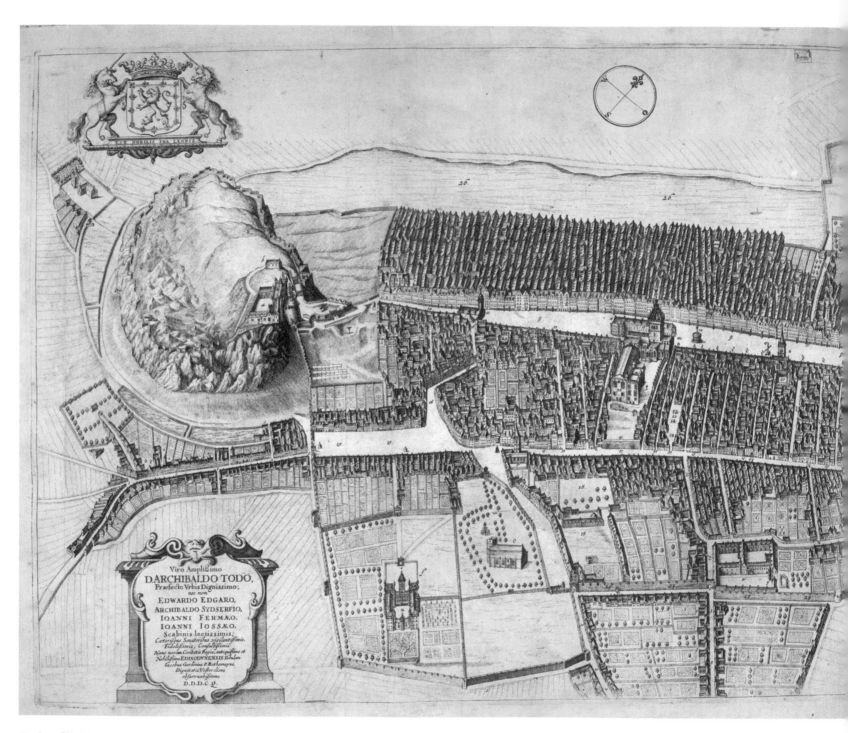

Gordon of Rothiemay's map of Edinburgh, 1647 (Trustees of the National Library of Scotland).

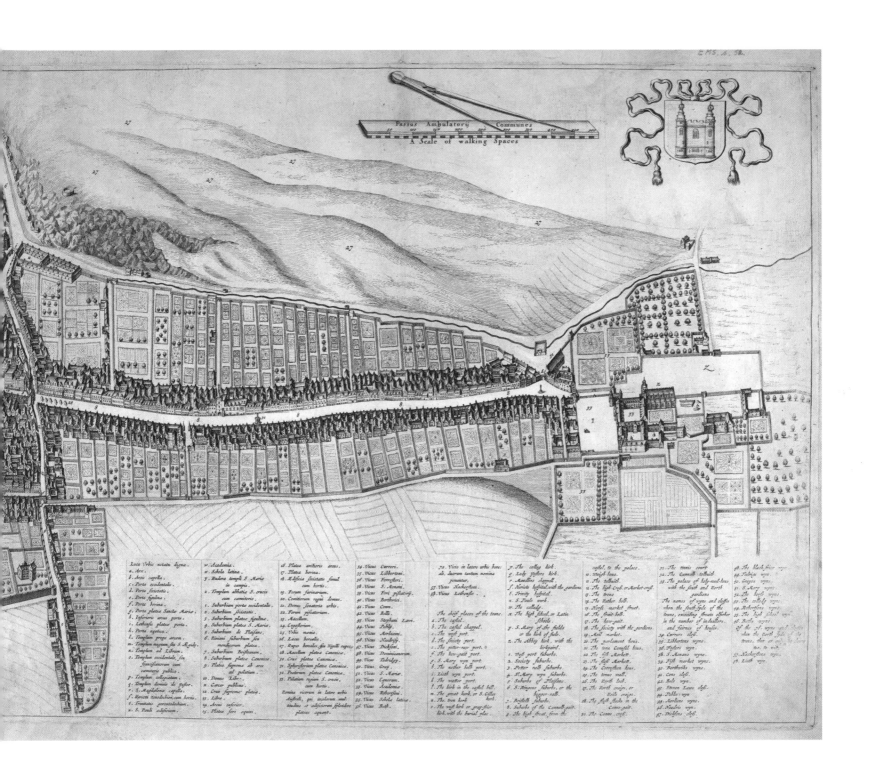

Passus Ambulatorij Communes
A Scale of walking Spaces

Canons Regular, who first founded the Abbey; and since the Abbey was converted into a Royal Palace, the prime Nobility built their Palaces in this Street, and those that were oblig'd to attend the Court, took their Lodgings here; so that nothing can be suppos'd to have suffer'd so much by the Union as this Street. On the South side, just with the Pend, George Heriot,[6] Founder of Herriot's Hospital, built a Square of Free-stone, with a good Garden behind it … A little higher, on the South side, is the Palace of the Duke of Queensbury, still in good Repair; consisting of a Front and two Wings, with good Offices and a handsome Garden behind. Over-against that, on the North side, is the Palace of the Earls of Winton, torn to pieces by the Mob, and now purchased by York Buildings. A little higher, on the South is the Palace of the Duke of Roxborough, on a large Spot of Ground, with a large Garden behind, but much neglected; And on the North, the Palace of the Earl of Penmure, in excellent good Order and very fine Gardens. And on the South, a little higher, is the fine Palace of the Earls of Murray of free Stone, with a pav'd Court in the middle. There is a very large Parterre or Flower Garden behind, with four hanging Walks or Terraces to the bottom, where there is a Bowling-green, and a handsome Pavilion or Pleasure-house; and above the back Entry a Stone Balcony, which gives a full View of the Park. A little higher you enter the City by a Gate, called the Netherbow; and this Suburb from the Palace hither makes half an English Mile.

Macky goes on to describe the houses built for the Company of Surgeons and the Physicians' Hall south of the Cowgate, both with fine gardens and, nearer Greyfriars, 'a neat Hospital for Girls, with a pretty Garden and Bowling-green'. He also mentions George Heriot's Hospital, where 'The Gardens are very well kept, consisting of a Flower Garden, an Orchard, and Kitchen Garden … The House and Gardens contain between nine and ten Acres of Ground'.

Royal Charters from 1188 onwards specifically mention gardens, not just in Edinburgh but also in Perth, Paisley, Innerwick, Haddington, Renfrew, Glasgow, Berwick and Kelso. A trawl through the National Archives of Scotland's land register of sasines also throws up legal documents relating to urban gardens the length and breadth of Scotland from the early sixteenth century. A typical one for Stirling in 1526 reads:

Instrument of resignation and sasine in favour of James Bennie of a lower garden lying in the barony of Bouchquhaderok, sheriffdom of Striueling, between garden of said James Bennie, on the east, garden of Alexander Lewingstourn, on the west, garden of Janet Norvel, on the north and the common burn, on the south, on resignation by said Janet Norvel, widow of John Robisoun, burgess of Striueling and Cristina Robisoun, her daughter.

And in 1670 another document states:

Instrument of sasine in favour of John Ros, sacrist and doorkeeper of the King's College, Aberdeen, of a tenement and garden which once pertained to Alexander Wadie, baker, lying on the east side of Old Aberdeen, following on charter, 3rd July, 1669, by Patrick, bishop of Aberdeen.

Throughout the sixteenth, seventeenth and eighteenth centuries, records of gardens of ordinary folk such as burgesses, bakers, spinners and smiths are mentioned, from Dumfries to Aberdeen.

In Dumfries, Mackay notes: 'This high Street is spacious, with good Stone Buildings on each side; those on the North side having their hanging Gardens to the River side.' At Berwick there is a 'very fine house , with good Gardens, built here for the Governor'. He goes on to describe Dundee as a beautiful, well-built city with wide, paved streets lined with trees from the harbour up to the town. On the west side he notes a 'handsome Hospital for decay'd Burghers, where they have a good Maintenance, and Gardens running down to the River side'. In St Andrews Macky, while noting the destruction of the reformers, reports that St Leonard's College had spacious and well-kept gardens behind the South Apartments. St Andrews had been at the centre of John Knox's reforming wrath and Faujas de St Fond was appalled at the destruction and vandalism caused: 'The fanatics, maddened into fury by the homicidal sermons of the gloomy Knox, had carried the force of destruction to men and things in this unfortunate

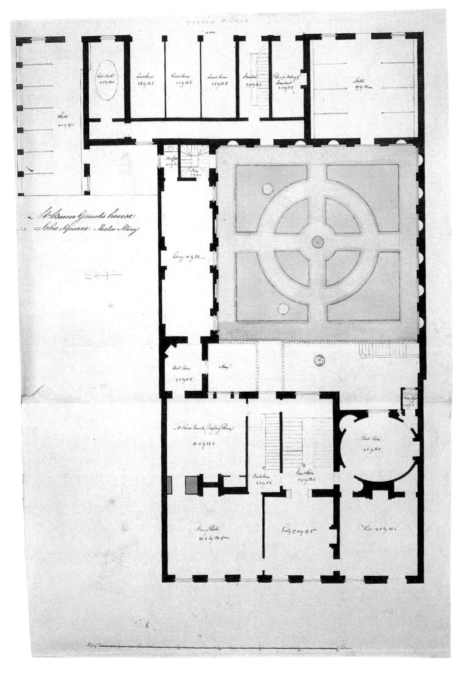

Robert Adam's design for Baron Grant's garden in Soho Square, London.

town.' As a Roman Catholic, he was equally upset that a church in St Andrews was turned into a gardener's house with a kitchen garden where the 'house of God serves as the home of the gardener and that he there keeps his carrots and turnips during the winter'.

Todd Longstaffe-Gowan has written an extremely comprehensive and well-illustrated book[7] on town gardens in eighteenth- and nineteenth- century London, where many Scots had settled and where the Scottish aristocracy had town houses. The Adam brothers maintained a stylish house in Edinburgh as well as one in London on St James's Park, where they would entertain characters such as James Boswell and David Hume and their aristocratic clients. The Adams were involved in designing architectural features for town gardens as well as designing houses in both cities. This was the golden age of house-building and garden-making both north and south of the border. Town houses became fashionable not just in the larger cities of Edinburgh, Glasgow, Stirling and Aberdeen, but in places such as Banff and St Andrews where town gardens were similarly laid out.

Town gardens were shown on maps in a rather haphazard fashion in previous centuries and only the larger houses have more detailed images portrayed in prints and paintings, but the Buildings Act of 1774 meant that standards in building were now laid down and this included the garden areas too. By the nineteenth century they were classified as: first, second, third and fourth-rate houses and J. C. Loudon applied the same labels to the gardens attached to them:

It may be observed here that the size or rate of the garden is not necessarily a criterion for the size and rate of the house; for, in the immediate vicinity of a town, it is very common to find a first-rate house forming one of a row of houses placed along a road, with a fourth-rate garden; and, farther in the country, it is equally common to find a cottage removed some distance from the road, and standing in a third, or even second, rate garden.

Again the gardens correspond to the class of person who occupied them: aristocracy, upper class, middle class and

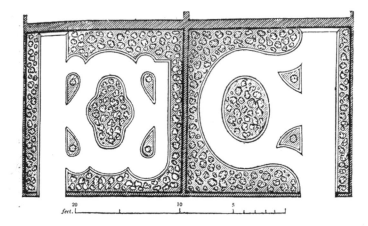

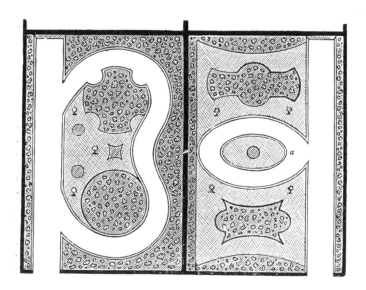

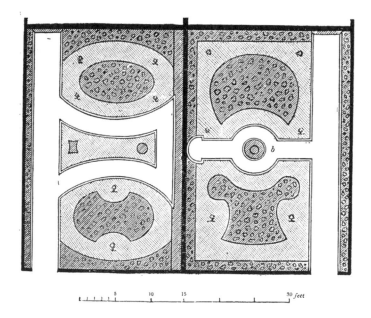

J. C. Loudon's designs for eight 'Fourth Rate Gardens'.

lower class each had their allotted place or required garden space. The poor town-dweller's mean strip behind the tenement would rarely have more than a privy, perhaps a wash house and a drying green and anyone employing a horse and cart in their trade would keep these in the enclosure too. Ordinary cottage gardeners are told exactly by the bossy Loudon what they should incorporate in their garden as well as in the composition of their dwellings (to include a porch, pantry, hen roost etc.):

In the garden should be a well, with a pump, if deep; unless some other source of good water is near.

A water-closet, placed in a hidden part of the garden, behind the house, so contrived that the visitor may neither be seen from the windows of the cottage nor the public road, with a going and returning or an incidental approach, instead of the direct cul-de-sac paths which commonly lead to such places.

A pigsty, attached to the north-east or south-west front.

A dunghill, or a small spot adjoining the pigsty, surrounded by a dwarf wall.

A niche in the wall of the south-east front of the house, to hold two or more beehives, with two iron bars, joined and hinged at one end, and with a staple at the other, to lock them up, to prevent stealing.

In the labourer's cottage garden of the period, we are told, it should be enclosed, if not with a wall then with a wooden 'close paled' fence or a hedge composed of holly, thorn, sloe-thorn or damson plum 'according to circumstance'. Added to which plum, pear, apple and cherry should be planted either against the wall or free standing in the hedge. Gooseberries and currants should be found a place and Loudon recommends that honeysuckle and roses should be placed around the porch, ivy over the water closet and scented clematis around the pigsty. Pot herbs and vegetables to be grown are 'of the basic kind; mint, thyme, parsley, potatoes, peas, turnips and beans'; and 'on no account' are 'forest trees' such as elm or ash to be included, 'as their invasive root systems would destroy the fertility of a small garden'.

Washington House, in the village of Ardler in Perthshire, is the home of Christopher Dingwall, the garden historian. The village was planned by George Kinloch, the 'Radical Laird',[8] in the 1830s as a model village where every house would have its own garden and space for a weaver's shed at the back. By encouraging freeholders to purchase a plot, the right to vote was extended, as only freeholders were allowed this privilege. Model villages had started to be built from the mid-eighteenth century, when many landowners followed Lord Kames' example and set about improving their estates and the housing conditions of their workers – not least because landowners had started enclosing the common lands, which greatly altered the equilibrium of country life. Spittalfield in Perthshire (1760) and Newtyle in Angus (early nineteenth century) are other examples. Ardler, or Washington as it was called on the plans, was typical in that the houses had no front gardens; this was to prevent the residents creating a midden[9] on the street.

In the town again, Loudon is to the fore with designs and ideas to suit both narrow front and back gardens. He changes his mind, as the century progresses, from his earliest designs of 1812 which consist of swirling beds filled with flowers surrounded by mown grass and gravel paths: by 1838 he is urging individuality where 'everything may be grown, though on a smaller scale, and even brought to perfection, that is cultivated in first-rate gardens attached to the mansions and palaces of the nobility'. The bedding-out craze was in full swing and Loudon advocates 'planting to produce symmetrical Masses of Colour' using 'showy perennials which are common and cheap' or 'planting with Bulbs succeeded by half-hardy annuals and greenhouse plants'. He also encourages his readers to install vases, urns, statues and sundials, geological specimens, small fountains or 'pieces of antiquity … such as a stone from some celebrated building'. It all sounds very frenetic and labour intensive.

Labour for town gardens was most often provided by contract gardeners who were employed by companies known as 'florists'. Florists were first set up in Edinburgh by French weavers in the eighteenth century in Picardy Row and they supplied plants as well as gardeners who would do the initial landscaping work and planting. Thereafter jobbing gardeners visited on a regular basis to tidy and water and replace wilted specimens, more often hiring out the plants. One of the most successful of these was James Cochran, who practised 'contract hire' and also 'flowers for the night'. Loundon explains that

All these, and other sorts of plants in pots, are also lent out by the market-florist, to decorate private or public rooms on extraordinary occasions, but especially for those midnight assemblages called routs. This is the most lucrative part of the grower's business, who generally receives half the value of the plants lent out, though many of them, and generally those of most value, are so injured by the heat as never recover.

Cochran set up in London's fashionable Mayfair, subcontracting to other nurserymen. By 1822 he was a highly successful florist, used by the aristocracy and high society, who only needed plants when they were in town occupying their houses for the season. Both the Earl of Bute and the Duke of Buccleuch were amongst many Scots who retained town houses in London and used his services. Established in 1770, the nursery of Robert Anderson in Broughton, Edinburgh, had a similar gardening shop called the Gilded Gardener, situated 'by the Cross on the north side'. From here, Anderson hired out to 'noblemen or gentlemen experienced gardeners of good character' and 'flowers for the night' in the shape of 'a great variety of flowers and flowering shrubs in pots, which may be lifted and transported at any season'.[10]

As Edinburgh expanded, larger houses were forming residential suburbs in places such as Fountainbridge and Dalry[11] that were surrounded by elaborate gardens and parks with gardener's cottages. Dalry was also the site of many nurseries and home to the Society and Fraternity of Gardeners in the Shire of Midlothian (which had begun in a building called the Gardeners' Hall in 1722). In the following century it became an area for prosperous citizens

Thomas Rowlandson's Florist, *1799.*

Thomas Rowlandson's The Jobbing Gardener.

House of Dean, an example of a prosperous suburban house and garden in Edinburgh c.1760 (National Galleries of Scotland).

and minor aristocracy to settle.[12] In 1816 an advertisement in the *Edinburgh Evening Courant* for a typical residence read:

> *To be sold or let for such time as may be agreed on. The house, offices and grounds of 'Grove' situated at Fountainbridge in the neighbourhood of Edinburgh. The house contains eight fire rooms besides kitchen, cellars, etc., with an excellent washing house and dairy adjoining, and the offices consist of gardeners houses, six stalled stables, byre and poultry house. The grounds consist of upwards of ten English acres and extend northwards from Fountainbridge to the Glasgow Road. About four acres are laid out in garden and pleasure grounds well stocked with fruit trees, and in the highest order. The remainder of the ground is divided into four parks, well fenced and surrounded with old trees under the shadow of which there is most delightful walks round the premises.*

On a smaller scale, but still surrounded by an acre of walled garden, Anna Buxton's town house in Edinburgh's Murrayfield was built in 1913 and is an example of the architecture of the Arts and Crafts movement. In 2004 it may be uncommon to have such a large area to cultivate in a town, but there are still such gardens in some of the residential areas of Edinburgh, built at the turn of the nineteenth century, that have survived the building boom of the twenty-first century. I think Loudon would have termed this a first-rate garden. It has a country feel from the moment you enter off the street, through the whimsical Arts-and-Crafts, green-painted, wooden porch. The microclimate afforded by the surrounding buildings and the enclosing stone walls provides a growing space for semi-tender species that is enviable to the country gardener in Scotland.

Books have always been Anna's interest. In 1986, the family moved from Rome to Edinburgh whereupon she

Anna Buxton, Murrayfield Road, Edinburgh.

switched from dealing in books about Italy to selling second-hand gardening books.[13] Her own personal collection includes first editions of John Reid's *Scots Gard'ner,* and *The Hortus Medicus Edinburgensis* by James Sutherland,[14] two of the earliest botanical books to be published in Scotland, printed in the seventeenth century. For many years Anna was Convener of the Friends of the Royal Botanic Garden, Edinburgh, through which she has explored her interest in plants, gardeners and gardening. Her own garden reflects the intellectual approach she takes and is filled with interesting and unusual varieties, many of which have been bought at the Botanics' annual auction of plants.

Anna's interest in evergreen plants is helped by the lack of wind that will scorch

Evergreens and cloud pruning in Anna Buxton's garden.

and burn many varieties growing in more exposed sites. This is not a garden filled with gloomy shrubberies inhabited by sooty laurels and conifers, as so often are found in town gardens; instead soft grey, green, blue and silver foliage plants contrast with shiny dark greens and pinky-purples. As much thought has been given to the shapes and textures of the leaves as to the colours. On the west-facing front of the house grow billowing groups of lavender, rosemary, choisya and a rare phlomis, *alba*, self-seeded *Teucrium fruticans*, yellow-flowered *Coronilla glauca* and a red herbaceous *Euphorbia dulcis* chameleon that stars in summer.

Recently, Anna has been experimenting with different kinds of asymmetric pruning. A twenty-foot-high *Cotoneaster cornubia* tree has been carefully shaped to create a waterfall of elliptical bright green leaves and spectacular red berries that cheer up the gloomiest December day. Some conifers have been 'cloud pruned' in the Japanese fashion, softening the normal rather rigid growth and showing off their needles in billowing cloud-shaped mittens, while others are trimmed into rounded columns of three or five per bush.

Winter flowers and berries are very much in evidence, one border near the back door bursting with scent from *Saccocia confusa*, skimma Kew Green, *Mahonia belii* and *Viburnum fragrans*. The giant seed pods of *Cardiocrinum giganteum* tower over them, unusually grown here in the gravel in the shade of a silver birch tree. Further along, the purple berries of calicarpa contrast with the fading cobweb flowers of *Hydrangea villosa*, which in summer has the tall purple orchid

Cotoneaster cornubia arches over the pond at Anna Buxton's garden.

Dactylorhiza mayalis growing at its base, contrasting with the large evergreen silver spears of the yucca-like *Astelia chathamica*. Anna's love of interesting leaves and colour is further shown by the bronze-leaved bergenia Margery Fish and tubs of heuchera 'plum pudding', with the tips of purple tulips pushing through, and the pretty, grey-leaved *Buddleia fallowiana* and a *Drimys lanceolata* which she has growing near the house.

Where there were once three greenhouses, there is now one good-sized frost-free structure. This is mainly used for growing pot plants for the house and for housing tender plants from the garden during the winter. Permanent residents include an exotic passion flower with hibiscus-shaped carmine flowers, mimosa and *Eupatorium sordidum* with large downy heart-shaped leaves. A central bed grows chrysanthemums for cutting in the late summer and autumn.

It is a very natural-looking garden with lawns, a woodland area, a wild-flower meadow, a winter garden, shrub borders and a pond surrounded by a rockery (no fish, as there are too many herons). Large, mature, graceful silver birches dotted amongst the other trees growing in the lawns around the house transport you to a rural idyll. Anna says that she was lucky to inherit a continuously well-tended garden when she moved here with good soil, few weeds and some lovely mature trees and shrubs.

It is noticeable how many new houses are going up in town gardens, shrinking the green space available, as property prices rise. As urban gardens increasingly become hard-landscaped extensions of a living space, Anna's garden is a luxury indeed.

A silver birch in front of the wild-flower meadow, Murrayfield Road.

Notes

1. Writing on the village of Glenluce, in *Observations made in a Journey through the Western Counties of Scotland; in the Autumn of 1793* (2 vols).
2. Including the Knights Templar – Temple Lands of Orchardfield.
3. The Nor' Loch, created from three burns by James II in 1460 as a defensive measure, was finally drained in 1820 and Princes Street Gardens laid out there. The draining process had begun in 1763.
4. *Flores canellae*, imported from the West Indies in 1600.
5. Chambers, *Caledonia*, vol. IV.
6. Jeweller to James VI and his queen, Anne of Denmark, whose love of jewellery made Heriot very rich indeed.
7. *The London Town Garden, 1700–1840* (2001).
8. George Kinloch of Kinloch was forced to flee into exile for his radical views in support of the workers of Dundee, prior to the Reform Act of 1832, after which he became MP for Dundee.
9. 'Midden' = rubbish dump.
10. As the Presbyterian Church had lifted its ban on dancing earlier in the eighteenth century, routs and balls were now regular occurrences, requiring 'flowers for the night' to decorate the assembly halls.
11. Dalry – Gaelic for 'King's meadow' – was the site of the royal farm outside Edinburgh in the twelfth century.
12. 'Dalry House, Its Lands and Owners' by John Smith, in *Book of the Old Edinburgh Club*, XX (1935).
13. Anna ceased trading in 2005.
14. … containing a complete list of the plants in the 'Physical Garden at Edinburgh'. See Chapter 1, on botanical gardens.

CHAPTER NINE

Artists and Designers

The pond garden at Newmains Farm.

ARTISTS AND DESIGNERS

'The scenery of a garden should differ as much from common nature as an heroic poem doth from a prose relation; and gardeners, like poets, should give a loose to their imagination, and even fly beyond the bounds of truth, whenever it is necessary to elevate ... to enliven, or to add novelty to their subject.'

SIR WILLIAM CHAMBERS[1]

When artist and designer Humphry Repton wrote the following, he knew what he was talking about:

The spot from whence the view is taken, is in a fixed state to the painter; but the gardener surveys his scenery while in motion ... The painter sees things as they are, the gardener as they will be.[2]

Repton was both a practical gardener and a landscape painter who took up landscape design to support his growing family. His famous *Red Books,* containing presentations to his clients of 'before' and 'after' watercolours, gained him numerous commissions. Repton was a landscape man and trees and views took precedence over mere flowers and colour. The painter Alexander Nasmyth (1758–1840) was also at the heart of the landscape movement, as well as embracing the concepts of the Enlightenment with regard to man's relationship with nature and the landscape. Nasmyth painted the scenes that the Rev. William Gilpin[3] came to Scotland to see, the picturesque and the bucolic. Originally a portrait painter, Nasmyth studied with his fellow Scottish artist Allan Ramsay in London. He later switched to landscape painting after travelling in Italy, before settling in Edinburgh, from where he travelled all over Scotland. His son James wrote[4] that his father was well aware of the inter-relation between painting, garden layout and architecture. This talent allowed him to project ideas for various clients who could see desired changes to their houses, gardens and the surrounding landscape, at the wave of a paintbrush, which could add a grove of trees here and a change of level there.[5]

Gardening can sometimes be described as 'painting

with plants' and many of the great garden designers started out studying art – Russell Page[6] and Gertrude Jekyll spring instantly to mind. Frances Macdonald, who is a keen gardener, was not allowed to go to art school as her Presbyterian parents thought it would corrupt her morals. Instead she trained to be a nurse, qualifying as a midwife, thus enabling her to achieve her other ambition – to go to sea and see the world. It was as an officer on board ship that

Frances Macdonald, Crinan, Argyll.

The cottage garden at Crinan.

At first the garden grew up around the cottage behind the hotel in which they live, but in 1980 Frances decided to investigate the land between their garden and the hotel. Once the copse of self-seeded trees had been cleared, the original terraces and paths revealed themselves within walls that had been built 200 years earlier to enclose a vegetable garden for the original inn. This gave her scope for expansion and a garden for the guests to use. Apart from yachtsmen, many of the people who come to stay at Crinan do so because it is a strategic base from which to visit the many famous gardens in Argyll.

Frances has used her artist's eye to create a riot of colour and texture around some of the original trees and shrubs that were uncovered during the clearance. A

Aquilegias and geraniums line a Crinan pathway.

Frances met her husband, Nick Ryan, whose love of the sea had caused him to join the *Queen Mary* at sixteen as a bell boy, later progressing into the catering side. Five days after their wedding in 1970, Nick took over management of three hotels in Argyll, including the Crinan Hotel, which he eventually bought in 1977.

As rarely happens, all the Ryans' dreams seem to have come true. They live by the sea, they have a boat on which they can go sailing, they own one of the best seafood restaurants in Scotland and they have a beautiful garden. Better still, Frances, in spite of her parents, has never stopped painting and is a successful artist who has had many exhibitions in Scotland and London.

Magnolia wilsonii at Crinan.

huge *Rhododendron fragrantissimum* and two griselinia trees were amongst the finds that thrive outdoors in these mild coastal conditions. Twenty years on, crinodendrons self seed amongst the many azaleas, while species of rhododendron, magnolia and a tender callistemon, the bottle brush tree from Australia, do well here too. Roses and honeysuckle clamber up the side of the steps that lead up to this garden and in the cracks grow ferns and hostas. Herbaceous borders provide summer colour after the spring shrubs have finished, while rodgersia and gunnera add interesting leaf colours. The cottage garden

has a different feel to it, filled with masses of Frances's favourite flowers, catmint, iris, lupins, poppies, herbaceous geraniums, agapanthus and lilies. Near the kitchen door grow herbs and a large bay tree and further up is an olive tree. Of all her many shrubs, she particularly likes the *Magnolia wilsonii*, not just for its cup-shaped white flowers but for the striking branches in winter. You have to be a bit of a mountain goat to scramble up the narrow rough stone steps and along stone paths to the top of the rocky hill, where a strategic bench rewards those who are out of breath. Sitting there, you can look down on the flowering canopy of the shrubs and trees clinging to the hillside, and out over the Crinan Canal to the beaches around Loch Crinan.

Frances says that Crinan is all about views and although she used to paint mainly flowers and still-life pictures, she has now turned to these views for her inspiration. Her seascapes are painted not only from the shore, but also from the deck of Ryan's Tarbert fishing boat, the MV *Sgarbh*, which she uses as a floating studio. To garden here successfully, you have to pay attention to the conditions; it seems there is a price to pay for being able to grow so many tender plants and that is the notorious midge. The gardening has to be finished by the end of June, otherwise, while working in the lush undergrowth, you become a gourmet meal for them. This is another good reason for heading out to sea with canvas and paints during the height of the midges' summer season.

Before the advent of the camera, botanical artists were much employed to record the finds of plant hunters. William Roxburgh (1751–1815) from Ayrshire, started out in a completely different field, studying medicine in Edinburgh before joining the East India Company as a surgeon. Roxburgh's hobby was plant hunting and from 1776 he roamed and collected in India, before becoming chief botanist at the Calcutta Botanic Garden. He left 2,500 botanical drawings. Another was Walter Hood Fitch (1817–92), who was born in Glasgow and apprenticed to a calico design company as a teenager. Sir William Hooker, then Professor of Botany at Glasgow

University, spotted his talent, paid off his indenture fees and took him to work in the herbarium. Fitch later went to Kew, where he produced over 1,000 engravings and 10,000 drawings. He is most familiar today as the illustrator of Bentham and Hooker's *Flora of Great Britain*. He wrote a book about botanical illustration, towards the end of his life, which was re-published in 1950 as *The Art of Botanical Illustration*.

Other Scottish botanical artists of more recent fame include the late Mary McMurtrie from Aberdeenshire, Liz Cameron from the Black Isle and the Lady Emma Tennant from Roxburghshire, all of whom have created beautiful gardens around their houses and used the flowers as inspiration for their work. Another is Ann Fraser, who is quick to point out that the garden at Shepherd House, outside Edinburgh, is very much a joint venture between herself and her husband Sir Charles. In Rosemary Verey's book, *Secret Gardens*, Charles Fraser acknowledges his wife's contribution as 'an eye for design and a knowledge of plants' and modestly wonders what his own is. Having visited Shepherd House, I think his contribution is crucial. He weeds, clips, cuts, tidies, cultivates the ornamental potager and makes compost. In just an acre there is so much crammed into the various different small garden rooms that if it were not kept tidy, the design would become blurred. Touches of humour, too, can be put down on Charles Fraser's side of the slate: topiary animals and birds, a huge box 'broody hen' laying an egg, a comical rabbit-like creature known as the 'millennium bug' and a clipped box dachshund.

Ann Fraser, Shepherd House.

Charles Fraser.

*Pots of flowers in
the knot garden at
Shepherd House.*

The entrance to Shepherd House is via a knot garden with clipped box hedges and 'sentries' of standard iceberg roses. It is a calm and tranquil space, the style reflecting the period of 1690 when the house was built, and earlier in the year it is ablaze with tulips that fit well with the Dutch gables of the house.

After the Frasers' four sons grew up, the playroom was pulled down to make way for a conservatory and it is through this that you enter the main, walled, garden. Lots of quite tender plants are grown in pots here; *Convolvulus cneorum*, passion flower and agapanthus that are over-wintered inside. For the first twenty-five years the garden was mostly a 'football pitch/cricket ground' and Charles grew vegetables in neat rows. Ann describes the creation of the garden as it is presently as 'a fifteen-year learning curve' that has evolved after much discussion and much enjoyable

hard work. The garden is an irregular triangle, but with a clever use of vistas and formal layouts, the first impression is one of pleasing symmetry. Outside the conservatory is a second knot garden made with clipped rosemary, santolina and more box, watched over by the previously mentioned broody hen. Steps lead up through a low wall, which is home to a pretty collection of alpines enjoying the good drainage and warmth of the stones. These lead you to a rectangular stone pond with a fountain where large goldfish hide amongst the water lilies. This pond is linked by a narrow rill to a smaller, raised stone pond with cascading water jets at the far end of a rose tunnel. From the bright sunshine of the first lawn and pond you follow the wide grass path and rill under tumbling roses 'Rambling Rector', 'Wedding Day' and 'Seagull', getting glimpses of further garden rooms to each side before plunging into a cool, green, shady area.

Ferns, hostas and other shade-loving plants create a green jungle here and, as you look back towards the first pond, the rill has the appearance in miniature of a river flowing towards its sea.

The high stone walls at this end of the garden are smothered in shrubs, trees and climbers, including white and mauve abutilons, *Rhododendron loderi* 'King George', lilacs and *Rosa rugosa* 'Roserie de l'Hay'. Around another corner a tiny orchard of apple trees plays host to more climbing roses surrounded by a skirt of fritillaries, which have naturalised in the grass.

Behind an eight-year-old yew hedge, in which a moon gate window has been clipped, is the business side of the garden – Charles's neat row of compost heaps, wheelbarrows and crocks for the bottoms of pots. Opposite this is Ann's working greenhouse filled to bursting with seedlings and cuttings. The garden is constantly changing and has even spilled out onto the road, with iris and *Alchemilla mollis* running along the base of the outside walls.

I asked Ann how she divided her time between painting flowers and growing them. It seems that flowers get painted inside during the week and gardened outside at weekends.

The clipped box 'broody hen' in the knot garden, Shepherd House.

Flowers are indeed a passion at Shepherd House.

In 1990, on returning from a year out painting in Florence, artist Sally Oyler and her husband, chartered surveyor Patrick Gammell, found that their savings had disappeared in a stock-market slide. They did however still own a run-down office building in Edinburgh's Haymarket, so they borrowed some money and set about renovating this Georgian house to let out as offices. They formed a company and called it the Uffizi Partnership, as *uffizi* is the Medieval Italian word for offices.

Sitting in their personal '*uffizo*', a sun-filled conservatory looking out over the

The rill running to the pond under the arches of climbing roses at Shepherd House.

Sally Oyler, East Lothian manse.

garden of their old manse near Haddington in East Lothian, the Gammells explain their successful formula of adding ultra-modern concepts within or around classically restored exteriors and features. This has led them on to another project, that of rescuing the Old Assembly Rooms in Leith. Sally, who trained as a graphic designer at Gray's School of Art in Aberdeen, says that she loves joining up the old and the new.

At home they have turned these same design skills to the garden of the old manse that Patrick bought twenty years ago, three years before he married Sally. Unfortunately, the walled garden, next to the twelfth-century church – which had originally contained the earlier manse building – had been sold separately. A few years ago the couple managed to buy it back and join up their 1820 manse with its old garden. The shape is extremely unusual, being

like a balloon with corners instead of curves. The mellow twelve-foot high walls follow the line of the burn in a dogleg with the land rising steeply at both ends. To get to it from the house, you descend a steep wooden stair down to the wilderness garden, which rambles around a pond full of water-lilies. Rugosa roses, bamboos, azaleas, rhododendrons, *Kerria japonica*, buddleia and sennecio grow here among dense ground cover of arum lilies, rubus and carpets of aconites. Along the burn the geans and willows have been pruned to let in the light and beech and birch trees have been added.

The neatness of the small intimate walled garden is in marked contrast to the wilderness. An ancient garden bothy (formerly used by the next-door church as a mortuary) is built into the wall by the entrance gate. Next to this is a small bee bole set into the wall that would have

The circular rose-covered trellis in the centre of the Gammell's garden.

contained a bee 'skep' so that the minister's fruit trees in the adjoining orchard could be pollinated by the bees kept there.

When designing the interior of the walled garden, Sally employed the help of Beryl McNaughton at Macplants in East Lothian. The first decision was what, if anything, should be retained from the jungle of stuff inside the garden. Beryl McNaughton advised clearing out everything with the exception of a handsome weeping silver pear tree, a large clump of bamboo and two apple trees. Sally then drew out the shape and decided on the colours and textures that she wanted and Macplants supplied growing material that would 'do the job'. An unusual circular rustic trellis was built to Sally's design; and placed in the middle is a standing stone weighing over a ton. She found the beautiful Golden Foliate Quartzite stone near Cumbernauld, although it originated in Ireland. It was craned into the garden over the wall and then rolled into the centre on wooden posts, in much the same way as ancient stones would have been moved. On top of the stone is a bronze owl sculpture by Sally, inspired by the tawny owls that inhabit the wilderness garden. The owl clutches a mouse in its talons. Growing over the trellis are masses of scented climbing roses, and clematis. The narrow curving beds are edged with clipped box and contain a mixture of geraniums and violas in purples and pinks. At the wide end of the balloon the curved wall encloses a stone terrace planted with grey-leafed and scented herbs and plants. In amongst the paving stones grows creeping camomile

The bronze owl sculpture by Sally Gammell.

that gives out a strong scent when crushed underfoot. As for the colours, there are strong deep purples with a blast of violent pink mixed with whites, apricots, buffs and peaches – all colours that I noticed she uses in her flower and animal paintings that I had seen in her studio.

Through a door in the right-hand corner, we are back beside the burn and across a wooden bridge where *Clematis montana* has completely engulfed a huge tree and most of the bridge. On the bank above is a wooden bench, which is the perfect place from which to watch the sunset and look down on the tranquil walled garden and the churchyard on the other side of the wall.

There is an old adage that if a couple can plan and plant a garden together without arguing, this is a true test of their compatibility. If you were to give two people an identical space and the same budget, they would invariably come up with two different schemes. Brian Lascelles has lived in the Bank House in Glenfarg (formerly the Bank of Scotland and the Manager's House) for twenty-five years and was already a passionate and knowledgeable gardener when he married Maggie Mitchell, the artist, eleven years ago.

Brian has an enviably encyclopaedic mind when it comes to the plants he grows, with a particular love of the strange and exotic with interesting leaves and flowers. The interesting contrasts of variegation, shape and texture married to his military sense of order and discipline have produced wonderfully controlled planting schemes of great originality. Maggie, when not painting her exuberant and colourful paintings, has joined Brian outside and together they have developed the garden over the last decade, with exciting new areas combining strong colours and shapes. She also has a deep spiritual feel for the elements and for spaces which contribute to the atmosphere. They dispute as to who is the 'head gardener' here, but it would seem to me that this is a marriage that works on every level.

Maggie and Brian Lascelles, The Bank House.

Spires of white lupins and eremurus lily contrast with the undulating clipped hedge at The Bank House.

They share a love of modern sculpture, and in particular water everywhere you look there are fountains, ponds, waterfalls – a burn and a small lake. You can hear the soothing sound of water, running, trickling, gurgling and splashing over stones and into basins, under bridges and flowing into more water. There are vistas and views designed to frame and enhance the many pieces that they have collected. These range from heads, pots, statues, seats, bridges, fountains, flows, arbours and tunnels.

To catalogue the immense range of strange and wonderful plants that are grown in the back garden would take up many pages. I particularly loved the fern on the terrace *Athyrium felix-femina* 'Victoriae' and the ferny *Maium anthamanticum* (which smells like dill) growing near the formal pond. This pond contains a fountain named *Green Fingers* by the sculptor Polly Ionides. Although it is their private part of the garden, it is open by appointment (all proceeds go to the Prison Phoenix Trust), so interested plants-people should go armed with a pencil and paper. When the main garden at the back of the house became full, so full that no weed could ever find the tiniest space to invade, the Lascelles acquired a further three acres across the main road in front of The Bank House and turned this into an open garden with free access for the public.

This garden defies its origins as a rough field and a coal-merchant's yard and is now a peaceful oasis. It is approached from the road down steps, in the centre of which runs a flow-form cascade made by John Wilkes. On either side are beds filled with the roses Rosa Mundi, Glenfiddich and Harry Wheatcroft offset with cascading catmint and lady's mantle to echo the water running down the middle. Between this and the burn is a meticulously planted *yin–yang* bed with central eyes of golden and dark yew. This again I thought very apposite for the marriage of these two remarkable gardeners as the *yin–yang* symbolises balance and the harmonious combination of opposites. The *yin* is planted in dark-coloured plants and the *yang* in pale plants, representing the male and the female elements of the design. Dark ajugas, heuchera and paeonies contrast with golden spirea, silver lanata and feathery grasses.

From here the visitor crosses a gaily painted Monet bridge, covered with honeysuckles, which leads over the burn and out onto a grassy mown area where people can picnic and children can play. To the left is a large pond that was made by damming the burn. This has a path winding around it

so that the stunning planting on the margins can be seen reflected in the still water. Simpler and more recognisable plants than those used in the back garden grow here. There are drifts of *Primula japonica*, meadow sweet, campanula, loosestrife, elsholtzia, mimulus and white foxgloves with architectural rodgersias and verbascums rising through patches of cranesbill and ornamental grasses.

To the right, a wild-flower meadow runs up a steep slope opening out onto a plateau with two rough wooden benches made by the chainsaw sculptor Nigel Ross. Fifty-seven varieties of native wild flowers thrive in the poor soil in this part of the garden; they grow in amongst the grass that is criss-crossed with mown paths.

There is good balance here in the contrasts between the

Bank House pond with fountain 'Green Fingers'.

art can be seen against the backdrop of the snow capped mountains of Ross-shire. They appear in small formal areas, as eye-catching punctuation marks in the middle, at the end of the water garden and as focal points for vistas. You almost get the feeling that the garden is inhabited by living people and that they move around, which indeed they do – sometimes they are there and sometimes they go off to be sold or to exhibitions, so it is full of surprises. Years ago, arriving for dinner, I had a shocking nocturnal collision with a larger-than-life Sherlock Holmes – he was en route from the studio to where he now resides in Picardy Place in Edinburgh. There are those, like the fountains, that have been specifically designed for the gardens. Another permanent stone installation, which

Gerald Laing and gardener Gus (Eric Angus) at Kinkell.

sophisticated and the simple, the stone and the water, the ordered and the tumbling, the plantsman and the painter; the private and the public garden, the *yin* and the *yang* – a perfect marriage of mind, spirit and matter.

There is a school of thought which holds that gardens should be thought provoking and they should contain not just plants, but structure, texture and movement. In our climate of long winters it is even more important to have things to look at that arouse the senses when everything is dormant. The sculptor Gerald Laing has created just such a garden around Kinkell Castle in the Black Isle, where his

Kinkell Castle.

*'American Girl' in the
miniature walled garden,
Kinkell.*

reflects his impish sense of humour, is Gerald's moon-gazing folly Pyramid. He swears it has, in common with other pyramids, a rejuvenatory effect and that when people come out of the sixteen-foot-high, rendered stone structure (now nearly all covered with ivy) they definitely look and act younger.

Scottish by descent and by repatriation, Gerald was born and raised in Newcastle. After a spell in the army he went and studied at St Martin's School of Art in London before heading for New York. There in the 1960s he hung out with the Andy Warhol set and 'surfed on the wave of the avant garde', experimenting with pop and abstract art. (Work from this period is very collected now and recently the pop star Jarvis Cocker bought his famous Brigitte Bardot screen print.) He moved to Scotland in 1969 and by 1973 had turned away from landscape-inspired abstract sculpture to pursue the figurative, only returning to painting in 2004.

Gerald is passionate about his house and garden. He lives there, he has a studio in the garden and he used to have his own foundry there as well.[7] The buildings have a sculptural quality and the planting around them is in harmony. Even the old studio, which is now a guest cottage, has its own garden full of scented shrub roses with creeping thymes and violas in the flagged terrace outside. From here you can gaze up at the monumental mass of the mountains or look down on the reflection of the top figure from *axis mundi* [8] dancing over the water in the pond.

The garden around Kinkell Castle has grown and evolved over the years since 1969 when Gerald restored the small but perfectly formed tower house, dating from 1594. Various garden rooms and areas have emerged and each one has a permanent or visiting sculpture. Entering the garden, you are greeted by the figure of *Girl Waiting*. When it snows she is dressed in a fetching white fig leaf and matching hat. By the avenue of pleached limes there is a sundial, which Gerald cast from a bronze he was commissioned to do for the retiring chairman of United Biscuits, Sir Hector Laing (no relation). This is the ultimate horticultural 'gold watch' and reflects Gerald's interest in mathematical calculations.

In the miniature walled garden sits *American Girl* – a stunning erotic bronze of his second wife, Galina. Adaline, the third Mrs Laing (also from America), is represented by a one-and-a-half-times life-size reclining nude at the end of the water garden, entitled *Mnemosyne*.[9] Adaline designed and planted the water garden, which is one of the best, not just for the soft colours but also for its lush planting around a series of ponds and falls made by damming the burn that runs past

The water garden at Kinkell with 'axis mundi' at one end of the pond.

'Mnemosyne' overlooks her garden.

the castle. Huge clumps of gunnera and graceful ferns arch over the water and there are masses of *Primula japonica* and aquilegia that self-seed under the shrubs and mingle with the hostas, hellebores and marsh marigolds. *Mnemosyne* has a contemplative air as she watches over her garden.

As in all the best gardens, there are jokes – recently Gerald built a raised platform in one corner and planted it with turf. He plans to be buried inside so that his friends can continue to dine with him, at the table that he has placed on the top – 'al fresco dining has become an uplifting experience in a room with a view'.

'A garden hyphenates man with nature', believes sculptor George Wyllie. As you stand at the window looking out across his hilltop garden in Gourock, towards Dunoon, he explains:

First you see the grass, then the roof tops and then the water. Shoot across the water and it does it all over again. Through the houses on the other side, up the rocky bits into sky, through the clouds and goodness knows what happens up there in the planet. The world is an open window – it's a bloody good planet!

As you get older, looking after a garden is more difficult but the views come free of charge. George points out that his small garden is at the centre of the larger environment that surrounds it, and as a result it looks enormous. He has a sculpture illustrating this theory in the Buchanan Galleries in Glasgow. His preoccupation is with stone, air and water combined with balance and energy, all elements that any gardener should take into account, but he says he is no gardener. He describes his garden as a 'useable space because of the efforts of my wife to treat it with respect; but I take liberties with it'.[10]

Driving along past the row of modest houses in the street where the Wyllies live, it would be difficult to pick out one from another. They all have neat front gardens and larger but equally neat back gardens with manicured lawns, cared-for beds of heather and roses, an obligatory cherry tree and the odd carefully placed urn or small pond. You suddenly spot the explosion of energy that is the Wyllie's garden. The plants and layout are much the same, but the arresting sculptures that spill out onto the street turn the short walk to the front door into a philosophical journey. Every piece tells a story or illustrates an idea or an event. 'A garden is important,' George says, 'as it is man's contrived way of connecting with the earth. Our spirit

George Wyllie, Gourock.

Spires and Skewered Stones overlooking the Clyde, Gourock.

George Wyllie: Standing Stones – on the move.

is in the hills but everything now is hurly burly and gravitates towards the urban and urban attitudes are very unbalanced in the way that they see nature and animals.'

George calls the pieces in his garden 'liberties', and in a way that is the perfect description, as they are very free. They fit into the garden and add many dimensions to it. On the lawn is a balancing spire that replicates the movement of a ship on a heaving sea, in all directions at once. This large, graceful arching collection of rods perfectly brings the sea below into the garden, but with a see-through, airy quality that does not have the density of a boat 'shipping green' as it ploughs and tosses through the waves. In contrast a purposeful battleship, *Emporus*, made of welded scrap metal, ploughs its way through a sea of daffodils and lamium in a menacing way.

Where the vegetable garden used to be is the 'Sculpture Park'. This is where George parks things until they find a home. In the centre is another moving spire, entitled *Equilibrium*, but this one sits in water. George's philosophical approach is thoughtful and thought-provoking, but always with a sense of humour: 'You must think what others need and make it work in the space.' He feels that it is important to retrieve the soul and recently he has been experimenting with pieces that reflect the Shamanistic ritual for banishing evil spirits. Several 'spires' made of silver birch with different configurations on the theme are 'parked' around the garden, and two stainless steel *Quivering Horses* stand by the fence where they quiver deliciously to show that the bad spirits have departed when you pat them.

George created an installation in 2003 to celebrate the new Scottish Parliament – a kind of twentieth-century standing stones. This 'garden' is in Edinburgh's Regent's Park behind the Parliament building and embodies the thirty-two parts of Scotland in the arrangement of a stone from each region. Using Hugh MacDiarmid's poem *Scotland* as instructions, much agonising went into their placement as well as the choice of contrasting textures and the balance of the grass, stone, metal and air around them.

George jokes that 'On the face of it my work is unsaleable, but if you can't excite yourself, how can you excite other people?' My favourite work is his graceful 22-foot-high aluminium safety pin which would look fantastic beside water, where it would reflect its title of *Just In Case* or *A Monument To Uncertainty*. If I had a lake I would commission a safety pin at once.

'Growing old is compulsory; growing up is optional' could be applied to the energy and enthusiasm contained in the garden of artist Valerie Fraser in the seaside town of Elie, in Fife. There are almost more animals than plants in Valerie's wonderfully eccentric and colourful garden, not to mention the installations, both inside the house and in the garden. They demand attention, being as imaginative and arresting as any flower border. There is so much to look at that it is difficult to know where to start. Valerie, who studied art at Edinburgh University, ended up in Elie around twelve years ago when her globetrotting years with her ex-husband in

George Wyllie, in the Sculpture Park.

the Far East, Europe and America came to an end. She was no stranger to the place, as her grandfather had a house there and family holidays hold happy memories.

The furniture in Valerie's garden room is all made from driftwood that she has collected on the beach below the house: a table, a cupboard and bookshelves. Some of the seascapes that she paints hang there with frames made from driftwood and bits of netting worked into the paint. Shells and small pebbles are worked in too, echoing the seaside. A large 'mermaid tank' made

Valerie Fraser, Elie.

from driftwood is full of shoals of darting iridescent plastic fish, decorated with glitter and nail varnish – the mermaid rises magnificently up through them, and the nets and shells that decorate the inside, displaying her multicoloured shimmering tail.

I mistakenly sat down on a sofa to take some notes and was instantly draped with dogs, on my shoulders, on my lap and under my arms. There were six tiny ones and three large ones; all were hauled off and shut up in various rooms. A notice on the door read, 'Three cats in here.' One section of the kitchen was almost completely filled with a huge birdcage on wheels containing twenty live budgies all singing along to the CD player. Floating along one wall was a colourful plastic blow-up shark wearing psychedelic dark glasses, while nearby was a giant plastic cactus. Valerie pressed a lobster

View to the bottom of the garden at Elie.

sitting on a shelf, which started to boogie and sing.

It seemed easier to talk outside, as there was less commotion, and we left all the animals inside. Outside there are more creatures both alive and decorative. The first installation to greet you on the terrace is a very elaborate large arrangement of stones with a waterfall. It has been built to resemble frogspawn and it is decorated all over with glittering Christmas baubles, jewels and hundreds of frogs with crowns on their heads. Further down, a scarecrow, dressed in brightly coloured flowing skirts and shawls, is holding a plastic gnome which waves gently in the breeze. They are guarding a pond and what at first look like real ducks swimming around on the surface turn out to be masses of decoy ducks and they too are part of the home guard. Apparently the seagulls used to

Dragons guarding a pot of grasses and shells, Elie.

snitch the coy carp and the goldfish in the pond, but since the introduction of the guards, they have stopped.

The trees in the garden have been pollarded, to make them look Parisian and in them, on them and around them, there are frogs, hippos, angels and dragons. One sycamore has eyes stuck on the trunk. There are creatures climbing up things or just perched in branches and niches in the stone wall. Flowerpots are planted with unusual combinations; in one, daffodils and ornamental cabbages, another is full of shells and in a third a plastic skull sits amongst tulips.

Valerie banished the small lawn at the top of the garden and replaced it with a raised beach of pebbles. Merging

white Skye marble chips with rose quartz has created the shimmering gravel paths that lead from there down to the pond. A bright-pink flowering currant bush grows with the large-flowered purple periwinkle to great effect beside drifts of aquilegias. Over the fence grows honeysuckle. Later in the year comes a great display of poppies, both the wild red ones and the exotic oriental perennials; and pelargoniums, overwintered in a small plant house in the garden, are bought out to flower providing hot reds and pinks. A large yucca plant grows beside a red Bhuddha on top of a pile of round brown and black stones. On top, one stone is painted with a flower to resemble a Bhuddhist

An installation of stones by Valerie Fraser's pond.

offering, bringing echoes of the three years that Valerie spent in Bangkok.

With so many pets it is fortunate that Valerie never wants to go away. 'Elie is an amazing place; I don't need holidays, every day here is a holiday'. That is, unless she is working on pictures that she exhibits at the RSA, the RSW, the Glasgow Institute and the Serpentine Gallery in London. The exit to the garden is guarded by a couple of crown-wearing lions placed each side of the door, after all the colour and activity, the outside street seems strangely quiet and dull.

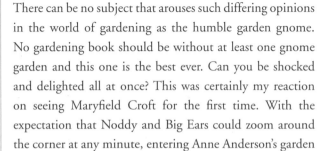

There can be no subject that arouses such differing opinions in the world of gardening as the humble garden gnome. No gardening book should be without at least one gnome garden and this one is the best ever. Can you be shocked and delighted all at once? This was certainly my reaction on seeing Maryfield Croft for the first time. With the expectation that Noddy and Big Ears could zoom around the corner at any minute, entering Anne Anderson's garden brings a smile to the lips and a lightening of the spirit.

As far back as 1797, Goethe, in his poem *Hermann und Dorothea*, describes a garden full of decaying gnomes where the lovers hide after the 'Salzburg Immigration'. They discuss how beautiful these two-and-a-half-foot-high fellows must have been when their paint was fresh and new. Gnomes were the preserve of the landed gentry in the nineteenth century. Around 1850 Sir Charles Isham, at Lamport Hall in Northamptonshire, decorated his huge bonsai rockery with gnomes he had ordered from Nuremberg in Germany. The collection of gnomes at Prior Park goes back to the late nineteenth century when the then owner, Sir Frank Crisp,[11] built an underground grotto and a mini Matterhorn mountain and peopled them with white terracotta gnomes imported from Switzerland.

Gnomes were an expensive luxury item until the advent of concrete when Prime Minister John Major's father and brother, Terry, had a workshop producing brightly coloured gnomes in the twentieth century. By becoming affordable they slid down the social scale into suburbia. Gnomes have always been associated in mythological cultures around the world with fairies, goblins and elves. In Scotland they are the 'wee folk', in Ireland leprechauns.[12] The true representation

The fairy garden at Maryfield Croft.

of a gnome, according to Anne Atkins, who started the Gnome Museum in Devon over twenty years ago, is a figure that is 'timeless, as ancient as the hills and as young as a child, combining the wisdom of ages and the innocence of a babe'. Atkins believes that the blame for their current bad reputation lies with Walt Disney who turned the gnome into a 'candyfloss, cutie-pie image' with his film of Snow White.

But I digress. Maryfield Croft is a kaleidoscopic cacophony of colour and sound and movement that put me in mind of my excitement when I first saw gaily decorated Jeepneys (taxis) tearing around the crowded streets of Manila. Maryfield is set in the heart of Aberdeenshire, with all its history of serious Protestant work ethic, a disdain for frivolity and a very old-fashioned sense of what and how people are supposed to be; a place where ostentation of any kind is frowned upon, where the bleak winds whistle and howl for at least nine months of the year and folk are muffled up in brown and grey against the elements. If Anne Anderson had been born in a different time and place, she would be travelling in India and South America, soaking up the colours and spirits of these different cultures and raising her consciousness, celebrating eclipses of the moon and dressing in colourful clothes. A notice at the entrance to her garden enjoins you to 'be happy, for every minute you are angry, you loose 60 seconds of happiness'.

That Anne is happy is very obvious in the pride with which she showed me around her creation, the loving way in which she described her animals both real and ornamental, her delight at my appreciation

Gnomes line the path to Maryfield's back garden.

of her jokes and sense of fun. She does not drive and she rarely goes out – this is her world. The plain harled cottage has gaily painted window surrounds, the grey stones of the dry stone dyke surrounding the garden are painted in primary colours, windmills whirr in the wind and bunches of plastic flowers flutter, wind-chimes of all shapes and sizes sing in the breeze. A plastic frog croaks as you walk past it and all the while hundreds of pairs of eyes gaze out from the windows – the gnomes are stacked four deep on the inside looking out – at the thousands of gnomes, pixies, animals and birds who are carefully arranged outside. A notice saying 'beware of the dog' leads the eye to a life-sized plastic Alsatian with a real bone placed beside him; and his companion border terrier sports a new collar every year.

There is humour, symbolism and meaning in each separate part of the garden. One part commemorates Anne's father and sister. Another, two of her dear departed dogs. Buckets and spades bring back memories of the seaside holidays of her youth. The swan garden is for her mother. Her favourite cartoon characters are also well represented and are arranged in tableaux: Mickey Mouse is driving over the roof. Budgie the Helicopter is flying guard over the bird garden, filled with nesting boxes to attract the many birds that Anne feeds and loves. The birds are quite unperturbed by the windmills and windchimes and seem to be quite at home with the squirrels and frogs. Superman in his buggy is driving around in one corner and a skull is placed for 'devilment' in a barrel full of flowers. Lots of butterflies signify freedom and peace.

Work begins in the spring in this garden and continues until everything is arranged to Anne's satisfaction. Faded people need to be repainted in her workshop, some every year. On quiet evenings the special gnomes and lighthouses are brought out from the inside to be outside where, sadly, they cannot stay all the time in case a light-fingered passer-by feels tempted. Real flowers are planted alongside the plastic ones. The aim is to finish it in time for the local show, when passers-by are welcomed in and allowed to sit and enjoy it all. She says that every year it is different and she is

always adding to the collection. 'I do it for the smiles and the happiness'. But where they all come from is not so clear – 'all over, some are gifts, they find me somehow'.

Not far from Maryfield Croft is the idiosyncratic garden of inventor and restorer, Major Mike Taitt. In 1985, two years after he retired from being a regular soldier in the Gordon Highlanders, Mike bought the farmhouse at Newmains and ten acres of hillside above the village of Oyne. Mike restored the ruined house himself, before turning his attention to the land. Initially he planted some roses, herbaceous plants and shrubs in the apron of garden at the back. What the rabbits

Mike Taitt, Newmains Farm.

The Bike Park in the silver birch wood at Newmains.

and deer did not eat his peacocks finished off and, as he was reluctant to dispatch them too, he is allowing the larger shrubs and small elder trees to take over. 'I am a tree man,' he says, and to this end he has planted mixed, mainly deciduous, woods covering seven acres. From the mown paths that meander through them you can enjoy the Bike Park, which contains a collection of antique bicycles rescued from skips. With his digger he has channelled the burns that flow down from the Hill of Bennachie behind the house and has made a series of ponds in the open areas within the new plantation. But his landscaping really began with the swimming pond that he dug for himself. Most people living in the hills of Aberdeenshire might not be thinking in terms of outdoor swimming pools – it never gets that hot – but Mike swims most days in the summer. The problem was that there was nowhere to change or sit.

This then was how he came to buy in 1994, a 1908 third-class Great North East Railway Company passenger carriage from a neighbour, for £100. The neighbour had bought it from the Inverurie Locomotive Works, where it had ended up after being retired from service when the Great Northern Scottish Railway sold off their rolling stock in the early 1950s. Although it had been home to the neighbour's hens, it still retained enough features to excite Mike to its possibilities. Railway carriages became a great part of farming heritage in this northeastern part of Scotland after the war, and most farms could boast at least one that was doing service as a chalmer,[13] bothy, henhouse or kennel.

First, Mike constructed a diving platform out into the pond that is reached

from a wooden-decked terrace in front of the railway carriage. In summer he can carry the table out from the kitchen/diner outside and dine with friends beside the water. A bottle cooler made from strategically placed rocks can be reached from the terrace. In 1998 the restoration of the Railway Carriage/Summer House was commended in an award for Rural Landscape Development. The certificate, proudly framed, hangs in the small entrance porch that has been added to the carriage.

The details are a delight: the lead down-pipe has the date 1996 on it; the old train lanterns hanging from the back give the carriage an air of almost being on the move until you notice the climbing rose 'Albertine', anchoring it to the ground. Around the pond the major has planted shrubby willows, broom and alchemilla, some gean, rowan, hazel and silver birch. Presently under construction is the 'viewing parlour', added so that the spectacular views of the surrounding hills can be admired from the warmth provided by the wood-burning stove. In it is a daybed based on one built in 1842 for the Dowager Queen Adelaide in her railway coach.

But the landscaping with carriages and water has not

The 1908 third-class railway carriage converted into a summer house with the Cupola Tree beside the swimming pond at Newmains.

stopped here. Finding that his ducks enjoyed his swimming pond as much as he did, he has dug a lower pond to lure them away. Another derelict railway carriage (a third-class carriage from Caledonian Railways) was acquired with plans to turn this one into a folly with a moving mural on cylinders worked by a generator so that you feel that the countryside in moving past the windows as you sit inside. The duckpond on the opposite side is more ambitious. Here Mike has built a crannog from living willow saplings to make an island for the ducks to nest on. This is six feet across, filled with large stones and earth, in which he has planted heathers and some silver birches. Further up is a larger island with a flat grass surface that he uses for golf-driving competitions from outside the summer house.

One of the most recent installations is a Hobbit House set into the bank. An old railway carriage door is set into the hillside and a chimney protrudes out of the turf above. By digging a large hole and setting a 500-gallon oil tank inside, Mike has created a wood-lined room with a wood-burning stove and a chair – much to the delight of visiting children.

Going back up the hill, you pass a half carriage stuck onto the end of a steading. Mike explained that he had cut it in half himself with a chainsaw and planned to add a viewing platform at the back, similar to the one on the Oriental Express. From it he will be able to admire the ancient Caledonian Pine beside the top pond by the house, watch who is coming up the road and look down on the 'umbrella tree' that he made from two metal cupola covers that were thrown out after his restoration of a local castle roof.

Events organiser and designer Pete Clark describes the modern house that he had built to his own design as 'Key West, Florida, in Colinton, Edinburgh'. Light, colour and atmosphere are very important in his designs and his garden is laid out so that it can be viewed from inside to optimum effect. Pete was born in Newark, New Jersey,

Pete and Val Clark, Colinton, Edinburgh.

which he describes as 'like the Gorbals, but with sun' and moved later with his Scottish parents to Key West, Florida, where they had a restaurant from which you could watch the gun boats and 'ciggy racers'[14] crossing to Havana. In 1966 he moved to Scotland to avoid being sent to Vietnam and after spells in Paris, Spain and California, he finally came to rest in Edinburgh when he married his Scottish wife. His first business venture in the 1960s was a clothes shop in Rose Street, from which he says that as a 'man of dreams' it was a natural progression to designing interiors and then to organising and designing large corporate events and parties. Plants, especially palms, play a major role in these designs so that he is sometimes left with orphan trees – they go back

Palm trees create Pete's 'Wee bit of Florida' in his Edinburgh garden.

to Colinton with him, further enhancing his 'wee bit of Florida' in Scotland.

The Braid Burn cascades into the garden as a waterfall and flows through under a bridge in the middle, before disappearing on its way to the Hermitage. Beside the water, Pete has created a sloping beach with real sand, which he buys from Mothercare, and around the sand he has planted palm trees. Pulled up on the beach is an antique boat, complete with ropes and oars, giving a spirit of adventure to the design. Continuing the nautical theme, on the rustic bridge he has hung two red and white lifebuoys. There are decks and gravel areas planted with cordyline palms and the low-growing *sempervivum* that continue the theme in other parts of the garden. With the use of sand and honey-coloured gravels, the atmosphere is imbued with warm colours and textures. Sitting in his favourite chair in front of the glass doors to the garden under a spreading palm tree, Pete gets a perfect view of the beach, the boat and the water, which he explains has an instant 'cheering-up' effect; it also explains why he designed his own house. 'The weather and the light in Scotland is terrible in the winter; I suffer from SAD[15] in old, dark houses and I have to be warm.'

So from each room in the house there is a planned view through huge windows onto a specific part of the garden that complements the interior decoration. The garden has been brought inside, where there are containers filled with both real and fake palms and cacti. Pete buys the latter wherever he sees them, because he is quite besotted with the plants. They are low maintenance and thrive on neglect, usually only dying from over-attention.

A boat is pulled up onto the 'beach' by the Braid Burn, Colinton.

The bathroom of the master bedroom is dominated by another vast palm tree and the flag from Scott Fitzgerald's yacht, bought by Pete at auction (he is an ardent fan of *The Great Gatsby*). Double doors lead out from the bedroom into the garden, where there is another deck and a water feature, to be seen from the bed.

To the left of the kitchen is the barbeque deck, which is viewed from the 'Navaho' bedroom that is decorated with leather-tooled cowboy boots, Mexican throws, and an ornate saddle and more cactus plants. An American-sized barbeque is built along the garden wall, decorated with numerous pot plants. More ideas for rooms and garden areas are constantly rehearsed in Pete's fertile imagination, not a million miles away from Alexander Nasmyth and his landscape ideas 'to be viewed from the windows'.

Nasmyth's son wrote in 1883 that his father was 'much employed in assisting the noblemen and landed gentry of Scotland in improving the landscape appearance of their estates, especially when seen from their mansion windows'. Given the Scottish climate, it is always a good idea to plan a garden as much from inside the house as from the outside.

The ten gardens that illustrate this chapter range from the conventional to the eccentric and on first glance they would seem to have little in common with one other. But they do: they are all very individual gardens, created by free spirits, individuals who are happy to express themselves without worrying what others think of them. Artists use their space in many ways, some using them as a gallery in which to display their art, an outdoor studio if you like. Others use their artistic skills to create a pleasing design, while some are using the elements in the garden to create artworks. The definition of art is as elastic as the many styles represented.

Notes

1. Sir William Chambers (1726–96), a Scotsman born in Sweden, worked for the Swedish East India Company, travelling widely in China where he studied Chinese gardens and buildings. He studied architecture at the École des Arts in Paris before being employed by the third Earl of Bute as a tutor to the Prince of Wales and later as architectural adviser to his gardening widow, Princess Augusta, at Kew. There he designed many Chinoiserie buildings, including the Pagoda and the largest stove house then known. He wrote *A Dissertation on Oriental Gardening* in 1772 with the hidden agenda of disparaging Capability Brown's humble educational background: 'Amongst the Chinese … their gardeners are not only botanists, but also painters and philosophers, having a thorough knowledge of the human kind, and of the arts by which its strongest feelings are excited. It is not in China, as in Italy and France, where every petty architect is a gardener … In China, gardening is a distinct profession, requiring an extensive study; to the perfection of which few arrive.' Chambers introduced the reader to many plants grown in China that were unknown in Britain, but his main attack was on the landscape movement.

2. Humphry Repton, *Sketches and Hints on Landscape Gardening* (1794).

3. Discussed in the Introduction, p.5.

4. In *James Nasmyth, Engineer, An Autobiography.* (London, 1883).

5. James Nasmyth (son) wrote: 'The Duke (of Atholl) was desirous that a rocky crag, called Craigybarns should be planted with trees, to relieve the grim barrenness of its appearance. But it was impossible for any man to climb the crag in order to set seeds or plants in the clefts of the rocks. A happy idea struck my father. Having observed in front of the castle a pair of small cannon used for firing salutes on great days, it occurred to him to turn them to account. His object was to deposit the seeds of the various trees amongst the soil in the clefts of the crag. A tinsmith in the village was ordered to make a number of canisters with covers. The canisters were filled with all sorts of suitable tree seeds. The cannon was loaded, and the canisters were fired up against the high face of the rock. They burst and scattered the seeds in all directions. Some years later, when my father revisited the place, he was delighted to find … trees flourishing luxuriantly in all the recesses of the cliff.'

6. Russell Page (1906–85) was probably the most prolific garden designer of the twentieth century, with an international reputation.

7. The foundry Black Isle Bronze is now based in Nairn and run by his son Farquhar.

8. A group of flying figures on a central axis, now at Tanfield House, Canonmills, Edinburgh.

9. Her pose is based on a sculpture on 110th St, Broadway, New York entitled *Mnemosyne* in memory of Mrs Schultz, who drowned in the Titanic (in reality – not in the film). Mnemosyne was the Greek goddess of memory and the mother of the nine Muses.

10. Daphne Wyllie died in 2004 after a long illness.

11. An expert on medieval gardens.

12. At auction, gnomes are 'novelty items', but do occasionally come up for sale. Mainly from middle Europe, Austria and Germany, they can fetch up to £3,000 for a good antique specimen. Sizes start at 'cake decoration' up to around three feet. The 'Gno' part of the word comes from the Greek word for knowledge. In the sixteenth century the meaning of gnome was sententious, moralistic, pompously formalising and from the German it implied maxims, proverbs and aphorisms. It is from Germany, too, that we get the connection with toadstools as there they have a mythical connection with forests. *OED* definition: 'A subterranean spirit or goblin in folklore.' They are further defined as 'a person with sinister influence, especially in finance' – hence the term, Gnomes of Zurich. Interestingly, they are also described as one of a race of diminutive spirits fabled to inhabit the interior of the earth and to be the guardians of its treasure. There must be a link between the Gnostic gospels, written by the Essenes about the original inhabitants of the earth who were driven underground. In Scotland the Picts were a persecuted minority: 'little brown men' who lived underground; in Ireland they were leprechauns. How far back gnomes go is difficult to ascertain, but they are entrenched in our mythical and literary history. The Gnome Museum web site is www.ndia.ndirect.co.uk/gnomes/museum.htm

13. 'Chalmer' = farmworkers' quarters (literally 'chamber', from Fr. *chambre*).

14. High-powered speed boats used to smuggle goods, principally tobacco, between Cuba and Florida.

15. Seasonal Affective Disorder – depression caused by lack of daylight.

Epilogue

Garden pavilion at Spedlins.

EPILOGUE

Gardens are about people, the way they live, and their needs and wants. From kailyard to woodland, from herbaceous border to decking, the plants and layouts reflect the people and the social reality. The garden is about necessity, food, status, acquisitiveness, recreation, but also about beauty, peace and happiness. It may have started out by being a place to aid survival and then moved through many eras to become a space just to be in or in which to gain strength from the earth. Scottish gardens are not just about rhododendrons and heather, any more than Scotland is just about tartan and shortbread.

In today's world, many gain more information from the screen than from books. Television gardening is influencing what can be found in our gardens. But is the concept of the garden as an extension of the house, composed of a series of rooms with different purposes, a new one? Some TV gardening shows concentrate on advice on how to create 'rooms' outside and would have us believe that it is. With brightly coloured decks, patios and kiddie-play areas replacing the vegetable patch and the herbaceous border, modern gardening, it seems, is not about sowing seeds. Instead, it is learning how to mix up orange- and turquoise-coloured cement for a funky outdoor terrace on which to entertain friends and enjoy the barbecue. Children no longer search for worms to put in jam jars, but instead frolic on hygienic bark chips which cover the ground around their swings, slides and playhouses. Ubiquitous water features burble and gush down perspex tubes into ponds surrounded by painted decking, lit with elaborate lighting schemes that make these spaces as useable by night as by day.

Specifically designed outdoor rooms, though, are far from being the new rock and roll of gardening; they are more an updating of an old idea. As early physic gardens, kailyards and monastic cloisters gave way to pleasure gardens; outdoor rooms were increasingly incorporated. In times gone by the garden was very much an extension of the house – all the consumer durables or 'white goods' that we so neatly fit into our kitchens were separate 'rooms' outside. Today you would employ Diarmud Gavin or Anne McKevitt to design your outdoor dining room just as in the past architects such as Sir William Bruce or Robert Adam designed laundries, icehouses and dairies.

Man has always been adept at embellishing his functional necessities, but nowhere more so than in the garden. Through the ages, once the house had been built and decorated, attention was shifted to building small and sometimes classical, sometimes eccentric, garden buildings with a function.

As well as growing-spaces, gardens were necessary for domestic activities such as hanging out the washing and storing food. Outdoor privies were essential and existed in all but the most humble abode. In the large households of the past, separate areas in the garden housed the dairy, the laundry and drying green, the doocot and the icehouse. Some boasted elaborate stone cunningaries where rabbits were bred for fresh meat, fishponds that were stocked with fish for the table, smoke houses to cook and preserve fish and meat in and elaborate game larders to hang birds and animals in to tenderise the flesh. Miniature tower houses were constructed in walled orchards to store the fruit, often with bee-boles in the walls for the straw skeps, so that the bees could pollinate the blossoms in spring and make honey. Elaborate orangeries, vineries and glasshouses,

Gothic laundry.

decorated with delicate ironwork and pillars, grew fruit and vegetables that were also a pleasure to visit.

Different rooms for different things – whether it be for food, function, ornament or recreation – have always been incorporated into gardens. Queen Mary's bath house, dating from the sixteenth century, now sits neglected, barely clinging to the edge of the garden at Holyrood Palace, as the traffic roars past it and on up the Royal Mile in Edinburgh. In the gardens of the past there were areas that were used for archery, bowls, jousting, ocasionally 'lion yardis', where lions and tigers were kept,

and 'Jouet courts' for tennis. Even when the Romantic movement swept most of the enclosed spaces away in the eighteenth century, walled gardens were re-created at a distance from the house, because they were still necessary for providing fruit, flowers, herbs and vegetables. Later tea-houses would be placed strategically for a welcome sit-down.

Having sorted out the areas in the garden for the necessities of life, further rooms for recreational use have always been incorporated. The ponds by the icehouses were used in winter for curling and skating, which spawned

Doocot.

Gardener's bothy set into the wall.

additional buildings in which to store curling stones and equipment. Fancifully embellished curling houses were sometimes classical, sometimes gothic or sometimes whimsically turned into shell-encrusted grottoes to disguise their functionality. Many of these ponds were later expanded to form serpentine lakes to conform to the Romantic movement in landscape design. Islands were added with the occasional ornate goose-house where birds could nest. Walks were constructed around these, planted with species shrubs and trees. Rustic bathing huts appeared to preserve the modesty of the ladies of the house, along with classical boathouses for the fishing dinghies. Grand houses by the sea might have oyster beds that could be looked at from an ornamental terrace embellished with statues, before one visited the pheasant-house beside it. Games such as tennis and croquet needed enclosures and

elaborate pavilions, where one might sit and watch and where equipment would be stored.

Gradually, as technology reduced the need for the functional outside and the lack of cheap labour spelled the demise of the recreational spaces, gardens adapted and changed. The fashion from the 1960s to the 1990s was for garden rooms too, but that was in the design sense that you moved from one room to the other, using trees, shrubs and hedges as the walls. This method of gardening creates different atmospheres and allows varied and dramatic plantings to happen without one clashing with another. In a small garden it has the effect of making it feel bigger and in a large one it creates more intimacy. Colour-themed gardens became the rage and for these it was necessary to isolate them within a garden room. Plants that all bloom at once can be used to maximum

Modern banqueting pavilion.

effect and once this garden is over, another garden takes its place, so that a patchy flowering effect can be avoided. Equally, the daunting task of weeding and tidying seems less if you are faced with one room at a time rather than finding the whole area crying out for attention.

So we have come full circle and are using our gardens as outdoor rooms again. Aided by outdoor heaters and sophisticated lighting, outdoor dining areas and extra rooms at the bottom of the garden are possible. Gardens are not just for growing things; they are for people to live in, too. Supermarkets may have replaced lakes, dairies and doocots; refrigerators are our icehouses and larders. Today privies and bath houses have moved indoors as bathrooms; ornate gate lodges have been replaced by burglar alarms. We have digital clocks inside and few sundials in the garden. Washing machines ousted wash houses and tumble dryers do the job of the drying green. Those garden rooms are all inside the house now, but new ones are taking their place.

Architecture and gardening cannot otherwise entertain the mind, but by raising certain agreeable emotions or feelings; with which we must begin, as the true foundation of all the rules of criticism that govern these arts … Gardening, beside the emotions of beauty from regularity, order, proportion, colour, and utility, can raise emotions of grandeur, of sweetness, of gaiety, of melancholy, of wildness, and even of surprise or wonder. In architecture, the beauties of regularity, order, and proportion, are still more conspicuous than in gardening; but as to the beauty of colour, architecture is far inferior…

Sundial.

In gardening as well as in architecture, simplicity ought to be a ruling principle. Profuse ornament hath no better effect than to confound the eye, and to prevent the object from making an impression as one entire whole … Thus some women defective in taste, are apt to overcharge every part of their dress with ornament.[1]

Kames placed poetry at the top of his list of the fine arts for 'its power of raising emotions'; next came gardening and architecture, and last painting and sculpture. So in the twenty-first century how would Kames, the great 'improver', have viewed garden design today and, conversely, how would his theories about gardening and architecture be viewed?

Ian Hamilton Finlay at Little Sparta.

Large-scale gardening in the twenty-first century is increasingly the province of landscape architects who, together with the architects, not unsurprisingly favour an architectural approach to gardening. There is a reluctance to include plants and trees that will grow freely and that cannot be kept static; it is their landscape design that they want you to see, so the plants have to complement, not dominate. Another change that has taken place is that of the garden as an *art form* with a message.

Of the last three gardens that I have chosen to explore, the first, Ian Hamilton Finlay's Little Sparta, is to do with poetry, art, wit, classical architecture and a battle with bureaucracy that has grown up around a farm bothy. The second, Charles Jencks' and his wife's[2] Portrack, is to do with landscape architecture, giving a contemporary twist to historical garden forms, linking these to science and cosmic speculation, all set around an old country house. The third is Scotland's new Parliament, where the landscaping is an extension of, and the linking of, a new public building to its surroundings. None of them has to do with the conventional idea of gardening as in growing flowers, fruit, vegetables and trees just for the sake of it, within a garden setting. These are gardens that convey messages, just as artists today require you to read the message in their work rather than just looking at that work for pleasure.

———— ⚬ ————

I went to see Little Sparta on the same day that I saw Portrack. Both are considered to be seminal gardens in terms of their originality and of exploring design concepts at the turn of the twentieth century. They have been endlessly described in the media and in each case they have a specific book devoted to them,[3] so I do not need to go into great detail. Neither relies on plants to create an effect and both contain messages and thought-provoking ideas, but that is where any similarity ends. I enjoyed them both but the feelings that they aroused in me were quite different.

Little Sparta brings the landscape into the garden and uses nature to explore and enhance philosophical ideas by placing poetic words and images in it. Over time it has been a family garden with areas named The Raspberry Republic and Allotment and a boating pond for the children, Lochan Eck. Intellectual themes are explored; the philosophy, religion and poetry of ancient Greece and Rome amongst others, while Hamilton Finlay's battle with bureaucracy is recorded in the *Battle of Little Sparta* and *The Log Pile*. Blood, sweat and tears went into the construction. This was done with simple materials, by hand, often on a miniature scale and not at great cost. It has been an organic progression, self-conscious but not challenging, it is peaceful and intelligent.

In the Portrack garden, by contrast, the landscape has been manipulated on a huge scale using both natural and man-made materials, requiring mechanical assistance at, presumably, enormous cost.[4] Having taken over her mother's garden near Dumfries, Maggie, with her husband, architectural critic Charles Jencks, began

Waveforms at Portrack,
Dumfries.

renovations by digging out the ponds as a place for their children to swim. Maggie was an admirer of the late Robert Smithson, who pioneered EarthArt[5] in the 1960s and '70s; so, instead of carting the soil away, it was decided to create raised earth-forms sculpted out of the spoil, to form the Snail Labyrinth, and the wave-shaped walkways, echoing some of Smithson's work. Portrack is constantly evolving with new areas and new meanings that show the link between science and gardening, covering many acres. In the former kitchen garden Charles Jencks[6] has made a physic Garden of the Senses, where metal helix shapes of DNA, and sculptures of the other senses, have taken over from the rows of cabbages. It is challenging in its complexity, a bit frightening and maybe too clever.

If you have no knowledge of the classical writing of Greece and Rome and are too young to remember the

The Garden of the Six Senses, Portrack.

Beehives, Little Sparta.

Huff Lane, Little Sparta.

Second World War, you can still take meaning from Ian Hamilton Finlay's garden art. His anger at injustice is tempered with humour; his knowledge of history, to make sense of life, is timeless. These, coupled with the Scottish art of the pun mean that, unless you want to have the origins behind the ideas explained, you can understand on a subliminal level.

Charles Jencks' garden, on the other hand, is very enjoyable on a visual level but unless you have a working knowledge of his cosmic principles, as in DNA and atoms, black-hole cosmology and all things scientific, the message

is obscure. His updating of historical garden ideas as in the labyrinth (*The Snail Mound*), the medieval physic garden (*Garden of the Six Senses*), the Italian Renaissance (*Universal Cascade*), the Landscape movement ha-ha (*The Symmetry Break Terrace*) and the 1960s EarthArt installation, (*Waveforms* and *The Snake Terrace*) are more understandable to garden enthusiasts. He has made what is, in places, a spectacular visual experience into a convoluted and rather daunting intellectual exercise that diminishes his achievement rather than enhancing it. In America they have a phrase 'baby steps', which is to say that when you

The Universal Cascade,
Portrack.

are looking, at an exhibition for instance, you learn as you go around. The myriad historical and scientific data that Charles Jencks, himself an American, has drawn from in creating his 'Garden of Cosmic Speculation' definitely requires baby steps to understand its messages.

Looking at a creation when you know nothing about it is much more exciting than having had it explained in advance. Sometimes it leads you to ask questions and so you search out information; first impressions produce spontaneous emotions. At other times it does not seem important to know why it was done in such a way and what

it is intended to tell you – it just is pleasing as it is. When you read a book you have to create the images in your head, especially if there are no pictures. If you see the film first then these are provided for you, leaving no room for the imagination. With gardens it is the other way around. Both Finlay and Jencks want you to read their gardens and not just look at them. A major difference between the two gardens is how they will grow and therefore change. Little Sparta is continually changing as the plants and trees grow and as the stone and wood weather. The spaces decrease as trees grow, taking up more room. At Portrack, on the other

Adam and Eve dance in the wood at Little Sparta.

hand, the garden is designed in such a way that it can be kept from any change forced by natural growth. Everything can be cut, pruned and clipped to retain the original design and proportions. This is not only the difference between poetry and science. It is also the difference between freedom and control.

Hamilton Findlay told me that he never thought of his garden as in any way extraordinary: 'I thought our garden was like all gardens and it was only latterly that I realised that it wasn't when I heard people talking about it.' He believes that 'nice, good gardens should be read rather than looked at'. But he was not trying to communicate anything. Taking another tack, Jencks has deliberately set out to create a garden that is extraordinary and doesn't want anyone to have their own ideas about it. He dislikes others writing about it, and encourages you to read the book he has written about its creation, before looking at it. I decided not to read either of the books about these gardens before visiting them. Maybe the telling thing, and why these two gardens are so very different, is that Hamilton Finlay let somebody else write the book about Little Sparta, while Jencks wrote his own about Portrack. A true artist must always expect criticism both positive and negative, it is the oxygen that any creativity requires. I enjoyed looking at both these gardens and now, having seen them, I am going to read them via the books – there are so many *points de vue* to explore.

In contrast, I was told all about the garden of the new Scottish Parliament building three years before I got a chance to see it with my own eyes. When I visited the site in September 2001, it was just a gleam in the design team's eye, a balsa wood model and a glossy brochure. The architect Kenny Fraser[7] told me, 'It is not a principle of design to look at what was there before, the park's history is not important.' He is obviously not a fan of Cicero, who warned 2,000 years ago, that 'cultures without history doom themselves to remain trapped in the most illusory tense of all, the present'. Christopher Dingwall, conservation officer for the Garden History Society in Scotland, said at the time: 'The Society was certainly disappointed at the undue haste which characterised the choice of site and the starting of work on the ground, which did not allow for proper historical assessment both documentary or archaeological of the former Queensberry and Moray House gardens whose history goes back 300 years.'[8]

Much has been written about the controversial designs and the spiralling budget costs of what the late Donald Dewar described as 'a signature building for Scotland'. But is the four acres around it a signature landscape? The 'external works' were due to be completed six months after the Parliament, in June 2003, at a projected budget of around £14 million.[9] The decision to shoehorn the new Parliament into an area which is at the core of a medieval UNESCO World Heritage Site, rather than on Calton Hill, where there was much more land available, can only be justified if the end result is seen as a spectacular celebration of twenty-first-century design. Looking at the nearly completed project in December 2004, it appears that the somewhat frenetic buildings could have done with more landscape space around them as a calming anchor and frame, particularly at the front where the plaza is too cramped for the scale of the building and gives you no chance to stand back from it.

The site of the former brewery sat on a labyrinth of aquifers and tunnels that required costly stabilisation. In gardening terms it is poor. The low-lying sheltered ground is a frost pocket and the compacted soil will take years to recover. But does this matter? I am constantly being told that 'architecture is the new gardening' and indeed both Fraser and Callas are adamant that their landscape is the same as the building – 'it should be viewed as an extension of that building'.

Kenny Fraser, landscape architect for the Scottish Parliament.

The Scottish Parliament Building.

Holyrood Palace, the surrounding parks, Moray House and Queensberry House have long had important gardens and areas that were used for recreational, ceremonial and practical activities, but above all they were there to impress. This all came to an end with the sacking of Holyrood by Cromwell's troops in 1650, although the Union of the Crowns in 1603 had already diminished the importance of Holyrood because the seat of power moved to London.

So with devolution and the return of power to Holyrood, will the parks and gardens impress once more?

Catalan architect Enrique Miralles drew the original concept sketches, in his competition entry, of an earthform that depicts a waving 'tail':

The tail is drawing in the people of Scotland and the Crags of the surrounding hills to symbolise a gathering place for the Scottish people to be and to sit down and discuss things. It will bring the people inside the land of Scotland.

The tail, which is five metres high at the tallest point, moves in the same direction as the historic 'closes'. Like a horse's flicking tail, it is a series of raised boomerang

The gabion walls of the walkways that flow through the green 'tails' at the Scottish Parliament.

Queensberry House and the MSPs' garden.

shapes planted with native grasses that will create 'a flow of green'. Walkways through these are constructed in precast concrete that curve up to form benches, while the retaining walls are composed of gabions.[10] The gabion walls, much used in motorway edgings to stabilise steep slopes, are composed of stone salvaged from the demolished brewery buildings that previously occupied the site. As gabions go they are pretty classy, but the stones are too good to be caged in this way and would have been better used as edgings instead of the dreary concrete that, even on a sunny day, looks drab. It is not a material that

ages gracefully – rather, disgracefully – and on a grey winter's day it recreates the depressing mood of a 1950s tower block.[11] The meadow grass on these tails is 'hydroplanted' with appropriate native plants to reflect those found on nearby Arthur's Seat and Salisbury Crags. Apart from gorse, the other plant identified for this purpose is the German 'sticky catchfly' plant.[12] One of the few colonies for this in Scotland is to be found in Holyrood Park. The planting in the MSPs' garden, an enclosed space behind Queensberry House that is viewed from the lobby through floor-to-ceiling glass is, to be polite, strange.

Given that materials for the entire landscape project were not specifically sourced in Scotland,[13] there is definitely no Scottish bias in the inspiration throughout, or in the choice of plants and materials, so there was a blank canvas available. But, whether through bad planting by the contractors, or by an inharmonious choice of plant material, given the aspects and site, the designers might have been better to leave out the plants altogether and concentrate on the architecture here.

Water has not been neglected and a series of angular-shaped ponds have been incorporated into the 'urban plaza' that divides up the Parliament buildings from the Palace of Holyrood. The designs are intriguingly described in the landscape plans (Stage D report) as 'the significant Theatre of Horse Wynd'. The 52-page document contains extensive computer-aided plans and diagrams developing Miralles' sketches, which are shown at the beginning and have changed little in the intervening years. It goes on to explain the significance of the water as

> *More than a pond, it is a mist that allows the reflection of the buildings. Still, reflective pools, lined with Caithness stone as a continuation of the ground plane, the water features aid security by presenting a threshold to vehicles, while providing a noble threshold to the public entrance.*[14]

With full-time public access to all the gardens, except the MSPs' private space, health-and-safety regulations have necessitated many changes to the original design, not least by voicing fears that people could fall off the raised grassy fronds of the tail or tumble into the ponds unless they were all fenced off. You will still be able to fall off the Crags above, though, where you get the best view of the layout, which is comforting. Further complications in the same vein, plus obvious concerns to do with levels, access and wheelchair requirements, did at times have the planning tail wagging the design dog and Fraser and Callas found this frustrating: 'In Barcelona we have the same bureaucracy, but it is not followed so stringently.'

How history will judge the gardens of the twenty-first century it is impossible to tell. Will travellers a hundred years from now see the messages that the designers intended to be read from the landscaping and sculpture incorporated in them? Maybe, like visitors to the ruined garden at Edzell today, they will puzzle over their meaning. Or will they just interpret them and form an opinion of the people who made and lived in them from where they will be standing in the twenty-second century? Will fashion have changed so much that they no longer exist, or will they be covered with a town, like the magnificent seventeenth-century gardens of the Earl of Mar at Alloa? Will they only be able to imagine what was there from written descriptions; and how will these descriptions differ one from another?

In this book, I have written about the enemies faced by the Scottish gardener, whether they be financial, climatic, from wars, predators, critics or, currently, health-and-safety inspectors.[15] As you wander the paths of history it becomes clear that, above all, it is fashion that destroys gardens. As for the creation of gardens, some can make them with what is to hand while others rely on wealth to control their environments. How two people deal with the same space is of continuing fascination. More, how two people see a garden is even more interesting. How one person wishes you to see their garden bears no relation to how you in fact do see it, or indeed the emotions that a garden can cause you to feel. It really all depends on your *point de vue.*

Notes

1. Henry Home, Lord Kames, *Elements of Criticism* (1761).

2. The late Maggie Keswick.

3. *Little Sparta: The Garden of Ian Hamilton Findlay*, by Jessie Sheeler (2003) and *The Garden of Cosmic Speculation*, by Charles Jencks (2003).

4. The Keswick family fortune from their trading company Jardine Matheson, was founded on smuggling opium into China. One of the founder's descendants celebrated this by building gateposts, decorated with griffins holding opium poppy seed heads, at his mansion, Aldross Castle near Alness.

5. EarthArt was pioneered in America during the 1960s and '70s by artist Robert Smithson, the father of 'installations'; he is best known for building huge spirals and labyrinth mounts in the landscape. The catalogue for a recent retrospective exhibition in Los Angeles explains that Smithson 'had a talent for employing scientific jargon in an artistic context … drawing on themes from religion, science, mythology, and popular culture. His oeuvre defied convention, utilizing non-traditional art materials such as mirrors, maps, concrete, earth and asphalt, moving art into the landscape.' Robert Smithson, MOCA California (2004).

6. Maggie Keswick died in 1995 of cancer. She left instructions and money to found the Maggie Centres for the nurture of cancer patients.

7. Kenny Fraser, took over the project on behalf of the Edinburgh architects RMJM who, in partnership with Joan Callas, from Enrique Miralles's Barcelona architectural practice EMBT, have designed and managed the landscaping. The work has been carried out by Bovis Lend Lease, with the planting contracted out.

8. See Chapter 8.

9. The Scottish Parliament said in December 2004 that 'the final construction cost for the landscaping is estimated at 13.4m, of which 0.6m is still identified as reserve. We also paid 0.5m for the transfer of the muster room (gardener's shelter), 0.3m on land purchase, 1.9m on fees and site management, and 2.6m went back to the Treasury as VAT.' The work was still ongoing at this time but my maths makes that around £18m.

10. Cages of wire filled with stones.

11. Instead of the concrete being sand-blasted to enhance the finish, it has been acid-etched, a cheaper process, which does nothing to give lustre to this most toxic and inorganic material.

12. *Lychnis viscaria*, a native of Germany, can be found all through Europe and Asia, but is rare in Scotland.

13. The trees came from Hillier's Nursery in the south of England, the concrete from Newcastle and the granite setts from Portugal.

14. During the building, the contractors used the ponds to store 'type one' aggregate which stained the Caithness stones lining the ponds to a uniform concrete colour, and now they have had to be painted to resemble the original stone.

15. Any garden that opens to the public on a regular basis has to incorporate health-and-safety measures, from providing lifebelts beside ponds to fencing off any area deemed to be 'dangerous'. Equally, disability access has to be made and designs changed to allow for this, irrespective of how this affects the creative design.

BIBLIOGRAPHY

Anon: *The Curiosities, Natural and Artificial of the Island of Great Britain*, 6 vols, printed for the proprietors, n.d. [c.1770], vol. 6.

Anthony, John: *The Renaissance Garden in Britain*, Shire Garden History, 1991.

Arnim, Elizabeth von: *Elizabeth and Her German Garden*, Virago, 1985.

Bannerman, John: *The Beatons, A Medical Kindred in the Classical Gaelic Tradition*, John Donald, Edinburgh, 1998.

Beith, Mary: *Healing Threads*, Polygon, Edinburgh, 1995.

Black, David: *All the First Minister's Men*, Birlinn, Edinburgh, 2001.

Boutcher, William: *A Treatise on Forest-Trees*, printed by R. Fleming, Edinburgh, 1775.

Brown, P. Hume: *Early Travellers in Scotland*, facsimile of 1891, Mercat Press, Edinburgh, 1978.

Chambers, Robert: *Domestic Annals of Scotland, from the Reformation to the Revolution*, 2nd Edition, 3 vols, W. & R. Chambers, Edinburgh & London, 1859.

Charmers, George: *Caledonia: or, a Historical and Topographical Account of North Britain from the most Ancient to the present Times, with a Dictionary of Places Chronographical and Philological*, 8 vols, Alexander Gardner, Paisley, 1887–1902.

Cooksey, J. C. B: *Alexander Nasmyth H.R.S.A 1758–1840 A Man of the Scottish Renaissance*, Paul Harris, Whittinghame House Publishing, 1991.

Cox, Euan: *A History of Gardening in Scotland*, Chatto & Windus, London, 1935.

Darwin, Tess: *The Scots Herbal*, Mercat Press, Edinburgh, 1996.

Defoe, Daniel: *A Tour Through the Whole Island of Great Britain*, Promotional Reprint Company, 1992.

Dickson, Camilla & James: *Plants and People in Ancient Scotland*, Tempus, Gloucestershire, 2000.

Dunbar, John G: *Scottish Royal Palaces*, Tuckwell Press, East Linton, 1999.

Dutton, G. F: *Harvesting the Edge*, Menard Press, London, 1995.

Elder, Isobel Hill: *Celt, Druid and Culdee*, The Covenant Publishing, 1938.

Ellis, Peter Beresford: *The Druids*, Constable & Robinson, London, 2002.

EMBT & RMJM: *The Scottish Parliament, Landscape Stage D Report*, Edinburgh, 2000.

Evelyn, John [William Bray, Ed.]: *Diary of John Evelyn … to which are added a Selection from his Familiar Letters …* , 4 vols, Bickers and Son, London, 1906.

Faujas de St. Fond [Sir Archibald Geikie, Ed.]: *A Journey through England & Scotland to the Hebrides in 1784 by B. Faujas de Saint Fond*, 2 vols, Hugh Hopkins, Glasgow, 1907.

Gilpin, William: *Observations on several Parts of Great Britain, particularly The High-Lands of Scotland* [1776], 2 vols, third edition, printed for T. Cadell and W. Davies, 1808.

Gow, Ian & Alistair Rowan: *Scottish Country Houses, 1600-1914*, Edinburgh University Press, 1995.

Grant of Rothiemurchus, Elizabeth: *Memoirs of a Highland Lady*, Canongate, Edinburgh, 1988.

Grieve, Mrs [C. F. Leyel, ed.]: *A Modern Herbal*, Penguin, London, 1980.

Hadfield, Miles, Robert Harling & Leonie Highton: *British Gardeners, A Biographical Dictionary*, A. Zwemmer, 1980.

Haldane, Elizabeth S: *Scots Gardens in old Times*, Alexander Maclehose, London, 1934.

Hales, Mick: *Monastic Gardens*, Stewart Tabori & Chang, New York, 2000.

Harvey, John: *Mediaeval Gardens*, B. T. Batsford, London, 1981.

Herman, Arthur: *The Scottish Enlightenment*, Fourth Estate, London, 2003.

Heron, Robert: *Observations made in a Journey through the Western Counties of Scotland*, 2 vols, printed by Morrison junior, Perth, 1793.

Historic Scotland, & Scottish Natural Heritage, Countryside Commission for Scotland & Scottish Development Department: *An Inventory of Gardens and Designed Landscapes in Scotland*, 5 vols, n.d.

Home, Henry, Lord Kames: *Elements of Criticism*, reprinted University Press of the Pacific, Hawaii, 2002.

Hunter, Thomas: *Woods, Forests, & Estates of Perthshire*, Henderson, Robertson & Hunter, Perth, 1883.

Hussey, Christopher: *The work of Sir Robert Lorimer*, Country Life, 1931.

Jameson, Fiona: 'The Royal Gardens of the Palace of Holyrood', In *Garden History* vol. I22, no. I, 1994.

Jellicoe, Geoffrey and Susan: *The Landscape of Man: Shaping the Environment from Prehistory to the Present Day*, Thames & Hudson, 1975.

Jencks, Charles: *The Garden of Cosmic Speculation*, Francis Lincoln, London, 2003.

Johnson & Boswell: *Journey to the Western Islands & A Tour of the Hebrides*, reprinted Oxford University Press, 1924.

Johnston, James B: *Place Names of Scotland*, John Murray, London, 1934.

Keay, John & Julia: *Collins Encyclopaedia of Scotland*, Harper Collins, London, 1994.

Lindsay of Pitscottie, Robert [John Graham Dalyell, ed.]: *The Chronicles of Scotland, by Robert Lindsay of Pitscottie, Published from several old Manuscripts.* 2 vols, printed by George Ramsay & Company, Edinburgh, 1814.

Little, Allan [Ed.]: *Scotland's Gardens*, Spur Books, 1981.

Lockhart, J. G.: *The Life of Sir Walter Scott*, 1771–1832, new and popular edition, Adam and Charles Black, 1896.

Longstaffe-Gowan, Todd: *The London Town Garden*, Yale University Press, 2001.

Loudon, J. C.: *The Travels of John Claudius Loudon and His Wife Jane*, 1831, reprinted Lennard Publishing, Harpenden, 1987.

Loudon, J. C.: *Encyclopaedia of Gardening*, new edition, Longman, Green & Co., London, 1850.

Lynch, Michael [ed.]: *The Oxford Companion to Scottish History*, Oxford University Press, 2001.

Malcolm, C. A: 'The Gardens of the Castle' [of Edinburgh], in *Book of the Old Edinburgh Club*, vol.14, pp.101–120, printed for the Members of the Club by T. & A. Constable Ltd., Edinburgh, 1925.

Martin, Martin: *A Description of the Western Islands of Scotland*, circa 1695, Birlinn, Edinburgh, 1999.

Maxwell, Sir Herbert: *Scottish Gardens*. Edward Arnold, London, 1908.

Minay, Priscilla: 'Eighteenth and early Nineteenth century Edinburgh Seedsmen and Nurserymen', In *The Book of the Old Edinburgh Club*, new series, vol. I, 1971.

Mitchell, Ann Lindsay and Syd House: *David Douglas*, Aurum Press, 1999.

Mitchell, Arthur: 'A List of Travels, Tours, Journeys, Voyages, Cruises, Excursions, Wanderings, Rambles, Visits, Etc., relating to Scotland', in *Proceedings of the Society of Antiquaries of Scotland, 1900–1901*, vol. 35, third series, vol. XV, pp.431–636, printed for the Society by Neill and Co. Ltd., Edinburgh, 1901.

Monro, Donald: *A Description of the Occidental i.e. Western Islands of Scotland, 1549*, Birlinn, Edinburgh, 1999.

Musgrave, Toby, Chris Gardner & Will Musgrave: *The Plant Hunters*, Cassell & Co., London, 1998.

MacCulloch, John: *The Highlands and Western Isles of Scotland, … in Letters to Sir Walter Scott*, 4 vols, Longman, Hurst, Rees, Orme, Brown, and Green, 1824, vol. I.

M'Intosh, Charles: *The Book of the Garden*, 2 vols, W. Blackwood & Sons, Edinburgh, 1853.

Mackay, Sheila: *Early Scottish Gardens*, Polygon, Edinburgh, 2001.

Macky, John: *A Journey Through Scotland. In familiar letters from a gentleman here, to his friend abroad. Being the third volume which compleats Great Britain. / By the author of The journey thro' England*, imprint: London: printed for J. Pemberton and J. Hooke …, 1723.

McKean, Charles: *The Scottish Chateau, the country house of Renaissance Scotland*, Sutton, Stroud, 2001.

McLeod, Dawn: *The Gardener's Scotland*, William Blackwood, Edinburgh, 1977.

Newte, Thomas: *Prospects and Observations; on a Tour in England and Scotland: Natural, Oeconomical, and Literary*, printed for G. G. J. and J. Robinson, London, 1791.

Nichol, Walter: *Nichol's Gardiner's Kalendar* (title page missing), Edinburgh, 1812.

Ochterlony, John of Guynd: *Account of the Shire of Forfar, circa 1682*, Forfar & District Historical Society, 1969.

Ottewill, David: *The Edwardian Garden*, Yale University Press, 1989.

Pennant, Thomas: *A Tour of Scotland in 1769*, reprinted Merlin Press, Perth, 1979.

Plant, Marjorie: *The Domestic Life of Scotland in the Eighteenth Century*, Edinburgh University Press, 1952.

Pliny the Elder: *Natural History*, Penguin, London, 1991.

Prest, John: *The Garden of Eden – The Botanic Gardens and the re-creation of Paradise*, Yale, 1988.

Reid, John: *The Scot's Gard'nr*, 1683, reprint Mainstream, Edinburgh, 1988.

Robertson, Forbes W: *Early Scottish Gardeners and their Plants, 1650–1750*, Tuckwell Press, East Linton, 2000.

Ross, Anne: *Everyday Life of the Pagan Celts*, B. T. Batsford, London, 1972.

Scott, Sir Walter [W. E. K. Anderson, Ed.]: *The Journal of Sir Walter Scott*, Canongate, Edinburgh, 1998.

Scott-Moncrieff, Robert [ed.]: *The Household Book of Lady Grisell Baillie 1692–1733*, Scottish History Society, Edinburgh, 1911 (2nd series, vol. 1.).

Sheeler, Jessie: *Little Sparta, The Garden of Ian Hamilton Finlay*, Frances Lincoln, London, 2003.

Steuart, Sir Henry: *Planter's Guide*, John Murray, London, 1828.

Steven, Maisie: *Parish Life in Eighteenth-Century Scotland – A Review of the Old Statistical Account*, Scottish Cultural Press, Edinburgh, 1995.

Strong, Roy: *The Renaissance Garden in England*, Thames & Hudson, London, 1979.

Taitt, A. A: *The Landscape Garden in Scotland 1735–1835*, Edinburgh University Press, 1980.

Taylor, Patricia: *Thomas Blaikie – The 'Capability' Brown of France 1751–1838*, Tuckwell Press, East Linton, 2001.

Triggs, H. Inigo: *Formal Gardens in England & Scotland*, 1902, reprinted Antique Collectors Club, Woodbridge, 1988.

Truscott, James: *Private Gardens of Scotland*, Weidenfeld & Nicholson, London, 1988.

Tsai, Eugenie [ed.]: *The Museum of Contemporary Art, Los Angeles - Robert Smithson - exhibition 2004*, University of California Press, Los Angeles, 2004.

Urquhart, Suki: *Chambers Roofed by Heaven, The Walled Garden in History*, unpublished ms.

Wordsworth, Dorothy: *Tour in Scotland A.D. 1803*, David Douglas, Edinburgh, 1804.

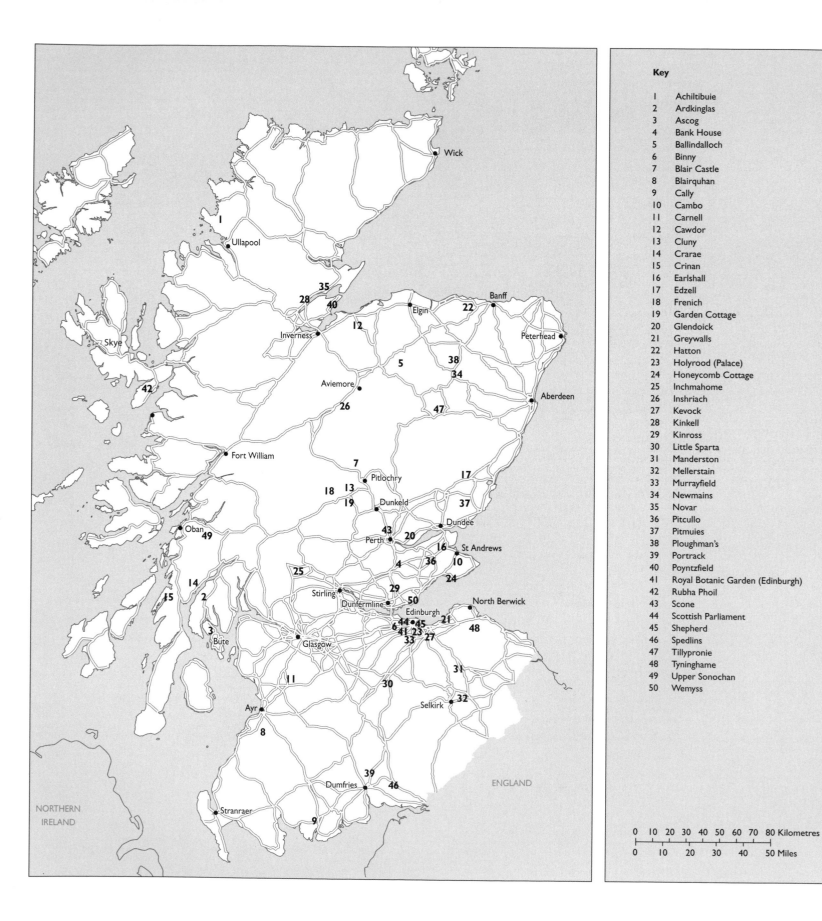

Key

1 Achiltibuie
2 Ardkinglas
3 Ascog
4 Bank House
5 Ballindalloch
6 Binny
7 Blair Castle
8 Blairquhan
9 Cally
10 Cambo
11 Carnell
12 Cawdor
13 Cluny
14 Crarae
15 Crinan
16 Earlshall
17 Edzell
18 Frenich
19 Garden Cottage
20 Glendoick
21 Greywalls
22 Hatton
23 Holyrood (Palace)
24 Honeycomb Cottage
25 Inchmahome
26 Inshriach
27 Kevock
28 Kinkell
29 Kinross
30 Little Sparta
31 Manderston
32 Mellerstain
33 Murrayfield
34 Newmains
35 Novar
36 Pitcullo
37 Pitmuies
38 Ploughman's
39 Portrack
40 Poyntzfield
41 Royal Botanic Garden (Edinburgh)
42 Rubha Phoil
43 Scone
44 Scottish Parliament
45 Shepherd
46 Spedlins
47 Tillypronie
48 Tyninghame
49 Upper Sonochan
50 Wemyss

The locations specified here are approximate

0 10 20 30 40 50 60 70 80 Kilometres

0 10 20 30 40 50 Miles

INFORMATION ON VISITING THE GARDENS FEATURED IN THIS BOOK

ABBREVIATIONS:

SGS Scotland's Garden Scheme Tel: 0131 229 1870
    Web: www.ngs.org.uk
(published annually giving details of opening times etc.)
HS Historic Scotland Tel: 0131 668 8600
    Web: www.historic-scotland.gov.uk
NTS National Trust for Scotland Tel: 0131 243 9300
    Web: www.nts.org.uk
AYR All Year Round

CHAPTER 1 PHYSIC, MONASTIC AND ROYAL

The Herbalists' Garden, Garden Cottage, Pitnacree, Perthshire
Open: May–October
The Herbalist's Clinic and Dispensary
Tel: 01887 840773
Email: TheHerbalistsGarden@hattenjack.com

Rubha Phaoil Forest Garden and Herb Nursery, Armadale, Isle
    of Skye
Open: AYR from dawn to dusk
Tel: 01471 844700
Email: sandyru@tiscali.co.uk

Inchmahome Priory, Lake of Menteith, Perthshire
Owned by the Stewart Society and administered by HS and is
    easily accessible by boat from the Port of Menteith, Perthshire
Tel: 0131 668 8600
Web: www.historic-scotland.gov.uk

Palace of Holyroodhouse, Edinburgh
Garden administered by HS, can be visited as part of a tour of
    the palace
Tel: 0131 524 1120
Email: bookinginfo@royalcollection.org.uk

Royal Botanic Gardens, Edinburgh, Inverleith Place, Edinburgh
Open: AYR
Tel: 0131 552 7171
Email: info@rbge.org.uk

CHAPTER 2 GRAND DESIGNS

Edzell Castle, north-west of Edzell, Angus
HS
Open: Spring–Autumn
Tel: 01356 648631

Kinross House, Kinross-shire
Open: Easter to October
Tel: 01577 862900
Email: jm@kinrosshouse.com

The Hercules Garden, Blair Castle, Perthshire
Open: April–October and by appointment in winter
Tel: 01796 481 207
Email: info@blair-castle.co.uk

Mellerstain, Gordon, Borders
Open: May–September (closed Tuesday & Saturday)
Tel: 01573 410225

Manderston, Duns, Berwickshire
Open: By appointment for parties AYR. Open days (house
    and garden) Sunday and Thursday from mid-May to end of
    September
Tel: 01361 883450
Email: palmer@manderston.co.uk

Earlshall, Fife
Open: by appointment
Tel: 01334 839205

Greywalls, East Lothian
Open: April – October
Tel: 01620 842144
Email: hotel@greywalls.co.uk

CHAPTER 3 – CASTLES AND WALLED GARDENS

Cawdor, Nairn, Inverness-shire
Open: May to mid October and AYR by appointment
Tel: 01667 404401
Email: info@cawdorcastle.com

Novar, Black Isle, Inverness-shire
Open: SGS

Pitcullo, Fife
Open: By appointment AYR
Tel: 01334 870239

Anonymous Fruit Garden
Not open to the public

Blairquhan, Maybole, Ayrshire
Open: By appointment AYR and from mid-July until mid-
  August
Tel: 01655 770239
Email: enquiries@blairquhan.co.uk

Ballindalloch, Grantown-on-Spey, Banffshire
Open: From Good Friday until the end of September, daily
  except Saturday
Tel: 01807 500205
Email: enquiries@ballindallochcastle.co.uk

Hatton Castle, Turriff, Banffshire
Open: By appointment AYR
Tel: 01888 562279
Email: jjdgardens@btinternet.com_

Spedlins, Dumfries
Open: By appointment June–August
Tell: 01576470224
Email: graydsgn@aol.com

CHAPTER 4 PLANTS AND COLLECTORS

Scone, Perth
Open: April–October
Tel: 01738 5523000
Email: visits@scone-palace.co.uk

Ardkinglas, Cairndow, Argyll (Woodland Garden)
Open: AYR
Tel: 01499 600261
Email: arkkinglas@btinternet.com

Crarae, Inveraray, Argyll
NTS
AYR
Tel: 01546 886614/886388
Email: fsinclair@nts.org.uk_

Upper Sonochan, Argyll
Open: By appointment
Tel: 01866 833229

Ascog Hall Fernery and Garden, Isle of Bute
Open: Easter to the end of October, closed Mondays and
  Tuesdays
Tel: 01700 504555
Email: enquiries@ascoghallfernery.co.uk

Cluny Aberfeldy, Perthshire
Open: March–October
Tell: 01887 820795
Email: Matcluny@aol.com

Cambo, St. Andrews, Fife
Open: ARY every day
Tel:01333 450054
Email: cambo@camboestate.com

Tillypronie, Aboyne, Aberdeenshire
SGS

CHAPTER 5 SPECIALISTS

Stoneyhill Road, East Lothian
Not open

Acorn House, Ballater
Not open

The Hydroponicum, Achiltibuie, Ullapool, Easter Ross
Open: Easter–October
Tel: 01854 622202
Email: info@thehydrponicum.com

Kevock Garden Plants and Flowers nursery
Open: By appointment and under SGS
Tel: 07811 321 585
www.kevockgarden.co.uk

Tanfield House, Edinburgh
Not open

Marginal garden, Bridge of Cally, Perthshire
Not open

CHAPTER 6 NURSERIES
Cally Gardens, Gatehouse of Fleet, Dumfries
Open: Easter–September (variable opening times) and under
    SGS twice a year
Tel: 01557 815029
Email: cally.gardens@virgin.net

Poyntzfield, Black Isle, Ross & Cromarty
Open: March–September and by appointment from October–
    February
Tell: 01381610352
Web: www.poyntzfieldherbs.co.uk

Binny, Ecclesmachan, West Lothian
Open: mid-January–end of November
Tell: 01506 858931
Email: binnyplants@aol.com

Inshirach, Newtonmore, Inverness-shire
Open: March–October; groups by appointment
Tel: 01540 651287
Email: info@drakesalpines.com

Glendoick Garden Centre, Perthshire
Open: 7 days a week, AYR
Tel: 01738 860260.

Glendoick Nursery and Gardens
SGS
Open: first and third Sundays in May annually, 2–5pm or by
    appointment
Tel: 01738 860205
Email: jane@glendoick.com

CHAPTER 7 GARDENERS
House of Pitmuies, Forfar, Angus
Open: April–October
Tel: 01241 828245
Email: ogilvie@pitmuies.com

Carnell, Hurlford, Ayrshire
SGS
Tel: 01563 884236

Wards, Stirlingshire
Not open

Frenich, Perthshire
Open by appointment mid-May to mid-September
Email: colinindia@eth.net

Wemyss Castle, Fife
Open: By appointment, sometimes under SGS and every
    Thursday (noon–dusk) from 1 May–mid August
Tel: 01592 651327
Email: wemyss@jepense.freeserve.co.uk

Tyninghame Walled Gardens, Dunbar, East Lothian
SGS

Ploughman's Hall, Old Rayne, Aberdeenshire
Open: By appointment May–September and under SGS
Tel: 01464 851253
Email: tony@ploughmanshall.co.uk

CHAPTER 8 TOWN AND VILLAGE
Murrayfield, Edinburgh
Open by appointment AYR
Tel: 0131 337 1747

CHAPTER 9 – ARTISTS AND DESIGNERS

Crinan, Hotel garden Argyll
Open: To guests AYR and under SGS
Tel: 01546 830261
Email: art@francesmacdonald.demon.co.uk

Shepherd's House, Inveresk, East Lothian
Open: SGS twice a year and Tuesday and Thursday 2–4 p.m.
Tel: 0131 665 2570
Email: ann@fraser2570.freeserve.co.uk

The Walled Garden, East Lothian
Not open

The Bank House, Glenfarg, Perthshire
Private garden: Open by appointment May–August
Tel: 01577 830275
Public garden: Open AYR

Kinkell, Black Isle, Ross & Cromarty
Open: By appointment AYR
Tell: 01349 861485
Email: kinkell@btinternet.com

McPherson Drive, Gourock
Not open

Honeycomb Cottage, Fife
SGS (sometimes)
Maryfield Croft, Aberdeenshire
Not open

Newmains Farm, Aberdeenshire
Open: By appointment AYR
Tel: 01464 851379
Email: mtaitt@freenet.co.uk

Craiglockhart Edinburgh
Not open

EPILOGUE

Little Sparta, Dunsyre, Larnarkshire
Open: By appointment from June to September, on Friday and
    Sunday afternoons
Tel: 0189 981 0252

Portrack, Dumfries
Open; Under SGS and by appointment (write to Charles Jencks,
    PO Box 31627, London W11 3XB)

Scottish Parliament, Edinburgh
Open; AYR

INDEX

Note: Page numbers in bold type indicate an illustration.